Once Upon a Time in Paradise

Once Upon a Time in Paradise

Canadians in the Golden Age of Hollywood

Charles Foster

THE DUNDURN GROUP
TORONTO

Publisher: Anthony Hawke
Copy-editor: Andrea Pruss
Design: Emma Kassirer
Printer: Transcontinental

National Library of Canada Cataloguing in Publication

Foster, Charles, 1923–
Once Upon a Time in Paradise: Canadians in the Golden Age of Hollywood / Charles Foster.

Includes index
ISBN 1-55002-464-7

1. Motion picture producers and directors—California—Los Angeles—Biography. 2. Motion picture actors and actresses—California—Los Angeles—Biography. 3. Canadians—California—Los Angeles—Biography. 4. Motion picture industry—California—Los Angeles—History. I. Title.

PN1998.2.F668 2003   791.43'092'279494   C2003-904046-1

1   2   3   4   5   07   06   05   04   03

THE CANADA COUNCIL | LE CONSEIL DES ARTS
FOR THE ARTS | DU CANADA
SINCE 1957 | DEPUIS 1957

Canadä

ONTARIO ARTS COUNCIL
CONSEIL DES ARTS DE L'ONTARIO

We acknowledge the support of the **Canada Council for the Arts** and the **Ontario Arts Council** for our publishing program. We also acknowledge the financial support of the **Government of Canada** through the **Book Publishing Industry Development Program** and **The Association for the Export of Canadian Books**, and the **Government of Ontario** through the **Ontario Book Publishers Tax Credit** program, and the **Ontario Media Development Corporation's Ontario Book Initiative**.

Printed and bound in Canada.⊕
Printed on recycled paper.
www.dundurn.com

Dundurn Press
8 Market Street
Suite 200
Toronto, Ontario, Canada
M5E 1M6

Dundurn Press
2250 Military Road
Tonawanda NY
U.S.A. 14150

Once Upon a Time in Paradise

Table of Contents

Prologue

When sound arrived in Hollywood at the end of 1927, it was the Warner Brothers picture *The Jazz Singer* that made all the headlines.

Jack Warner, head of the studio, was born in London, Ontario. But he was not alone in Hollywood. Hundreds more Canadians were already in place waiting to show that they had the knowledge and the voices to make this new medium into the success everyone dreamed it could be. In the years ahead they were joined by hundreds more Canadians. Not all became stars, and not all were successful, but those who did reach the top are worth remembering.

Whether you believe Jack Warner's claim that he was the first to produce a sound film, or whether you prefer to accept the word of Louis B. Mayer, head of the biggest studio in Hollywood, Metro-Goldwyn-Mayer, that his genius Douglas Shearer was the first to put real sound on film, or whether you want to think that director Allan Dwan should be called the first real name in sound because, well ahead of Warner, he had filmed a newsreel with sound for Movietone News in the summer of 1927, there is no doubt about one thing. They were all Canadians.

The Academy of Motion Picture Arts and Sciences was created by Louis B. Mayer. In 1926, before sound arrived, Mayer called all the big studio heads in Hollywood together and laid before them his plan to raise the image of the film industry in the eyes of the picture-going public.

There had been many scandals in the motion picture industry in the years before 1926, and Mayer felt it was time to do something to stop the bad headlines that had upset too many people and hurt the industry. Some films were banned, others were never shown, because they starred or featured people who had hit world headlines in an unsavoury manner. It should be mentioned that no Canadians were ever involved in these major scandals.

The Academy of Motion Picture Arts and Sciences ruled before the 1926 award ceremonies that *The Jazz Singer* was ineligible to get any award since it was "unfair that silent films should have to be compared to this early arrival on the sound scene."

Records show that Louis B. Mayer, who had always feuded with Jack Warner, was the mover of the motion to keep Warner's film out of the competition.

In a strange gesture, the Academy did allow *The Jazz Singer* to compete in two categories, Writing and Engineering Effects. How the decision was made to award the first year's statuettes was never revealed, but there can be no doubt that Mayer had considerable influence in the awards. Unlike the present Oscars, when only the company handling the ballots knows the results until the envelopes are opened on stage, the members of the Academy board did know the results long before the actual ceremony.

When it became obvious that the sound film everyone was talking about wasn't even going to take home the coveted statuette in either the Writing or the Engineering Effects category, the Academy members, over the protests of Louis B. Mayer, voted to give a special award to Warner Brothers for *The Jazz Singer*, described in the citation as "the outstanding pioneer talking picture which has revolutionized the film industry."

Mary Pickford, reminiscing in her eighties, said with a laugh, "It was once said that Mayer had ten votes for every one we got to cast." That may have been stretching things more than a little, but there can be no doubt that Mayer's power in Hollywood allowed him to pressure voters to cast their ballots the way he wanted them to vote.

All the people listed above were Canadian, if you will agree that Louis B. Mayer deserves to be called Canadian since he arrived in Saint John, New Brunswick, at the age of only eighteen months with his refugee parents from Russia and remained in his new hometown until he reached his late teens.

Louis B. Mayer, Douglas Shearer, and Mack Sennett, still King of Comedy in Hollywood when sound arrived, were all given star treatment in *Stardust and Shadows*, along with fifteen more Canadians who played major roles from the very beginnings of the industry in New York to the arrival of sound in Hollywood.

One more thing before we get around to talking about *Once Upon A Time In Paradise*. Were you aware that in the second, third, and fourth years of the Academy Awards three Canadians won the Best Actress Oscar (even if it wasn't called an Oscar until the third year of the ceremonies)?

Mary Pickford was named best actress in 1928–29 for her role in *Coquette*, her first sound film. The film was made by United Artists, the company she, along with her husband, Douglas Fairbanks, and comic genius Charlie Chaplin, controlled.

Norma Shearer was nominated twice at the 1929–30 ceremonies for her performances in *The Divorcée* and *The Love Parade*, both MGM films. *The Divorcée* won her the statuette.

Marie Dressler gave the winning Oscar performance in the 1930–31 awards. For MGM's *Min and Bill* she took home the award that was, for the first time, officially called the Oscar.

The remarkable life stories of Pickford, Shearer, and Dressler were all included in *Stardust and Shadows*.

You will discover in this book that Jack Warner, who found an excuse to not attend the meeting to form the Academy, never got over his hatred of Mayer, but he did later get many Oscars to take home to his studio and was still going strong long after Mayer had been dethroned.

I found at least fifty Canadians worthy of remembering. It was not easy to select the fourteen stars you will find on the pages ahead. Many of the films they made are available on VHS and now on DVD. You may be astonished at some of the things they achieved.

Bobby Breen, a singing star at nine in Hollywood is, at seventy-six, still singing and enjoying a successful career in Florida.

Yvonne de Carlo survived well into the glory days of television, and now and then can be seen making a guest appearance on one of the top dramatic series.

David Manners, a big star in the 1940s, lived until he was ninety-six in 1998. His fame has lasted because of horror films like *Dracula* and *The Mummy*.

I met and spoke to all but one of the Canadians whose stories are told in this book. Berton Churchill died one year before I first set foot in Hollywood, but I found many big stars happy to talk about the achievements of this remarkable actor.

Walter Pidgeon, whom I first met while serving with the British Royal Air Force in the Second World War, remained a friend until he died in 1976.

The personal knowledge I gained directly from these Canadians has been augmented by many years of research on both sides of the Atlantic, in Canada, the United States, and England. I have left out a lot of stories that were nothing more than rumours that could not be substantiated.

Hopefully you will learn from reading this book that we in Canada have a great deal to be proud of in the exploits of these remarkably talented men and women in the film capital of the world.

After my first book was published I was asked by some people why many of the stars and technicians I profiled deserved to be called Canadians, because they left Canada for the United States in their teens or earlier. I anticipate the same question will arise over some of the men and women whose life stories are on these pages.

The answer is very simple. Most of the stars were proud to be called Canadians because Canada was the land that provided refuge to their parents from wartorn countries where there were no opportunities and little hope of living an acceptable standard of life. They may have left Canada in their teens, or even younger, but those whose parents found refuge here loved Canada for what our country did for their families.

Please enjoy my memories. They were written because every Canadian in the book did many things to make Canadians proud of them.

Charles Foster, 2003

Ben Blue

Charlie Chaplin told a Los Angeles newspaper in 1948 that he hated Ben Blue more than he had ever hated any other man.

But Lou Costello, the funny man of the superb comedy team of Abbott and Costello, said he adored Ben Blue and wished he had just a few of his talents.

Frank Sinatra said he looked forward to working with Ben Blue. "He is the only man I know who can do the same act with dialogue or in mime and still be excruciatingly funny."

That unique ability came to Blue when he was working in vaudeville. One night he suffered from laryngitis and couldn't speak. "So I did my entire act in mime," he said. "They loved it so next day I changed my act to half stand up comedy the other half mime."

Blue officially died on March 8, 1975. But this wasn't his first time dying. The *New York Daily News* announced his death in their edition of February 6, 1958.

After his obituary was printed in 1958, about a dozen stars, led by Judy Garland, Gene Kelly, Fred Astaire, Red Skelton, June Allyson, and Jimmy Durante, purchased the largest birth notice ever printed in the *Daily News*. Almost half a page, it announced the arrival of a new comic, the reincarnation of Ben Blue, who would, said the stars, take over the deceased Ben Blue's life and career.

In the 1970s Red Skelton recalled the incident. "The *Daily News* at first refused to accept the advertisement, but we had every studio notify the paper that if they insisted on rejecting the ad they would instruct their advertising companies to place no more film ads in the *Daily News*. The paper executives quickly changed their minds!"

Controversy of this kind swirled around comedian Ben Blue throughout his fifty-eight years in show business.

Blue was born Benjamin Bernstein in Montreal, Quebec, on September 12, 1901. "My parents told me I was laughing when I was born," he once said. "Since it pleased them then I guess I just took naturally to being a funny man."

He never did become the box-office star that many predicted, but in most of the twenty-six feature films he made in Hollywood it was usually Blue the audiences remembered as they laughed their way out of the world's theatres.

Why did Charlie Chaplin hate him? In 1956, in London, he explained:

> My hatred was rather tongue-in-cheek. I hated him because he was funnier than me. He could do every trick in the book, create every expression known to man, and the only time we ever appeared together in public he got the last laugh. I stole more than a few ideas from him during my career.
>
> I would have loved to have Ben Blue under contract, to appear in every film I made, but I was scared that the picture would no longer be a Charlie Chaplin comedy but a Ben Blue comedy. It's disgraceful that he never did become a big star.

Blue, very much alive in Hollywood in 1956, laughed when told of Chaplin's confession. "Now my life is complete. This is the first time Chaplin has admitted that he didn't devise every gag he used himself. But me funnier than Chaplin? That's the funniest thing I have ever heard."

Lou Costello watched Ben Blue in one film and had a clause put in all his contracts that Blue must never be given a part in an Abbott and Costello comedy.

"The man is brilliant," said Costello. "He didn't need a straight man, he was both feed and comic rolled into one. If I was asked to name the best comic in the film industry in the forties I would say Ben Blue without hesitation."

So why was Ben Blue never a star?

Judy Garland, with whom he appeared in *For Me And My Gal*, is on record as saying, after she read of Ben Blue's supposed death in 1958:

> I have always loved comedy, but nobody at MGM could see me doing a comedy routine. Ben Blue, who I

adored, tried to convince Louie Mayer that he and I would make a perfect team, but Mayer vetoed the idea that Ben presented to him.

The great asset of Ben Blue is that everyone improves their own performance when working with him. He was so easy to team up with that I have to believe that he was never, to my knowledge, given starring roles because producers liked what he did to other actors who he supported. He will be sorely missed in our industry. Given the right lead role at the right time in the late 30s and 40s he should have been a major star today.

His father, D.A. Bernstein, a lifelong resident of Montreal, was known internationally as a renowned expert on antique furniture. As a child, growing up in the antiquated world of his father, Blue gained a vast knowledge of the world's finest furnishings. His father said, "[Benjamin] contradicted me when he was only seven when I declared a specific table to be from such and such a year. He said, 'No dad, those legs were not in fashion for at least two more years.' He was right, I had blundered, but I was grateful some of my knowledge was rubbing off on him. It looked certain that Benjamin would be following in my footsteps in the world of antiques."

But Benjamin didn't. At eight he won a contest in a Montreal theatre as a stand-up comic. "He was hooked," said his father to the *New York Times* in 1919. "The only legs he looked at after his Montreal debut were the legs of chorus girls. Antiques were definitely out."

By the time he was fifteen, Benjamin Bernstein had appeared in dozens of musical shows, dramas, and comedies presented by amateur companies in the Montreal area. He had also tried out for several professional shows that rehearsed and had their pre-Broadway runs in Montreal. They all thought him too young, despite agreeing that he had considerable talents as a comedian. He later recalled:

The first real interest came when George M. Cohan came to town with his new Broadway-bound revue. I walked into Mr. Cohan's dressing room after fooling the

stage doorkeeper that I had been hired to sweep the
stage after rehearsals. I told Mr. Cohan that I could
dance as well as anyone in Canada and wanted a part in
his show. He asked me to demonstrate so I did a few of
my own original steps. "You are hired," said Mr. Cohan.
"Your salary will be fifteen dollars a week and until we
reach Broadway your rooms and food and travel will be
paid by me. After that you are on your own. You'll have
to find your own place to live, and if I were you I'd brush
up on my cooking skills. You won't be able to afford
many meals in restaurants in New York. Bring your parents to the theatre in the morning. They'll have to co-
sign your contract." My parents were a little hesitant at
the idea of me travelling with a theatrical company
when I was only fifteen, but Mr. Cohan charmed them
into agreeing to let me go on tour and then to New York.

He joined a talented group of dancers and a choreographer with
considerable Broadway experience who admitted he had never seen
some of the steps that Benjamin Bernstein displayed.
Blue recalled:

The choreographer called me on one side at the lunch
break on my first day and asked where I had learned my
unusual steps. I decided to be honest and tell him the
truth that I had never had a dancing lesson in my life, that
I had just created some steps that came naturally to me.

At first he considered taking me to Mr. Cohan to be
fired, then he smiled and asked me if he allowed me to
stay would I teach him a few of the steps I had demon-
strated. That night we remained in the theatre after
official rehearsals had ended, and after three hours I
had him chuckling with glee as he mastered more and
more of my steps that were unique.

Next day Mr. Cohan was on stage when we were
rehearsing. He watched for a while and took the chore-

ographer on one side. We could all hear him say clearly. "This is brilliant. Those are great steps, completely original. I want you to teach me a few of them."

And so, at fifteen, in my first show, I had not only taught the choreographer how to dance but the great George M. was also using the steps I had invented. I let the choreographer take all the credit. It was enough that I was in the show. At fifteen I was headed for Broadway.

In New York Benjamin Bernstein attended as many matinees of other shows as he could. He said:

In those days different productions had afternoon shows on every day of the week, and when we didn't have a show ourselves I headed for the nearest theatre that did.

Performers of that era, even the most unimportant like me, had business cards printed that listed the show they were in. Dozens lined up with these cards at theatres for matinees for it was an unwritten rule of the theatre that any performer requesting admission be given any unsold seat in the house at no cost.

I saw more than thirty shows while the Cohan Revue was on Broadway, and the seats never cost me a cent.

One of those theatres was the New York Palace. "Vaudeville was at its height and everyone on the national vaudeville circuit hoped one day they'd play the Palace," he said. "Seeing the great acts on that wonderful stage spurred me to dream that one day I would not only play the Palace but that I would be top of the bill."

His dream of fame made him change his name from Bernstein to Blue. "I looked at the Palace marquee and suddenly realized that Benjamin Bernstein wouldn't fit in the area reserved for bill toppers," he said. "I counted the letters and discovered that the maximum being used was fourteen letters. It was easy reducing Benjamin to Ben but what about a second name. The names of the headliners were always in blue. So I became Ben Blue, just like that."

When he was seventeen, with no immediate prospects of another show, he approached the aging owner of a dancing school in New York that was just about to close its doors. "I convinced the lady that I could put the school back on its feet in less than three months if she would give me half the profits for the next three years," he said. "Though I had no training I knew I could teach the students how to dance much better than the existing teachers."

Blue coined the school's new slogan, "Walk In and Dance Out." Within a month he was earning more than $400 a week. The owner, who had promised him big things, now demanded that he quit the job. "You're earning far too much money," she said.

Blue recalled, "When her 225-pound brother, a wrestler, came to see me, I didn't argue anymore, I got out. I went out on a vaudeville tour and was delighted, when I returned to New York to hear the school had gone bankrupt."

Years later, when he was top of the bill at the Palace Theatre in New York, Blue introduced a skate-less skating act that brought howls of laughter from audiences everywhere. His glided around the stage on shoes that allowed him to move across the wooden floor as though it were ice. He always refused to tell other performers what he smeared on the soles of his shoes to simulate the actions of ice skating, and when he died the secret died with him.

The skating act became so popular that he was invited to make a six-month tour of England, France, and Italy. "I even had the King of England in to see my show one night in London," he recalled. "I saw him laughing and was very honoured when he came backstage to meet me."

Over the years that followed, Ben Blue the vaudevillian, with his sad face, rubber limbs, deadpan mime, original dance steps, and brilliantly timed comedy routines, topped the bill at New York's Palace Theatre twenty-four times, more than any other performer on record.

He played in major Broadway stage musicals, including the famed *George White Scandals*, a popular revue that the producer changed each year. It was there he met his future wife, a dancer in the show. Axie Dunlap and Ben Blue were still happily married when Blue died in 1975.

Axie Dunlap worked with him in his nightclub and vaudeville acts, and she played many roles in the early comedy films with Blue before retiring to raise their two sons, Tom and Robert.

Often Blue's tours as a vaudeville performer took him to the West Coast and Los Angeles. In 1926, while appearing in Los Angeles, he was approached by Hal Roach, then one of the comedy kings in Hollywood. Roach had found many stars, like Laurel and Hardy and the youthful performers in the Our Gang comedies. Blue recalled:

> He told me there was a future for me in the movies ... It was the end of my tour so I decided to see what he had to offer. If it didn't work out there were plenty of night-clubs in Los Angeles so I figured it was time Axie and I put down our roots in California.
>
> I made about a dozen one-reel films for Roach before Jack Warner of the Warner Brothers studio waved at me from his car as I was leaving the studio one day. He asked if I would meet him next day for what he called "a lucrative discussion."

At Warner's studio Ben Blue became a popular comedy man in dozens of short one- and two-reel comedies. "But I wanted more," he said.

> Sound films had arrived and suddenly I found myself doing comedy routines with more than just mime. Lots of lines, and my voice recorded well.
>
> But I had agreed to go out on a three-month vaude-ville tour with George Burns and Gracie Allen. When we returned to Los Angeles, late in 1934, George Burns drove me over to Paramount Studios, where he was scheduled to start a new film. I owe my entire career to George and Gracie. They convinced Paramount that I should be given a role in a new film scheduled to start shooting in two weeks.

College Rhythm wasn't a major film, but it got me a lot of attention. Paramount liked what I did and signed me to a long-term contract.

Memorable films he made with Paramount included *Turn Off The Moon, Top Of The Town, High, Wide and Handsome, Artists and Models, Thrill of a Lifetime, The Big Broadcast of 1938, Paris Honeymoon,* and *Coconut Grove.*

Blue remembered:

A representative of Metro-Goldwyn-Mayer rang the doorbell one night at my apartment when I was being pestered by Paramount to sign an extension to my contract. He asked when my next day free came around, and said before I re-signed with Paramount, I would be wise to visit Metro-Goldwyn-Mayer studios to see Louis B. Mayer. Now I'd been in some pretty big company by that time. Stars like W.C. Fields and Dorothy Lamour were now my personal friends, Jack Benny was a regular visitor for lunch, but Louis B. Mayer. I never thought in my wildest dreams that he would ask to meet me.

"I'm not too sure they always came to see Ben," said his wife Axie. "Even though I say it myself I'm one of the best cooks in California." That was a statement that Blue remembered with delight much further down the road in his career.

Two days later Ben Blue was standing in the secretary's office outside Louis Mayer's office. "I was actually shaking. Somehow I sensed that if I could convince Mayer to put me under contract I'd be set for life," he said. "Well, I did satisfy him, although he never cracked a smile when I dropped in bits of my facial expressions and moves that made audiences howl with laughter, but he put a contract in front of me and asked me to sign for five years. I didn't even read it, I just signed, and I was right, it was the best thing that could ever have happened to me."

With his Paramount contract due to expire in two more months, Blue spent all his spare time at MGM meeting the producers, directors, and stars. "As a Canadian I was excited when Mayer told me he was from Saint John, New Brunswick, that the studio's most successful producer, his nephew, Jack Cummings, was also from New Brunswick, Canada, and the studio's biggest star, Norma Shearer and her brother Douglas, of major importance in the creation of sound films, were both from Montreal," he recalled. "It was a little like going home!"

His first film at MGM was *Panama Hattie* with Red Skelton and Ann Southern. Both stars became his friends for life. Red Skelton talked about that friendship in 1975 when Ben Blue died:

> He was one the few genuine people in the film industry in Hollywood. If he told you he would do something, he did it, even if he had to go to a lot of expense to fulfill that promise. I don't believe Ben ever told a lie in his entire life. He and I spent hours just throwing lines back and forth between us. If anyone was listening they were soon doubling up with laughter. I shall miss him. Many other stars and the little people at the studio, in the cafeterias and set builders, will miss him.

"Judy Garland asked for me to be in *For Me And My Gal* with her and Gene Kelly," said Blue in 1967. "I'd seen Judy at the studio and remember once making her laugh loudly at an expression I made to her in the studio commissary. Other actors told me it was the first time in months the depressed Judy had smiled in public. The way they treated that girl I don't know how she survived. They popped pills in her mouth half-a-dozen times a day."

MGM gave Ben Blue some great supporting roles. "I worked with Kathryn Grayson, Gloria de Haven, Van Johnson, June Allyson, Jimmy Durante and Lucille Ball," he recalled. "It was a little like reaching heaven without having to die to get there. I heard that Jack Cummings had demanded that I be in all his musicals. Finally I was in the big time."

In *Thousands Cheer* he got rave reviews from critics who only mentioned Kathryn Grayson and Gene Kelly after they had finished their applause for Ben Blue.

The same thing happened in *Two Girls and A Sailor*. Although he was never given star billing he received star treatment from the news media over the name stars of the film, Van Johnson, June Allyson, and even Jimmy Durante.

"Durante was like a father to me," he said. "He asked for an extra scene with me that was the hit of the movie."

But still Blue couldn't get star billing on any of the films. Louis B. Mayer told Hollywood columnist Hedda Hopper that Blue was more use where he was. "He has such a superb approach to every scene that his mere presence makes everyone else in the film work harder to handle his brilliance."

There was lots of time to spare between films, and Blue, with his new exposure to filmgoers raising his vaudeville salary sky-high, took every opportunity to go back to the stage circuit. Nightclubs in the Hollywood area paid him immense money to make personal appearances. "I recall getting $10,000 a week at one of the biggest clubs," he said.

> I had discovered that what the vaudeville audiences wanted was nothing like the sophistication the night-club audience demanded. So I devised two completely different routines and often the theatre managers across the country where I was appearing would encourage local club owners to book me in for late shows after the theatre was closed. They found those club goers came to the theatre next day and were quite astounded when they saw a very different type of Ben Blue.
>
> I made great money and was able to buy a lovely fourteen-room home at 917 Roxbury Drive in Beverly Hills. I actually went to the bank and paid for the house in cash. Even then a lot of realtors didn't trust actors enough to accept a cheque. Beverly Hills was the place to be then as it is now and I felt I'd moved up in the world. One of my neighbours was Jimmy Durante. Would you believe his house was smaller than mine.

"But I still wasn't a star," he said in 1962, "and for the life of me I couldn't figure out what I had to do to become one."

In 1944 Louis Mayer offered Blue to the Hollywood Victory Committee to travel overseas to entertain servicemen and women:

> I went to Africa, free China, India and Burma with Ann Sheridan, Mary Lande, Ruth Denas and Jackie Miles. You can't begin to imagine the thrill I got when I heard the applause from those GIs so far from home. Of course they all wanted to get as close as they could to gorgeous Ann Sheridan, but more than anything they wanted to find a reason to laugh. I was out there more than six months. We appeared during rainstorms and not one of the thousands of GIs, soaked to the skin, left the open-air arenas. Sometimes after the shows I talked for several hours to the men and women. I must have signed about twenty thousand autographs on scraps of paper, shirts, hats, anything they had that would take a signature. I also did my act to audiences of perhaps two dozen people or less in the field hospitals that had sprung up everywhere. To see them smile was wonderful.
>
> In the mid-thirties it was obvious people had noticed me. Letters started coming in dozens every day. Axie was kept busy answering the mail that by 1937 had reached close to four hundred letters a week. It cost us a fortune sending out autographed pictures, but it was worthwhile. People started to talk about me and I knew we had done the right thing settling in Hollywood.

He proudly claimed to any newsman who would listen that the most important find of his life was discovering that dozens of people in Hollywood, including Mary Pickford, Louie Mayer, Jack Warner, and others, were, like himself, born in Canada. "It gave me a warm feeling in my heart. I started a Canadian club in my home and many young actors came to visit and got their first taste of the real Hollywood. When my mother and father came to visit me in Hollywood," he recalled, "I was able to introduce them to every Canadian in the city and Mary Pickford threw a party in their honour at her beautiful mansion, Pickfair, on Summit Drive in Beverly Hills. That was their first realization that I'd made it in the entertainment industry."

One of Ben Blue's favourite comedy spots was a devastating impersonation of Charlie Chaplin. On three occasions Chaplin sued to stop him performing his routine. "On the first occasion I accompanied my lawyers to court," said Chaplin. "But that was enough. I didn't attend any future sessions. Ben Blue arrived in makeup and did an impromptu Chaplin routine for the judge who laughed loudly at it. Then he looked at me in my perfectly tailored suit, silk shirt and tie, without my moustache. 'I'm not sure,' said the judge, 'who is suing who.'"

Chaplin won his case, but Blue ignored the court injunction and continued his comedy impersonation. Chaplin sued twice more, winning both cases, but Ben Blue ignored those court orders too. Finally one judge said, "Enough. This is wasting the court's time. They're making us look like fools in the newspapers." He blocked Chaplin's fourth attempt in court. "I never did try again," said Chaplin. "Ben Blue lost the cases but won the audience."

But Blue loved the lawsuits. "They're great," he said. "I get more free publicity every time he sends his lawyers to court. I was front page in the newspapers just at the time I had opened my new Ben Blue's night club in Santa Monica and the crowds rolled in every night to cheer and laugh at my impersonation."

Chaplin admitted he went to one of the nightclub shows. "Without my moustache nobody recognized me. I cringed in my seat at his beautiful imitation. I can tell you now," he said in 1956, "that I picked up one or two ideas from Ben Blue's show. If he is still alive, I hope he won't sue me now!"

"Chaplin picked up comedy bits from me," said Blue when told of Chaplin's statement. "That's incredible. The man was a genius. If he picked up anything from me it was probably his own comedy that I had stolen from him years earlier. Chaplin was and is the greatest comedian the world has ever known."

But Blue's comedic abilities never did translate into the business world. He opened dancing schools in St. Paul, Minnesota; Chicago, Illinois; and Dallas, Texas. Because it was impossible for him to be at the schools in person more than once or twice a year, they failed, costing him almost half a million dollars.

In 1943, when he returned to the United States after his tour of U.S. Army bases, he bumped into Sammy Lewis, owner of the famous Slapsy Maxie's nightclub in Hollywood. The club had just closed its doors because it couldn't get enough stars to appear on its stage at salaries the club could afford.

"I told him to open up again and I'd appear there for as long as he wanted," said Blue. "The deal was simple. I was to get twenty-five percent of the gross take at the club. The first week Sammy took in $3,000 and I waited for my $750 in vain. Sammy had so many debts he could only give me $300."

So Blue approached the club owner with another deal. "For $1,000, which I would pay him immediately, I would get fifty percent of the club take. But even when the money reached $5,000 Sammy could still only pay me $300. I'd been conned into giving him $1,000 and all I got in return was the $300 that I was getting before I invested."

Blue refused to give up. "The audiences were big, they loved my act so I convinced Sammy to move the club to 5665 Wilshire Boulevard. We leased the premises for $1,000 a month with an option to buy after 10 years. It was a big club, biggest in Hollywood. Our gross receipts jumped to $36,000 a week."

But Blue never got more than $5,000 a week. The club flourished, but a major problem put him deep in debt.

"I was a gambler," he said. "I started betting on boxing, that was an obvious first step since Slapsy Maxie's was named after Slapsy Maxie Rosenbloom, a great boxer. Then I started going to the track and often I had lost my $5,000 before I even got it."

The club closed its doors in 1947. "When the war ended there wasn't the same need for entertainment. Returning GIs were more concerned with buying homes and getting married," he recalled. "So I swore off gambling and returned to the movies. *My Wild Irish Rose* was my first big film at Warners. It had Dennis Morgan and Arlene Dahl as its stars but my name was in quite large type too. It wasn't expected to be a big hit but, if I say it myself, audiences loved me and the film was a box-office bonanza."

But Ben Blue never forgot the memories of his father's success and knowledge in the antique world. He had furnished his Roxbury Drive home in quality antiques. "So many that we fell over them walking around the house," he said.

He opened an antique shop in Hollywood and found most of the stars he had worked with in films soon became his best customers. "I was honest with them all," he said, "no inflated prices and no phoney pieces. The store, in which I served each customer myself became a huge success and once again I had money to burn."

In 1948, after making a second successful film at Warners, *One Sunday Afternoon,* again with Dennis Morgan, he accepted a one-year contract to play the music halls and the vaudeville theatres of Australia, New Zealand, and England. The tour was a major success both artistically and financially. "I loved working to a live audience," he said. "But something else was looming on the horizon that took over my life for the next ten years."

The "something else" was television. "All the shows were done live in those days," he recalled. "If we didn't have an audience it felt like we had. Stage hands laughed out loud. And producers quickly realized that the television viewers liked the sound of laughter and so we were able to do our shows in old theatres with an audience."

In 1950, Frank Sinatra, a major star on records and in movies, agreed to make his first weekly TV series. "I wouldn't sign the deal until the producers guaranteed that they would put Ben Blue on the payroll," said Sinatra in 1958. "I knew that if things went wrong on the live show I could count on Ben to get us out of any difficulty that might arise."

The Sinatra television show ran for two years. Blue's reputation soared as more and more people bought television sets. "The money was good, Sinatra was extremely easy to get along with and we became good friends. He was right, I often had to improvise a few things when the show ran too short or when a piece of scenery fell down unexpectedly. It was like vaudeville's reincarnation. Those were good days in the television industry."

When Benny Goodman signed for television with his Sextet, he too demanded Ben Blue as the comedy man of the show. "I saw what happened to Frank [Sinatra]," said Goodman. "Ben was the standby bucket you put under the sink when the pipe leaks. He never missed an opportunity to get in the picture. Sometimes I think he pushed the scenery over so he could ad lib."

So many stars asked for Blue that on several occasions he did two live shows in one evening. "I remember once when they changed the time of rehearsals so I could run from one studio to another to appear live in the *Colgate Comedy Hour* and the *All-Star Revue* the same night," he said. "It was a lot of fun and though I had passed my fiftieth birthday I was fit enough to give all the energy the work required."

In 1957 Ben Blue prepared to get back into the nightclub world. He bought a large building at 2210 Wilshire Boulevard in the heart of Santa Monica. "Half-a-million-dollars refurbishing made the property into a beautiful new nightclub which I called Ben Blue's Nightclub," he said. "People had been stopping me on the street for years asking for my autograph or just to chat. I'd made friends from Broadway, vaudeville, nightclubs, movies and now television so I figured I had enough friends to fill the club six nights a week. I hadn't put on much weight. I think I looked twenty years younger than fifty-six, my real age."

Blue was right. In the five years it remained open more than half a million patrons attended his comedy show. It became known as the place to go at night. He recalled, "All the stars I had worked with came down to see the show and audiences could usually count on seeing at least one big star there every night. I remember one Saturday night in 1958 when Jimmy Stewart and his wife, Frank Sinatra and his wife, Gene Kelly and his wife were all in the club." He added, "And you know something, not one of those stars ever asked for special seating or for free meals and drinks. I was thrilled that they had come along as friends and felt the show I gave them was worth paying for."

But in 1962 the strain of creating new shows every week took its toll on Ben Blue. He announced he was closing the club forever.

That last night scalpers were selling reservations for as much as $1,000 at the doors. Judy Garland, Red Skelton,

Gene Kelly, Fred Astaire, Peter Lawford Jimmy Durante, Dorothy Lamour, Lucille Ball and Kathryn Grayson were all present. The show, usually ran about two hours, but on this last night it ran almost four. I gave them everything I had got some I didn't even know I'd got. All those stars I just mentioned joined me on stage for the finale. We sang "There's No Business Like Showbusiness," and most of them were in tears. I know I was.

For several years Blue shunned the movie studios in favour of television and personal appearances in the clubs of Las Vegas and Reno.

"I also learned how to play golf," he said. "Once I had mastered the basics I played with some of the best. My partners were people like Bing Crosby and Oliver Hardy."

In 1963 he received a terrible shock. "The tax man claimed I owed nearly $300,000 from the Santa Monica club operation," he said. "My

Ben Blue had the unique ability to perform his stage act in two different ways: one with dialogue, the other completely in mime. How this happened is a remarkable tale.

accountant had let me down badly. A U.S. district court agreed with the tax people and my accountant had left town probably with some of the money. The court authorized the government men to take up to $300,000 of my assets. I had to sell $100,000 of my antiques in the house to meet the demand."

But the judge who found him guilty of tax evasion showed a touch of humanity. "I will fine you only $1,000," he said, "and because of the good things you have done and the laughter you have given the world I will suspend payment of the fine indefinitely. I can do nothing about the assets you must forfeit but I only hope the government will use discretion in its demands from you."

"They did," said Blue in 1971. "I was able to raise the money and they gave me time provided I would sign over a large chunk of my earnings every time I played in Vegas."

In 1963 Ben Blue returned to the film industry that had made him a star on television, in Las Vegas, and on Broadway at the Palace Theatre. Producers remembered him when the all-comedy film *It's a Mad, Mad, Mad World* was being planned. Sid Caesar was to be the star, along with Ethel Merman and Mickey Rooney. Once again Ben Blue was chosen to be a supporting performer.

"But it was my spot, a classic routine, a running gag, throughout the film, of a man trying to catch a horse but always failing, that people remembered," he said.

Ben Blue never lost a single day's work. It was his proud boast that in more than fifty years of performing he never missed a show through illness or any other reason.

In 1966, Canadian director Norman Jewison chose him to appear in *The Russians Are Coming, The Russians Are Coming.* For the first time Blue got equal billing with comics like Jonathan Winters, Carl Reiner, Joey Bishop, and Art Carney. Once again his performance was chosen by critics as memorable in a film that had few highlights.

Three more films followed in 1967. In *A Guide For A Married Man* he appeared with Lucille Ball and Walter Mathau. His old friend Gene Kelly directed. In 1975, when Blue died, Ball said that both she and Gene

Kelly had told the producers that they wanted Ben Blue in the movie. "I believe Gene actually said he would not direct unless Ben was included in the casting."

For the first time in almost thirty years Ben Blue returned to Paramount to make *The Busy Body* with Sid Caesar, Anne Baxter, and Jan Murray. A huge sign was hung on the front gates of Paramount Studios to await Blue's arrival. More than two hundred studio personnel gathered around to cheer him on the first day of shooting. The sign read, "Where have you been all these years Ben?"

One more film, *Where Were You When The Lights Went Out*, followed. Ben Blue joined Doris Day, Robert Morse, Steve Allen, and Jim Backus at MGM before officially announcing that he was calling it a day. "But if all the days are as gorgeous as Doris," he said, "I may have to rethink that decision." When his comment was printed, Doris Day arrived at his front door with a huge bunch of roses. Ben, who opened the door, was shocked. "Thanks" was about all he could muster. Doris had the last laugh. "They're not for you Ben," she said. "They're for Axie who will have to put up with you every day from now on."

After retirement he returned to his home on Roxbury Drive, all his debts were paid, and he had money in the bank.

"All I'm going to do now is relax and play golf," he said. One of the rare Hollywood personalities to have his number in the Beverly Hills telephone book, he talked at length to whoever called, and if tourists rang the doorbell he usually invited them in for a cup of tea or coffee.

The stars he had worked with through the years often dropped in for a chat. "But, sadly," he said, "the number dwindled as they died one by one,"

On January 1, 1975, he spoke at length to a newspaper writer who called to ask him what his resolutions were for the year ahead. "I have plans to play golf until March," he said. "I got an eighty-one last week. That's the only thing I've ever taken seriously in my entire life. If I break eighty I may give golf up as well."

"I'll call you sometime in March," said the writer, "to see if you made the seventy-nine."

Ben Blue never received the call. On March 8, 1975, he lay down for a rest after lunch and never again awakened.

Red Skelton told the *Hollywood Reporter*, "One of the greatest funny men of this century has gone on to better things. I don't know if there is vaudeville up there in heaven, but if there is, Ben Blue will be a star there just as he was on earth to all those who had the good fortune to know him and work with him on this earth."

Ben Blue said he had only one regret in his life. "I see all my friends the stars with their names on the Hollywood Walk of Fame. I never did receive that great honour although Lassie and Rin-Tin-Tin made it. But then, I never really was a star, was I?"

Bobby Breen

Good Wishes
Bobby Breen

At seventy-six, Bobby Breen, who was a major singing star in Hollywood sixty-six years ago, looks back on his past with pride. Today he is far from being retired, and he is still an in-demand entertainer looking ahead to a long-term future filled with music.

At four he was singing professionally at the Silver Slipper Club in Toronto. At nine he was in Hollywood making the first of the ten films that made him into a superstar in the golden years of the film industry.

Bobby Breen was born Robert Borsuk on November 4, 1927, in Montreal, Quebec. Before he was two, his parents, refugees from the revolution in Russia, moved to Toronto, where his father, Hyman, and mother, Rebecca, ran a confectionery store at the corner of Bathurst and Dundas Streets. The family lived in three rooms above the store.

"It wasn't easy for them," he said recently.

> There was a great deal of anti-Semitism in Canada at that time and refugees from countries in Europe were treated with suspicion, even hostility. They had tough times. I still remember one occasion when the police came to the store when someone falsely accused them of selling cigarettes. But they persevered and made a remarkable success out of their lives and in doing so gave me, and my brother and sisters, a chance to achieve our own goals.

Bobby was one of four children given life by the Borsuks. Three were born in Kiev, Russia. Gertrude, born in 1911, Michael, 1913, and Sally, 1918, came to Canada in 1927 with their parents, who felt the growing country would give them opportunities they could never have in Russia.

Both Hyman and Rebecca loved music, and this love of the classics and the popular music of the era rubbed off on the four children. "There was always music around us in the home," said Bobby.

Gertrude was a competent singer, but chose not to enter the entertainment world. Michael, at one time the youngest cantor in the temples of North America, became a professional singer, touring the theatres and concert halls of Canada and the United States.

The Borsuks expected Sally would become the musical star of the family. Blessed with a superb voice, she planned to make a career for herself as a singer. When Bobby was born in 1927, she had, at nine, already won acclaim in the Toronto musical world.

Theatres in Canada at that time held weekly talent shows, and Sally, who entered every contest she could find, regularly brought home first-, second-, and third-place awards, usually winning monetary prizes ranging from five to ten dollars, which helped pay for her music lessons.

In 1931, when Bobby was only four, he accompanied Sally to one of the weekly contests. A shortage of participants that particular week led Sally to suggest to the contest presenters that Bobby be allowed to enter. The organizers had doubts about letting anyone as young as four enter, but finally agreed.

That night Bobby Borsuk received his first standing ovation. Unaccompanied by the theatre pianist, since he had brought no music with him, he enchanted the audience, won first prize, and an illustrious career had begun.

Over the months that followed, Sally, previously a regular first-place winner, never complained when she was pushed into second place by her four-year-old brother.

In 1936 she is on record as saying:

> I was only thirteen and considered myself a good singer, but it was obvious to me that my talent paled beside that of Bobby. I went to see the manager of the Silver Slipper Club in Toronto and somehow convinced him to come to a Toronto theatre the following Saturday to hear Bobby sing. A week later his name was in lights outside the Silver Slipper Club. Dad had to get a special permit to allow him to appear. It stipulated that he had to be out of the club before nine o'clock and that a chaperone must be with him at all times. I don't think they realized I was only thirteen when they agreed that I would be allowed to be his chaperone.

The Silver Slipper Club management reported to the *Toronto Globe* that they were getting the biggest early evening crowds in the club's history, for nobody wanted to miss young Bobby Borsuk's performance. Long before he was scheduled to appear they said it was standing room only at the club.

At four, accompanied by the Silver Slipper Club band, Bobby Borsuk made his radio debut. This led to a two-year engagement at the famous Savarin Restaurant in Toronto.

"I was there until I was seven," he recalled recently. "I can still hear the applause from the people who filled the restaurant every night." Once again his parents had to get a special permit to allow him to sing in the restaurant. Once again Sally, now sixteen, was permitted to be his "adult" guardian each night.

Sally, by now, was ready to give up her own hopes of stardom. Convinced that Bobby would become a much bigger star than she had ever dreamed of for her own future, she devoted all her time to promoting his singing career.

"She got a job singing and dancing in the chorus of a musical show playing in Toronto, and this money, together with what I was earning, enabled me to get the best vocal coaches available in the city," he said.

When Bobby was eight and Sally seventeen, she convinced her parents to allow her to take Bobby to Chicago, where she felt there would be more opportunities to enhance the young singer's professional career. Bobby said:

> It succeeded beyond all our wildest hopes. She got me
> an audition with the manager of the Oriental Theatre
> in Chicago, and I was given a two-week booking at that
> famous theatre. It was there I met my first big film star.
> Gloria Swanson was making a personal appearance to
> introduce her latest film, which was being premiered at
> the Oriental. Sound films had revolutionized the
> motion picture industry, but audiences still clamoured
> for the live shows that were presented usually before the
> feature film.

Bobby Breen with his sister Sally, whom he credits with making his
Hollywood career so successful.

Gloria Swanson is on record as saying, "He is the most outstanding
child singer I have ever heard, he should be in Hollywood."

But Hollywood was still more than a year away. With the money
they had saved and that earned in Chicago, plus a letter from the
Oriental Theatre manager to Boris Morros, the musical director for
Paramount Theatres and one of New York's most important managers,
they stepped aboard a train for New York City.

"Sally found a two-room apartment that was cheap and close enough
to downtown so we could walk to the places where she hoped I would find
work. That way we saved on trolley-car fares," recalled Bobby. He went on:

> Despite the letter of introduction from Chicago it was
> two weeks before we were able to get Boris Morros to
> hear me singing. Sally and I sat in his outer office day
> after day, but he walked right past and ignored us. But
> one day he stopped and called us into his office. He did-
> n't even let me finish my first song, 'Boulevard of

Broken Dreams,' before telling Sally he would give me a
two-week contract at the showplace of the Paramount
Theatres in New York City.

Bobby Borsuk never did meet Boris Morros again, but he recalled
reading after the Second World War that Morros was revealed as a major
spy working for the Russian government, seeking information about
Hitler and Germany. He is said to have used some of the performers and
talent scouts he sent to Europe to gather secret information. "Good
thing I was too young to travel abroad," said Bobby.

Sally worked at many jobs to keep the wolf from the door. "Even at
sixteen she was a cocktail waitress in night clubs," he recalled.

With a little money in hand, Sally enrolled Bobby in the
Professional Children's School in New York. It was a move that opened
another very important door.

Harry Richman, a major Broadway musical star in the 1930s, needed a child actor for his new stage show, *Say When*. He called the school,
and more than forty hopeful stars attended the audition. After listening
to every one of the youngsters, Harry Richman hired the youthful
Bobby Borsuk on the spot.

Before the show opened, Harry Richman told the New York papers
that "Bobby Borsuk is a second Harry Richman, only better."

Unfortunately, the show was one of Richman's few failures on
Broadway, and after only six weeks it closed its doors. But it stayed in the
theatre long enough for one of Harry Richman's co-stars, Bob Hope,
not yet in the film world, to recognize the youthful singer's talents.

"I don't think I had ever heard a voice so clear and beautiful," said
Hope in one of his autobiographies. "His on-stage personality was
delightful. I didn't have much power in those days in the industry so all
I could do was mark his name in my book of future stars."

Eddie Cantor, then in New York hosting one of the most popular
national radio shows of the era, saw Bobby in *Say When* and told Sally
that he too was convinced that Bobby Borsuk was destined to become a
star. "I can't use him in my current show," he said, "but I won't forget
him, you can count on that." Three years later he would keep his word.

In April of 1935, with only a few contacts in Hollywood, Sally, still just seventeen, decided that all the praise Bobby had received in New York suggested California was the place to be to enhance his career.

"We put all our money together and went across to California by train," said Bobby. "Sally's first move was to enrol me with Dr. Mario Marafioti, the vocal coach who had made operatic star Grace Moore into a film star."

Sol Lesser, a major producer at the RKO Studios in Culver City, heard Bobby while he was singing at Marafioti's. "He put me under a long-term contract. I can't recall how much money I got each week, but Sally was content, and that satisfied me. I remember it was enough to bring my mother and father down to California from Canada and we were able to buy a nice home at 345 McCarty Drive in Beverly Hills."

Working in a film studio was a totally new experience for nine-year-old Bobby Borsuk. "Although I must credit Sally with getting me to the top of the musical tree, and I shall be eternally grateful to her for giving up her own career to help me achieve my own goals," he said, "I remember with fondness the Italian-born actor Henry Armetta, the star of my first film, *Let's Sing Again,* for making me feel so at home in my new surroundings that the work became easy and pleasant. He went out of his way to make my first film a pleasure. Thank you Henry, wherever you are!"

Before shooting began, producer Sol Lesser changed Bobby's name from Bobby Borsuk to Bobby Breen. "Although most of the top studio heads like Louis B. Mayer and Jack Warner and most of the top producers were Jewish there was still a lot of anti-Semitism in the United States. Mr. Lesser discussed my name with my parents and Sally and before I knew it I was trying to remember to answer when people called me Bobby Breen."

A few years later Bobby Borsuk changed his name legally in the courts to Bobby Breen. "I had been Bobby Breen for several years so it seemed the sensible thing to do," he said. "I don't think I would answer today if someone called for Bobby Borsuk to stand up and take a bow."

The huge success in 1936 of *Let's Sing Again* brought Eddie Cantor back into his life. That year Cantor signed Breen to a three-year contract to appear each week on his top-rated weekly radio variety show now being aired from Hollywood. "I had one song every week, and parts in skits. I recall meeting Deanna Durbin, then a big star at Universal, but we never did sing together."

Appearances on the Cantor Show and guest spots on the popular Jack Benny radio show, along with the success of *Let's Sing Again*, followed that same year by *Rainbow On The River*, brought Bobby thousands of letters from fans. The entire Borsuk/Breen family spent many hours every week trying to answer the mail and keep up with the demand for autographed photographs.

Fans sent him gifts galore. "The most unusual present I received from a young fan was six live ducks," he recalled. "We loved them and kept them at home for a long time."

For his third film, *Make A Wish*, producer Sol Lesser brought Oscar Strauss, a member of the famous waltz family in Vienna, to Hollywood to write special songs for Bobby. "I remember meeting him," said Bobby. "It was exciting to be honoured by this fine composer."

In 2003, looking back on his four-year Hollywood career, from early 1936 to the end of 1939, Bobby Breen has many pleasant memories.

> Although I was very young I still remember clearly the people who helped make my film career enjoyable. Perhaps the nicest man I ever worked with was superstar Basil Rathbone. He always had time to talk to me. He showed me the way to get the most out of every part I played. Despite his importance he always treated me like an equal. I also enjoyed working with the great film comedian Charlie Ruggles. He too taught me a lot of things that helped make my career successful and the work so easy.

He also credits veteran actress Margaret Hamilton, who played with him in *Breaking the Ice*, with giving him many helpful acting tips. "She was kind and never too busy to help me with my role," he recalled. Margaret Hamilton went on to everlasting fame three years later when she played the Wicked Witch of the West in *The Wizard of Oz* with Judy Garland.

Bobby Breen with Charlie Ruggles in *Breaking the Ice*, one of the
young singer's first films in Hollywood.

The California state government kept a close watch over the careers and
education of the many young performers working in the Hollywood
studios. "I had a tutor on the set and every day I had to study with him
for at least three hours," he recalled. "But it was a great life and I don't
regret one minute of it."

Between films he attended the Third Street School in Los Angeles.
Hyman and Rebecca Borsuk made certain Breen's life was as near normal as possible for a youngster his age. They, and Sally, insisted he be
enrolled in an ordinary school. "It wasn't a great success. Most of the
other children were a little jealous of the fact that at nine I was already
a star. But I tried hard to be an ordinary student and I think eventually

I won over most of the other kids to my side. It wasn't easy," he recalled. "The teachers were very fair with me and I received absolutely no favouritism. I really had a very normal childhood. My parents, and Sally, made sure I was never allowed to get big ideas at so young an age."

When school was out for the summer and he had no films to shoot, Bobby Breen went out on personal appearance tours with Eddie Cantor. "They had to get special permission for me to travel away from California and of course Sally, then still only eighteen, always came along as my chaperone."

He recalled one important date that almost didn't happen:

> I was booked to go into the Radio City Music Hall when I was only ten but New York regulations regarding the appearances on stage of juveniles were very strict. We learned that the only person who could waive the rules was Mayor Fiorello La Guardia.
>
> I was taken along to see the mayor in his palatial office. He was a wonderful man, very kind, and I was told always found time for young people like me. They sat me on his knee for a photograph and then he signed a special waiver allowing me to appear at the Music Hall.
>
> But the problem still wasn't completely solved. At ten, with Mayor La Guardia's approval, I could appear on stage but wouldn't be allowed to sing. It didn't make much sense for me to just stand there so the theatre management came up with a brilliant solution. I recorded my songs with the music hall orchestra on a disc a few days before the show opened. Every night I stood centre stage and just mimed the song. Fortunately the disc didn't stick or skip, as they did so often in those days, and my first non-singing role brought the house down. The audience stood up and cheered. I don't think anyone knew I wasn't actually singing.
>
> This is the first time I have ever told anyone this secret and the fact that I really never did sing on the stage of Radio City Music Hall.

Breen always found time to sign autographs at the film studio, at the radio studio, and at the stage doors of the theatres where he appeared.

"Sally always made sure I stayed there until the last autograph was signed," he said. "There were no troubles in those days. The autograph seekers were polite, no pushing, no shoving. I must have signed many thousands of autographs but I enjoyed meeting every one who had enjoyed my films and live performances."

Bobby Breen sympathizes with today's young stars who need bodyguards to get them from place to place, rarely, if ever, being allowed to stop and sign autographs. "Things are so different now. There are so many people out there today with weird ideas. The stars today need to be protected from people who might be dangerous and the real fans rarely get to meet the people they admire. We had nothing horrible like that when I was in Hollywood or on tour."

In 1942 he teamed with two of the former stars of the Our Gang series, Alfalfa Switzer and Spanky McFarland, in a film called *Johnny Doughboy*. It cast the trio as child stars trying to make a comeback in their teens by forming a troupe to provide entertainment for the armed forces. It wasn't a success and he returned to Beverly Hills High School, where he had enrolled at twelve in 1939.

"Of course everyone knew me, but I was determined to be as normal a student as possible," he recalled. "I must have succeeded because I was chosen by the other students to be president of the school's student council. I really tried all my life to act like a normal person not a star."

For six consecutive years he was the California State Oratorical Champion. "The movie work had given me the confidence I needed and I was proud to be named champion."

After high school Breen attended a military college with the sons of Charlie Chaplin, Charlie Jr. and Sydney. "It taught us discipline and I have used that discipline throughout my career," he said. "Military College was probably the best thing that could have happened to me."

At sixteen he left the military college and was accepted into the University College of Los Angeles. At UCLA he majored in drama and music, successfully graduating before he was nineteen.

Throughout his career he had continued his musical training, and at eighteen he was an accomplished pianist. "I appeared at a lot of concerts as a pianist not a singer," he recalled. "The highlight of my life was an appearance I made as soloist with the Los Angeles Philharmonic. That was a special occasion I'll never forget. To be cheered for something other than my singing was very satisfying."

The Second World War was at its height when he graduated from college, and for a while he decided to put all thoughts of his singing career on hold. "I volunteered to join the United States Army when I was still only eighteen, and producer Josh Logan, then a captain in the U.S. Army, teamed me with Mickey Rooney, Red Buttons, and actor Broderick Crawford," he remembered. "We toured the army camps in England and across Europe. It was an exciting time and although I wasn't in the front lines of the war I think I helped bring a lot of good thoughts from home to those who had been actively in the forefront of the war."

Bobby Breen received a Bronze Star for his military work, and when discharged in 1947 he was still only twenty years old.

After his release from the army he attended the American Academy of Dramatic Arts in New York City. "It was just around the time when television was in its experimental stages," he recalled. "I had the idea at that time of working behind the scenes as a director or cameraman, but I was still singing and that brought me a regular fifteen-minute variety show in New York and later in Cleveland, Ohio. It was a good experience."

In 1948, the front pages of many American newspapers announced that Bobby Breen and the pilot of his small plane were missing from what should have been a routine two-hour flight from Waukesha, Wisconsin, to Hayward, three hundred miles north. His manager reported the plane as being overdue nine hours after the official time he was expected to land in Hayward. He said he had had no word from Breen and his pilot, Kenneth Thompson of Drummond, Wisconsin.

In Beverly Hills, Breen's parents said they were shocked at the news but hoped that the authorities would soon find the plane and the duo would be unhurt.

The story made the national radio newscasts and newspapers for several days before Breen and Thompson called from a small motel in Glidden, Wisconsin, to say they were alive and well. "Our plane was forced down in a field near Glidden," said Breen. "We were almost out of gas and had to hitch a ride to a nearby hunting camp."

The hunting camp had no telephone so Breen and Thompson couldn't immediately notify the authorities that they were safe and unhurt.

"Two days later we were able to move into Glidden and from there we called to say we were OK," said Thompson. "Bobby couldn't get through to his parents in California so he sent a telegram saying there was nothing to worry about."

Wisconsin law enforcement officials were unhappy about the story. Colonel B.J. Moeller, deputy wing commander of the Civil Air Patrol at Milwaukee, said about eighteen private planes took part in the search for the missing plane. "More than 200 people were involved. It cost us about one thousand dollars."

Bobby Breen denounced people who suggested the whole thing was a publicity stunt and that at no time were the two men in danger. He denied the accusation and offered to pay the costs of the search. The story finally died down and no more was heard of the suggestion that Breen and Thompson should be prosecuted for creating a hoax. No charges were ever laid.

Today Bobby Breen recalls the trip as an unfortunate incident. "Neither I or Kenneth Thompson wanted [that] to happen," he stated. "We were able to land, almost out of fuel, in a small field and neither of us was injured. I want to make it quite clear that if the intent had been to create publicity I certainly would have told my parents so they would not have been faced with the news that I might be dead. No, this was no publicity stunt, just a vacation flight that turned very nasty."

Ready to continue his singing career, he found Hollywood had changed dramatically. "Sol Lesser had left RKO and was only working now and then. There was really no place for me in the films of that era."

He looked around and went right to the top. "I contacted the William Morris booking office and told them I was preparing an act for theatres and nightclubs. There were plenty of theatres playing vaudeville and hundreds of night clubs, that had sprung up everywhere during the war, in every city, large and small."

The William Morris office was enthusiastic, and Breen's singing career began again. "The audiences were often people around my own age who remembered the films I had made as a kid and were more than ready to accept my new adult program."

In 1952 he met and married his first wife, the former Jocelyn Lash, a New York model. In 1958 the marriage ended in divorce. Jocelyn and their son, Keith, went out of his life. "A lot of things were said on both sides that I don't look back on now with any pride," he said. "It was not a friendly divorce, Jocelyn didn't say the nicest things about me, but for quite a number of years now I have been in touch with Keith at his home in New York City. We keep in contact through the Internet, and I am very satisfied that things have finally got straightened out."

Bobby Breen and Ned Sparks, both Canadian-born, were
together in the film *Hawaii Calls*.

When the Beatles' album *Sergeant Pepper's Lonely Hearts Club Band* became a multi-million seller, Bobby was surprised to receive calls from friends telling him his picture was on the montage on the front cover.

"How they chose me, or where they got the picture, I have no idea," he said recently. "But it didn't do my career any harm."

For ten years he was kept busy. "I worked all the best clubs, all the best theatres," he said. "My tour of the British Isles was a highlight. The Moss Empires theatre circuit was the prestige theatre circuit in England and Scotland and I played on every one of their stages. Audiences loved my new act that had flashbacks to the songs I sang as a kid blended with contemporary music from the forties and fifties. There were people waiting around the stage doors for my autograph every night. It was a very special time in my life."

He recalls particularly playing at the Chez Paree Club in Chicago. "Top of the bill was Sophie Tucker. She was a great entertainer but very demanding," he remembered. "She had to know the words of every song I was planning to sing and if they clashed with any of her own songs they were out. Our audience was a tough one. I remember many characters from the gangster era out front night after night. Good to look back on now but a little frightening at the time."

When he was starring at the Elmwood Supper Club in Windsor, Ontario, just across the river from Detroit, Michigan, an unexpected visitor arrived one evening.

"I knew of him," he recalled.

> Everyone knew the Motown sound and its creator Berry Gordy. But I'd never seen him so was surprised when he came backstage to talk with me. He had succeeded beyond his wildest dreams with black entertainers like the Supremes, but wanted to break into the white market. "I'd like to talk to you about a recording contract," said Gordy. After the Windsor engagement I had a week out so spent the time at Gordy's beautiful home in Detroit. He let me hear several songs he thought I could handle, and we actually went into his

studio and made tapes of several of the numbers. I was the first white performer he had put on record.

But for once Gordy had made a mistake. "They never did get released," Breen said. "I think he realized that my singing was not compatible with the Motown sound."

By the late 1960s, most of the theatres had ceased to run stage entertainment along with the film shows. Many of the big nightclubs had closed their doors.

"But I never really had a lean time," Breen recalled in 2003. "The Morris office kept me busy. Fortunately my voice was now a powerful tenor and my style changed as the years went by. I always kept up to date on the musical trends."

In 1971, while appearing at a club date in New Jersey, he suffered a setback that for a while looked like it would destroy his successful career. Contact lenses sent to him at the club arrived damaged and cracked. Not wanting to miss a show he wore them and the following morning was rushed to hospital with lacerated eyeballs. For several days he was almost blind. Happily, the doctors worked wonders and a week later he was back on stage performing.

While appearing in New York City he was introduced to Audrey Howard, then president of the renowned City of Hope charity that today operates a national medical centre in Duarte, California. It was then, and is today, one of the most successful research centres for cancer and other life-threatening diseases. More than 300 physicians and scientists and 2,500 other employees work towards the goal of finding a cure for cancer and other diseases. City of Hope, a Comprehensive Cancer Centre, is located on 112 beautifully landscaped acres just northeast of Los Angeles. "The centre is proud that eighty-eight cents out of every dollar received from individuals or corporations goes to patient care and research," said Audrey. "The annual operating budget is more than three hundred million dollars a year."

"Audrey wanted me to appear at one of the City of Hope charity concerts," Breen recalled. "Unfortunately I was booked elsewhere on the date of the concert. But I must have made an impression on her, she certainly did on me, and when we met again a few months later in Florida it was obvious to both of us that we should be together."

Bobby Breen married Audrey Howard thirty years ago and today they operate a theatrical agency in Florida that books the biggest stars in the industry and uses a lot of the profits from those shows to help young, up-and-coming entertainers get a foothold in show business.

Living in a beautiful home near Tamarac in Florida, they have staged hundreds of shows aimed at the thousands of retirees living in the southern part of the state.

"Most of them, like me, aren't too happy with today's music, like rap," Breen said. "Like me they look back at happier and more melodious entertainment, so we give them that kind of show."

Over the past thirty years they have presented performers like Milton Berle, Al Martino, Morey Amsterdam, The Four Aces, Cab Calloway, the Four Freshmen, The Diamonds, The Drifters, the Ink Spots, and so many more they have lost count.

"All the condominiums down here have rooms in which these big names can play," he said. "Most bring four musicians with them and we add six of the best musicians in Florida so they are backed up by a top-quality orchestra."

But it isn't only the veteran entertainers that occupy the mind of Bobby Breen Enterprises. "We look everywhere for new talent, young singers, musicians and comedians. When we find one with potential we give him or her a chance to appear with the big name artists," he said. "We have given a great number of performers their first opportunity to be seen and heard."

One thing Audrey and Bobby Breen don't allow is profanity and vulgarity on stage. "Our shows are aimed at audiences who remember when comedians were funny without being dirty," he said. "If a young performer can't do a show without dirt he will never get a booking from us."

Since the Berry Gordy recording session in Detroit, Bobby Breen has never again entered a recording studio. "My voice is still strong and clear, but I've never considered seriously making another record. Perhaps I should," he said.

Not satisfied with booking other entertainers, Breen can be relied on to raise his own voice in song whenever the opportunity arises.

"I appear at perhaps a dozen concerts a year," he said. "Although I sing contemporary ballads these days, you'd be amazed how many times I get a call from the audience to sing 'Rainbow on the River,' a beautiful song I sang in my second film of the same name. It brings back a lot of memories for me and from the applause I know it does the same for members of my audience."

Sally, the sister who made his entire career possible, married happily and died in 2002 at the age of eighty-seven in her home in Beverly Hills. "Going to her funeral was the saddest day in my life," said Bobby Breen. "I wonder where I might have been today had it not been for her determination and belief in me."

Mickey, fifteen years older than Bobby, is the only remaining Borsuk alive. "He gave up his singing and became a very successful salesman," said Bobby. "I last saw him at Sally's funeral, but we were never close and I don't hear from him these days."

In 2002, Bobby Breen, who had never had a day's illness in his life, was shocked to learn from his doctor that three of the arteries to his heart were 75 percent blocked. "They told me I must have bypass surgery on the arteries immediately if I was to stay alive," he said. "They knew I was scared so they got me into the hospital on the pretext that I was going to be given an anaesthetic so they could do more tests. When I woke up the operation was over. It was a great success. Within a few weeks I was feeling better than I had in the past five years."

Bobby and Audrey Breen have videotapes of all the films Bobby made in the 1930s. "We watch them now and then," said Audrey. "They were pleasant memories to Bobby and you don't like to forget the good things in life."

What is his reaction to the films, more than six decades after they were made? "He thinks they were pretty good, " said Audrey. "I think so too!"

The tapes came in useful some years ago for Paul and Ronnie, the two sons of Audrey from an earlier marriage. "They used to show the films to their friends," she said. "Even though they charged admission to the showings there was always a waiting list hoping to be invited."

The 78-rpm records that Breen made while he was starring in the RKO musical films have also not vanished completely. Several were best-sellers. One, "Rainbow on the River," became a number-one hit.

"When Sally died in Los Angeles we found she had kept quite a lot of Bobby's records that were big hits back in the thirties. Now we have them here in Florida." Audrey recalls.

CDs of songs and singers from fifty or sixty years ago are big sellers these days. Deanna Durbin, Bing Crosby, and others are selling more records today than they ever did in their heyday. The Breens have been asked several times to allow their discs to be remastered and released on a CD.

"So far we haven't agreed," said Audrey. "But who knows, when we have time we may dust them off and get them professionally re-recorded. I think a lot of people would like to hear Bobby as he was then. Even today, when he makes a personal appearance, there are calls from the audience for 'Rainbow on the River.'"

Has Bobby Breen, the man who has been a star for seventy-two of his seventy-six years on this earth, anything to say to hopeful young performers just starting on the road to fame?

"The way to fame is simple," he said. "You have to give the public what they want and when you give it make sure it is always the best you have got. If you don't they will soon forget you. Too many young performers today don't know how to handle success and failure. You need that knowledge to be sure you aren't cheated by unscrupulous agents who will take every cent of your money if you don't take care."

He gives credit to his wife, Audrey, for the financial success of their production company. "Her father was a renowned accountant in New York to such people as Walter Winchell," he said. "His knowledge of accounting became her knowledge and today I never have to worry about financial matters."

Late in 2002 he received an unexpected call from Australia. "A radio interviewer did an hour-long program with me for airing in a country in which I never did appear," he said. "Now and then the phone will ring from someone who knew me many years ago. It is always pleasant to hear from the people who were so important to my career."

But Bobby Breen, still a star at seventy-six, says that while he enjoys memories he will never stop looking at tomorrow. "That's where all the good things are," he said. "You should never lose sight of tomorrow."

Jack Carson

In 2003, CBS Television would like us to believe that *Everybody Loves Raymond!* That is the name of the popular television series that many times has led the audience ratings.

Sixty years earlier, in 1943, before TV arrived, CBS radio proudly proclaimed *Everybody Loves Jack*, as their popular radio show of that name first came on the air. From the thousands of letters that arrived at CBS studios every week, everybody did indeed love Jack.

Jack Carson, star of the show that bore his name, watched while the ratings soared. It broke audience records regularly during the four years it was on the air. Hollywood's biggest stars, like Robert Taylor, Cary Grant, Ginger Rogers, Doris Day, and Ingrid Bergman, lined up to do guest spots on the show. Unless a star had some pull with Jack Carson, the waiting list of famous people was said to be six months long. Greta Garbo said in New York in 1972 that she loved the show and wanted to make a personal appearance in 1944, but Louis B. Mayer, boss of MGM studios, refused permission.

"Jack Carson was one of the kindest men I met in my Hollywood years," she said. "But Louis B. Mayer was afraid that he would make me look foolish on the show. I tell you now that I would have been great in comedy, but Mr. Mayer said 'no.'"

Hedda Hopper, in a column printed in the *Chicago Tribune* in 1950, said Jack Carson sent out more than twenty thousand autographed photographs to fans each year. She added, "Jack Carson assured me that nobody was ever hired to sign the pictures. He claimed to have signed every one himself."

Jack Carson had been successful in vaudeville, and by 1943 he had appeared in more than forty movies, mostly at RKO Studios. He was with Ginger Rogers and Red Skelton in *Having A Wonderful Time*, with Rita Hayworth and James Cagney in *Strawberry Blonde,* and with Edward G. Robinson and Jane Wyman in *Larceny Inc.*

When his radio series began he was receiving equal space on movie posters with the likes of Ginger Rogers, Fred Astaire, Humphrey Bogart, and James Cagney.

Despite his rugged good looks and genial attitude he had become known worldwide as "the man who never gets the girl."

"Ginger Rogers was the first girl I lost in a film, but we got along so well during filming that she asked RKO to hire me to be the guy who lost her in her next five films. Then I lost Doris Day to my good pal Dennis Morgan in five more films," he told Sidney Skolsky, the *Hollywood Citizen-News* columnist, in 1950.

Ironically, ten years after Jack Carson's death in 1963, Doris Day told the world that Jack Carson may have lost her on the screen, but in real life she and Carson had a torrid romance going for more than three years while their films were being made.

"My life might have been much more satisfying had I been given the sense to marry Jack," she said. "But the world thought of me as the girl next door and unbelievably still a virgin. Studios never let our romance become public. My wholesome image was far too valuable to them at that time. In Hollywood they only count dollars."

Jack Carson was born John Elmer Carson in Carman, Manitoba, on October 27, 1910. His father, Edward L. Carson, was regional director of a successful insurance company.

When the company decided to expand its operations into the United States, Edward Carson was sent to Milwaukee, Wisconsin, to open the company's first office outside Canada.

Before his family left Canada, when Jack was only twelve, he had already made his mark in his high school's drama group in Carman. If a press release dated July 1940, from the publicity department of RKO Pictures in Hollywood, can be believed, "Eleven-year-old Jack Carson won a gold medal as best actor when he appeared in a school play that won first prize at the Manitoba provincial schools drama competition in 1921."

The press release goes on to say that eleven-year-old Dave Willock, who was appearing in the same play, *My Manitoba Home*, won the silver medal in the competition. This mention of Dave Willock gives the press release some credibility, because Carl Willock, another insurance salesman, moved with his son, Dave, to Milwaukee in 1922 to join the Carsons. Later, after they both graduated from college, Dave Willock became Carson's partner in a very successful comedy team that played large and small vaudeville theatres everywhere in North America, including the Paramount Theatre, the New York showplace where every act hoped one day to get a booking.

Jack and Dave completed their high school studies together in Milwaukee at the Hartford Avenue School, before being enrolled together by their parents in St. John's Military Academy in Delafield, Wisconsin.

"They felt we needed discipline," said Carson in 1950 to Hedda Hopper. "Our entire lives revolved around making people laugh and some of the ways we did it did not sit well with our parents." Both boys graduated from St. John's Academy at the same time and together enrolled at Carleton College in Northfield, Minnesota.

Jack Carson remembered his academy days in a story written by Paul Harrison in July 1941 for the *New York World-Telegram*:

> In high school Dave and I were a team in sports and drama, we followed this by creating a comedy routine when we were at the military academy. I recall at our final graduation ceremonies the academy principal, who I had always considered a pompous old ass, became my hero when he invited us to do our Willock and Carson comedy act in front of the packed auditorium, a routine that had, though I say it myself, the audience roaring with laughter.
>
> We got a standing ovation and when, later in the ceremony, Dave and I went up to collect our graduation certificates, both of us received a second standing ovation.

Many years later, when Jack Carson was a star in Hollywood, he received a letter from the academy principal asking him to speak at the next graduation ceremony. He enjoyed his return to Milwaukee so much that he volunteered to return every year until the principal that he now admired retired.

Jack Carson and Dave Willock went on together to Carleton College and graduated with honours. Twenty years later when he returned to Carleton to speak to the graduating class, Jack Carson had much to say.

"I'm thrilled to be here," he said, "But I want to hope that those of you here making the move today from college to the tough world outside were better students than I was. I graduated, but I must tell you now it was because I played in and conducted the school band, was a standout on the football field and took part in school drama productions."

To the horror of the Carleton teachers and the dean sitting on the stage behind him, he added, "I wasn't dumb but if I got 50 percent on any paper I wrote I had to wonder if the teacher marking my work had been told to make sure I graduated. I weighed 220 pounds and stood two inches over six feet. When I tell you I played Hercules in a leopard skin in the college drama group you may well be wondering if I scared all my teachers so much they were afraid to flunk me."

In Milwaukee Jack Carson became friendly with a local radio sports announcer who covered the university games. Years later that friendship paid dividends for them both. The sports announcer was actor and singer Dennis Morgan, who later teamed with Carson in many successful movies.

Perhaps regretting the years he had wasted at Carleton College, Jack Carson read every book he could find, from the Bible to the classics to the best-sellers of the era. He became the scholar his teachers years before had hoped for. He studied every newspaper he could read, and Sidney Skolsky wrote in the *Hollywood Citizen News* that "Jack Carson is probably the best-educated and erudite actor in the film industry."

"Thank you," wrote Carson in a letter to Skolsky. "I want you to know I didn't have to go to my dictionary to see what erudite meant."

In 1931, free from college, Jack Carson and Dave Willock decided to put a comedy act together and try their luck in the vaudeville theatres that were flourishing across North America.

"We tried our act out at a local talent contest and won first prize," said Carson in 1943 to Skolsky. "We were lucky that a booking agent from one of the smaller theatre circuits was out front. He grabbed us as we left the stage and offered us a twenty-week contract. The money was enough to let us eat occasionally, travel the cheapest route between cities, and that included hitchhiking more than once, and stay in rea-sonably clean rooms. So we signed."

Willock and Carson had created an act in which they sang, danced, gave impressions of important men of the era, and added a slick, fast-paced comedy routine that took them quickly from the small theatres to the most important. "But we never did play the New York Palace," he said to the *New York World-Telegram* in 1941. "If they ever open it again I shall get Dave Willock to join me and see if we can create an act worthy of the top vaudeville theatre in the world."

But Willock and Carson never did team up to do vaudeville again. Dave Willock became a newspaper reporter and daily newspaper editor in Milwaukee. However, when Jack Carson started his four-year radio show in 1943 he called Willock and offered him a contract as one of the show's writers. Willock wrote a character for himself, named Tugwell, into the show and he became a major part of the show's success as a performer and writer.

When vaudeville died and sound movies arrived in Hollywood, the act of Willock and Carson broke up. Dave Willock felt the vaudeville theatres would soon be closing their doors and he wanted to get a more secure job that would enable him to get married. "We had saved quite a lot of money and were ready to gamble our lives on something new," said Carson.

While touring, Jack Carson had met a young dancer, Betty Alice Linde. They prepared a song and dance act that for a year got good bookings on the prestigious Orpheum Theatre circuit, one of the biggest of the few remaining live theatre chains. Carson recalled:

> In every town we played we told the local newspaper that I could play any instrument that they cared to bring along. I wasn't such a great musician but in college I had studied music, actually conducted the marching band, and had tried out every instrument they played just for fun.
>
> Some of the instruments they brought were astounding, but only once when an Indian brought in a native reed pipe did I fail to play it. That cost us fifty dollars.
>
> The act of Linde and Carson lasted more than a year before I decided I wanted something better. But I didn't want to lose Betty so I married her.

Jack Carson was such an honest taxpayer that the United States tax
office used him in commercials to urge others to also make equally
honest returns. "They paid me," said Carson. "I'm probably the
only taxpayer who ever got a dividend for being honest."

The act played its last show in Kansas City. Carson convinced the
manager of the city's Tower Theatre to hire him as master of ceremonies
for the weekly talent show the theatre presented.

"I stayed there for almost a year and watched every movie the theatre showed. I started to wonder if perhaps Hollywood might have
room for me. I didn't imagine myself as the handsome hero who always
won the girl, and looking back on my career I was right," he told an
unnamed writer in the *Los Angeles Times* in 1946.

In 1936 Jack and Betty bought a new Model O eight-cylinder
Hupmobile, one of the fanciest and most exclusive cars of the era, and

set out for Hollywood. The car remained with him for the next six years, but he wasn't around in 1963 to see the car play a farewell performance in his life.

One of the few contacts Carson had in Hollywood was former vaudevillian George Stevens. Stevens had left the vaudeville circuit after finding some success directing a number of plays in New York, and by 1936 he was a highly regarded film director at RKO Studios in Culver City.

"He had nothing for me when I first contacted him. But he promised to help me whenever a part became available, and later he did play a major role in my Hollywood career," Carson told Hedda Hopper. "Fortunately for me I got a small part in a stage play directed by Ben Bard. He had been a successful silent movie actor and was then a dramatic coach showing people how to move from silents to sound films."

A Hollywood agent named Frank Stempel, looking for unknown performers, saw the play and asked if he could represent Carson. The Stempel-Carson team remained together until the day Carson died. "He believed in me and you don't forget a man like that," said Carson in 1956.

Frank Stempel had an additional talent that Jack Carson looked back on with satisfaction twenty years later. "He invested fifty cents of every dollar I earned in land and property in the growing area of Beverly Hills and the Hollywood Hills," he told Sidney Skolsky. "He knew what he was doing and astounded me many times with the figures that showed his success as an investor. Thanks to Frank Stempel I will never again be short of money."

Stempel answered his office phone one day in 1937 to hear the voice of George Stevens. "I am starting a new film, *Vivacious Lady*, with Ginger Rogers," he said. "I need a husky guy to play a rather important role in the film. Could Jack be available next week?"

Jack Carson said many times to many different writers that *Vivacious Lady* was the turning point in his career. "Ginger Rogers, already a star, came over to me on the set one day and said she liked the way I handled myself and how willingly I took advice from the director," he said. "She told me that she had several more films coming up and with my permission she would ask the producers to give me a role in every one. And she did!"

At Ginger Rogers' request, RKO Pictures put him under a short-term contract and used him over the next two years in more than twenty films, his roles getting bigger each time as his fan mail count started to skyrocket.

It was the start of a career in which he became known to audiences worldwide as "the man who never gets the girl."

Ginger Rogers said in 1953 that she believed her attention to Jack Carson caused the breakup of his first marriage. "I liked Jack, but there was nothing between us. RKO insisted on publicizing us as a team and we were seen together at first-nights of movies, at clubs and anywhere else the studio publicists could think of to get us photographed together."

Jack Carson tried hard to convince his wife, Betty, that the stories were just publicity, but she refused to listen, moving out of their apartment and filing for divorce.

"The divorce was civilized," Carson told Sidney Skolsky. "We just agreed the marriage should end. We had discovered we had little in common. Betty tried to start her own career as an actress. Unfortunately it never got off the ground although I did try to help."

Jack Carson and Ginger Rogers played together in five more films, *Stage Door, Having A Wonderful Time, Carefree, Fifth Avenue Girl,* and *Lucky Partners.* With each film his roles became bigger and his name larger on the posters.

Asked why she always lost Jack Carson in her films but was seen at nights with him on many occasions, Rogers said, "Sometimes what you see on the screen is not accurate. Jack is a loser to nobody. I adore having him around."

Carson's film work brought him to the attention of radio show producers. In one year he was chosen to do guest spots on twenty different comedies and variety shows.

Jack Carson's years in Hollywood, both on and off stage, were impeccable. In his entire career the only mystery attached to his life happened in 1939 when he was appearing in *Destry Rides Again* with Jimmy Stewart and German actress Marlene Dietrich.

Jimmy Stewart told this story to Hedda Hopper in 1979 after she asked him for facts about an incident that was rumoured to have happened in 1939, forty years earlier, but was not mentioned in Dietrich's autobiography, *My Life Story,* published in 1979.

Stewart gave this written statement to Hedda Hopper but always declined to elaborate on it when asked by other writers.

"I believe it is time to put to rest the rumours that have been around for many years about an incident on the set of *Destry Rides Again,*" he wrote. He went on:

> Although the incident was hushed up at the time and Universal had the power then to hush things up they didn't want printed, I'll tell you the story as I know it, for my friend Jack Carson, although involved, was in no way to blame for the incident.
>
> Somehow a stranger had managed to get into the studio and on to the set where we were filming. I was doing a scene with Marlene when he came out of the shadows and rushed at her, a knife in his hand, shouting "Death to all Germans."
>
> Jack Carson saw him coming and blocked the way so he never did reach Marlene. Jack was about 250 pounds and a former football star so he easily halted the charge of the intruder. The man aimed his knife at Jack and Jack responded by hitting the man in the jaw with one of the best punches I have ever witnessed.
>
> The intruder went down like a sack of potatoes, hitting his head on a concrete block. One of the stage crew then ran to the intruder, obviously planning to hold him down if he started any more tricks. But I heard him say to our director, George Marshall, "This man is dead." The set was cleared immediately and an hour later we returned as though nothing had happened. There was no body on the floor and nobody spoke about the incident. I asked George Marshall if he knew what had happened after we all left the set. He

told me that everything was taken care of and it would be better if nothing more was said about the incident.

In Hollywood stories like this spread like wildfire, and I was called by several writers seeking information. I told them all what George had told me to say, "I don't remember any incident on the set."

So the story was never printed. Jack Carson was a hero and not in any way to blame. Was the man dead? He certainly hit his head on the floor very hard. I didn't know then and I don't know now. I have no idea what happened to him, or his body, and I really don't want to know.

George Marshall had died in 1975 and none of the other people on the set that day would admit any such incident happened. Jack Carson told newspaper writers that he remembered no such incident. So is it just another Hollywood story, or did Jack Carson really punch an intruder so hard that he died?

Before his own show was aired, Carson was signed to the popular *Signal Carnival* radio variety show. The show introduced him to Kay St. Germaine, a featured singer on the program.

"I was master of ceremonies," he said. "Kay wasn't too enthused at first by the way I introduced her. She thought the humour I put into each introduction would hurt her image as a serious singer. In fact we feuded quite a bit about that, but when her fan mail started to grow because of her new relaxed image she accepted the fact that perhaps she had been too serious in the past." Carson continued, "I thought she was a wonderful person, but she didn't think too much of me. We weren't really friends until one day she came over to me on the set and said, 'Jack, you and I should have dinner together tonight.' Within days we were looking at each other very differently, but it took me six months to summon up the courage to ask her to marry me."

At that time under a five-year contract with Warner Brothers, Jack's hoped-for quiet ceremony was thwarted by Jack Warner, head of the studio. Warner gathered every one of his huge roster of stars together, and the quiet wedding became a major publicity stunt for the studio. The ceremony was held in September 1940 at the Beverly Hills Hotel.

"The only good thing about it was that Jack Warner paid all the bills. There were stars there I had never met," said Carson. "But Warner insisted on Kay and I having pictures taken with every one of them. We were there nearly three hours having the publicity shots taken."

Jack Carson, in the middle of a picture, was given no time out for a honeymoon. "I was horrified when, twenty-four hours later, Mr. Warner came to see me and told me to have Kay in the studio at nine next morning wearing her wedding dress. I asked what this was for, and Warner said, 'Some of the pictures didn't turn out as well as we hoped. We'll rebuild the wedding set and retake the pictures again in the morning.'"

The publicity campaign by Warner Brothers was a major success. Pictures were printed worldwide. "They even sent out a photograph of Ginger Rogers crying as she was looking at my wedding pictures," he recalled. "I called her and apologized, but she laughed. 'It was good publicity for both of us,' she said."

With his salary increasing every year, and his income from Frank Stempel's investments bringing large dividends to the family, Kay and Jack bought a home at 16133 High Valley Place in Encino.

"It isn't a big house, just seven rooms," Jack told Hedda Hopper. He continued:

> Neither Kay or I want the spotlight at home. We have no pool, no boats and no servants. The brick wall that surrounds the children's yard I built brick by brick myself. When Winston Churchill came to Hollywood I was one of the fortunate people who met and talked with him. It was just after I married Kay and Mr. Churchill told me that my house would not become a home until I had personally put every brick together to create something for the family. He told me he relaxed by building brick walls at his home in the country outside London. I never forgot that and laid every brick of the wall myself. I wrote and told Mr. Churchill that I

had followed his advice and would you believe he replied and sent me a painting he had done himself. I had it framed and it hangs in a place of pride in our living room. Now if only I could learn to paint!

Kay and Jack Carson had two children. Jack Jr. was born in 1941, and Catherine arrived in 1944.

A story put out by Warner's publicity department that Jack Carson one day hoped to become a pilot brought an unexpected response:

I was called to the telephone in the studio and found myself speaking to Howard Hughes, a man I had never met.

"Are you working this weekend?" said Hughes.

"No," I said.

"Then give me your home address and I'll pick you up at nine for your first flying lesson," said Hughes.

And that's how I became a pilot.

Jack Carson never owned a plane of his own, but he regularly flew with singer Allan Jones, who owned his own light plane. "Allan lent me the plane whenever I wanted to fly by myself," he said. "I became a good pilot and when America went into World War II I volunteered to join what was then the U.S. Army Air Corps. Would you believe they rejected me because at six foot two inches I wouldn't fit into the cockpit of most of the wartime planes."

According to Jack Carson this is how he officially became a star. Hedda Hopper reported this story.

"I was under contract to Warner Brothers. I was recognized as a feature player but not a star," he said.

So I walked into Jack Warner's office (you could do that in those days) and we talked about the situation. When we had finished, Mr. Warner said, "Jack you can from now on be called a star. I'll give you a new five-year contract, double your salary and give you star billing on future films." We shook hands, I left the office and floated on air back to the set where I was working. He kept his promise and that's how I became a star.

When he had time between films he accepted as many as possible of the hundreds of requests for him to appear in clubs and theatres or to just make personal appearances for charity.

"I loved the feel of talking to a live audience," he said. "I went to many cities where the money the club offered didn't even pay the expenses of getting there, but to meet the people who had made my career so satisfying was much more important than money."

He tried to join the U.S. Army but was told he had flat feet, and again he was rejected.

An avid golfer, he joined the Lakeside Golf Club, close to the Warner studio. For five years he was the club champion, dethroning Bing Crosby. "That was a great day," he said in 1956. "He was a much better golfer than me, but I had a lot of luck and won the trophy. Bing never challenged me after that which is probably why I won the championship five times."

When the Hollywood Canteen opened its doors to the thousands of servicemen and women visiting or serving in California, Jack Carson was behind the reception desk greeting each of the visitors with a handshake.

"I went there at least five times a week," he recalled in 1953. "I washed dishes, mopped the floor after the last guest had gone home, or acted as master of ceremonies to introduce the many stars who went there to meet the service people. I was astounded and delighted at how many people knew me by name. Most of the films I had made were escapist movies and obviously that was what the service men and women enjoyed."

One night when the great trumpeter Harry James and his orchestra were on the stage in the canteen, a serviceman approached Jack while he was signing autographs.

"I saw you once in Rochester, New York, Jack," he said. "You invited people to bring any instrument on stage and you would play it. I'd like to challenge you to show you can play every instrument in the Harry James Band."

Carson took the serviceman on stage and told James the story. "He was more than willing to see if I could beat the challenge. I had no difficulty in getting a tune out of every instrument and when I sat behind the drums the entire band joined me and we ended the show with a rousing version of 'When The Saints Go Marching In,'" he recalled. "All the band stood up and applauded me, but I must admit that Harry James didn't offer me a job in his superb orchestra."

In 1945, Kay told Jack quietly one night that she felt they should get a friendly divorce.

"I was stunned," he said. "We had never had a quarrel, and so far as I knew were doing just fine."

Kay explained to the *Hollywood Citizen-News*:

> Jack was so dedicated to his work that he had little time for his family. But his biggest problem was his generosity to others. If he heard of any actor down on his luck, or a former vaudeville performer needing help, Jack went to their homes and handed out thousands of dollars, never considering whether he could afford it or not. I argued with him constantly over this and for the children's sake we decided to divorce. We settled our financial difficulties in a sane manner. We both signed an agreement that Frank Stempel would give us equal shares of Jack's income from film work. Anything else, like the radio shows and personal appearances he would keep for himself so I moved out of the house and Jack agreed the children should be with me.

Jack Carson always considered the failure of this marriage to be one of the greatest mistakes of his life. "I loved Kay and knew we must always remain friends. I visited her and the children at least once a week for many years. They knew we were divorced but never saw us fight or argue. They both grew up to be fine teens and young adults and I hope I can say I contributed to their intelligent attitudes toward life."

During the 1940s Jack Carson often vanished from the Hollywood scene for several weeks. His wife, Kay, would never tell anyone where he had gone. Years later, just before his death, Jack Carson explained that he had joined the Clyde Beatty Circus as a clown. "Nobody knew me," he said, "but they loved me and my routines. It was the greatest gift any man could receive, wholehearted acceptance by strangers."

In 1952 he accepted an offer to star on Broadway at the Ziegfeld Theatre in a revival of the George Kaufman and George and Ira Gershwin musical comedy *Of Thee I Sing*.

The show was expected to run for a limited three weeks but was so successful that it continued for fifteen weeks until Carson finally said he had to leave the show to fulfill other commitments in Hollywood.

Before leaving for California he said this to the *New York Times*:

> To my dying day I shall always remember the cheers and applause and standing ovation I received when I first walked on stage on opening night. Maurice Levine, the show's musical director, saw the tears start to run down my face. He yelled at me to catch and threw the silk handkerchief from his tuxedo at me. Fortunately I caught it and quickly dabbed my eyes. Then I did an unforgivable thing in the theatre, I faced the audience, bowed and said "Thank You" before summoning up the strength to get back into my character to continue the show.

That same year he married actress Lola Albright, whom he met in New York. "The marriage lasted six years, but during the last four we just sat in silence at home. I was blinded by her beauty and realized we had both made a mistake. She didn't fit into the home I loved," he said. "She wanted a glamour palace and I wanted a place to relax. When she hired two servants to look after us in the house and a gardener to tend the flowers and lawns I loved, I knew the end was near. Lola wasn't cut out to wash dishes and iron clothes. Fortunately once again our lawyers handled the divorce quietly and we parted with dignity."

When television arrived in Hollywood, Jack Carson was in demand from day one. He made his debut on NBC's *Alcoa Theatre* and followed this by regular roles on ABC's *U.S. Steel Hour,* an award-winning drama series. Later, on NBC's *Saturday Night All Star Revue,* he rotated the host role with Ed Wynn, Danny Thomas, and Jimmy Durante.

For three years he lived alone in the house he called home. "I had lots of visitors, often threw parties, but when they were all over I washed the glasses and ash trays before going to bed. Suddenly I realized I was very lonely."

In 1961 he married for the fourth and last time. Sandra Jane Tucker, introduced to him by Jack Whiting, who had appeared with him on Broadway in *Of Thee I Sing,* turned out to be the kind of wife he thought he would never find. "She wasn't ashamed to wash the dishes, or help weed the garden," he said. "She fit perfectly into my idea of a perfect married life."

Jack Carson many times turned down opportunities to direct films starring himself or others. He said directing was not his cup of tea. In 1962 he changed his mind and agreed to go back to Milwaukee to direct a summer stock season production of *Light Up The Sky* at the Swan Theatre. His friend William Bendix was to be the star. "Bill convinced me to direct," said Carson. "The show was a success but I quickly knew that I was meant only to be a performer."

Carson refused all chances to become an independent producer. "I don't believe an actor should produce, write or direct the films in which he is going to appear. Judgement gets warped when you have so much control. An actor's job is to act and that I think is what I do best."

In 1964 he accepted an offer to star in the summer stock play *Critics Choice* at the Playhouse in Andover, New Jersey. During the final dress rehearsal he collapsed on the stage. Taken to hospital, he was told that he had stomach cancer and would only have at the most six months to live. Six weeks later, with his wife at his side, he quietly entered a hospital away from Hollywood for an operation the doctors warned him would probably not help at all.

The operation confirmed the earlier diagnosis. One of his kidneys was cancerous and the cancer was spreading. Doctors and hospital staff were sworn to secrecy and he returned home to Encino.

Jack Carson was said never to have lost a friend throughout his life.
So many of Hollywood's biggest stars wanted to attend his funeral
in 1963 that invitations had to be given only to his special friends.
The mourners were the elite of Hollywood.

"He told me what the doctors said," said Sandra, "but made me promise to tell no one until he was ready to announce it himself."

His final public appearance was on the Walt Disney television program *The Wonderful World Of Colour* in September of 1962.

At Christmas that year he arranged a party to which only a few of his closest friends were invited. None were told he had only a short time to live.

One of the guests, Sidney Skolsky, asked if he had any regrets about his career.

"Only one," he said. "I didn't object to losing the girl in almost every film that I made, but always hated the fact that I lost because the script made me out to be a big dumb guy. If only one writer had made me lose the girl because I was mean and vicious I would be completely happy today."

Skolsky said Jack Carson was in good spirits but seemed very tired. "After I left the house and was driving home I suddenly sensed that he hadn't long to live," he said. "I could have written the story for next morning's paper but you don't betray a man like Jack Carson who had never betrayed anyone in his life."

Jack Carson died in the home he loved on the morning of January 2, 1963. He was only fifty-three. At his side was his wife, Sandra, and Frank Stempel, the manager who had been his agent and financial advisor and close friend for more than twenty-five years.

Friends who attended his funeral all paid tribute to his way of life. "He always found it difficult to say no," said actor Sonny Tufts. "His generosity is legendary in this city where most people hang on to their gold."

Tufts arrived for the funeral driving the sleek 1936 Model O Hupmobile in which Jack Carson had arrived in Hollywood twenty-seven years earlier. "When Jack decided to sell the car I bought it," he said. "I only wish he could have been alive today to see how I have cared for his old car."

At the request of Sandra Tucker, Kay, his second wife, attended the funeral with their two children, John, then twenty-one, and Catherine, seventeen.

Others among the 150 people who had requested and been given invitations to the service in the Wee Kirk o' the Heather chapel in Forest Lawn Memorial Park were Ginger Rogers, Humphrey Bogart, Doris Day, Jimmy Durante, Jack Warner, Dennis Morgan, Judy Garland, Van Johnson, Joseph Cotton, Elizabeth Taylor, Richard Burton, Mickey Rooney, Danny Thomas, George Gobel, Raymond Massey, Joan Collins, Frank Stempel, and Carson's vaudeville and radio partner, Dave Willock.

Outside the small church in the grounds of Forest Lawn more than one hundred other people gathered to listen quietly to the service. A crowd estimated at more than five hundred, there to pay their last respects to an actor everyone admired and loved, lined the road inside the cemetery that led to the church.

"I saw many stars in that line," said Sonny Tufts. "They had not been invited to the church but they wanted to pay their tribute to a great man among men."

The Carson family had been members of the Hollywood Presbyterian Church for many years. Dr. Raymond Lindquist, pastor of the church, led the service:

> No one will ever know the many times Jack Carson came to my help when I heard of people in need. He would never allow his name to be used. He believed God had put a spark of response in every man and that it was man's purpose to discover it, use it, and nourish it. If we leave this church today with our heads held high and our minds attuned to the way he spent his life, promising to follow in his ways, we are saying that we are better people from having been given the privilege of knowing this wonderful man.

The next morning all the Hearst newspapers in the United States printed a black-edged, full-page column under Hedda Hopper's byline. She started the article by saying, "No words of mine are adequate to express the thoughts of Hollywood at the sad loss of actor Jack Carson. So I have asked other people who knew him to say it for me."

On the page were more than fifty personal tributes from the biggest stars in Hollywood.

The final one, from Humphrey Bogart, said simply, "The world has lost a giant in Hollywood, a land of pygmies. Goodbye Jack!"

Berton Churchill

tagecoach, starring John Wayne, made in 1939, was a major box-office success, but to the amazement of fans around the world it won only two Academy Awards. Thomas Mitchell, the veteran Hollywood actor, took home the trophy as Best Supporting Actor. The background musical score also earned an Oscar.

Five other nominations, for Best Picture, John Ford as Best Director, Best Black and White Cinematography, Best Film Editing, and Best Interior Decoration, brought no more awards to the movie which had earlier been named Best Film of the Year by the New York Film Critics.

Berton Churchill, whose performance as the pompous absconding banker had earned him rave reviews from hundreds of critics and moviegoers, failed to receive an Oscar nomination.

Over the years, millions of film enthusiasts who have bought video-cassettes of *Stagecoach* have disagreed with the decisions of the Oscar voters back in 1939.

In reviews of the film, stories posted on the Internet, and letters to print and on-line film newspapers, the comments are almost unanimous. Berton Churchill should have won the Best Supporting Actor award.

Berton Churchill, born in Toronto on December 9, 1876, was sixty-three when *Stagecoach* was made. Never once did he star in a film, but he was in constant demand by directors who quickly realized that his mere presence in a film could raise it from mediocrity to audience satisfaction. In both 1935 and 1936 he appeared in more than forty feature films.

He told the *New York Times* in 1940, when he returned to the city to appear in a new stage play, that many times he arrived home from a day's shooting to find his wife waiting on the doorstep waving a script that a director or producer had delivered during the day. "Often it meant I had to stay up long after midnight learning my dialogue for a scene in a film I had never, until that moment, heard about but which was to be shot the next morning," he said.

Actors like Tyrone Power, John Garfield, and Clark Gable said after his untimely death in 1940 that on several occasions they had only agreed to make a film if Berton Churchill was also given a role in support of their main characters.

During the Second World War, Clark Gable, then a member of the United States Army Air Corps, told the *London Daily Mail*, "We have a great man in Winston Churchill in charge of this war, but if another Churchill, actor Berton, could have been side-by-side with him this war would be over in no time. He directed without being the director. He was such a perfectionist that every decision he made was based on solid reason. That's what we need now to win this war, just reason, solid reason." He added, "But Berton Churchill, who was the real star of the picture *Parnell*, which officially starred Myrna Loy and myself, died three years ago when he was only sixty-four. A sad loss to the film industry and a great loss to the United States."

Berton Churchill won only one award in his entire stage and film career, but when he arrived home after the awards ceremony he locked it in a cupboard and refused to allow it to be shown to anyone or put on display.

Why did he dislike the award so much? That story comes much later in his illustrious career!

Churchill was in high school in Toronto when his parents decided to move to Newark, New Jersey. His father, Richard Churchill, had received a lucrative offer of work there with a real estate company, so Berton Churchill graduated as valedictorian from Newark High School.

It was the era when many of the plays and musicals heading for Broadway tried out their productions in Newark theatres before heading for New York City.

"In 1893 and 1894 I used to stand around the stage door collecting autographs of the many famous stars who were in town for one or two weeks," he recalled in 1910. "I loved what the theatre stood for, entertainment and relaxation, but I had no idea that one day I would be part of the acting profession."

He refused the opportunity of going to college and accepted his first job as a typesetter in the composing room of the *New York Daily News*.

"It was exciting to read the news almost as it was happening," he recalled in 1930. "It gave me my first ambition to be one of those newsmakers. I dreamed that one day the typesetters and page make-up men would see my name among the headlines."

Churchill travelled by ferry to New York City every day and often worked until two or three in the morning setting last-minute news stories.

"There were no ferries at that time of the morning so many times I slept on a bench in the waiting room until the call came that said the first ferry of the day was ready to sail."

When a friend from his high school days mentioned that she was joining the William J. Florence Dramatic Society in nearby Jersey City, he decided to travel with her by trolley car with her to see what acting was all about.

"I had to give up my job at the *Daily News* but found another one quickly with an evening paper so that I could be home in plenty of time for the drama group's rehearsals," he recalled.

It was this point in his life that he began his interest in union activities, an interest that stayed with him throughout his life. "I realized that most people not in managerial jobs were grossly under paid. I attended union meetings," he said, "and soon discovered my theatre interests being revived by the sad stories of chorus girls who attended the meetings. They told how they had to live in squalor while the stars were living in luxury. I wasn't able to do much about it at the time, but vowed that one day I would be able to help them."

The newspaper became so upset with his constant demands for better money and working conditions for the composing room personnel that they promoted him to pressroom foreman, in charge of the entire production staff of the paper.

"I lasted three weeks," he recalled in 1939 to the *Workers' Weekly*. "I discovered that though I may have deserved the promotion I was really moved up the ladder to management so I would stop my campaigning for better pay."

He quit the paper and moved to a large general printer in New York, where he continued his union activities.

"By this time I had appeared in several plays presented in Jersey City and Newark by the Florence Dramatic Society ... In 1896 someone first noticed me," he told the *Workers' Weekly*. "I still have the review the Jersey City newspaper gave of my performance. It said simply, 'The play is awful, and should be allowed to die. One of the actors, Berton Churchill, a young man of twenty, should be nurtured into the stardom he will surely one day attain.' I haven't had too many bad reviews in my career, but this was the first good one and I hope it will be buried with me one day."

In New York, the Berkeley Lyceum was the place to which young actors from the amateur ranks graduated. They presented different plays each night with youthful actors, all hoping that one of the important New York producers would drop by and recognize talent when they saw it.

Churchill recalled, "We were actually paid a pittance for our acting. But it was enough to convince me to give up my newspaper job. My father and mother often came across to the city to see how I was doing in my small one room apartment, and without fail they always dropped a few dollars in an envelope before they left. Those dollars kept the rent paid and me in business as an actor."

When there were no rehearsals he worked during the day at a nearby amusement centre, Luna Park:

> I was a "barker" shouting out exciting things about the sideshows that weren't exciting at all. It was then I realized I had an impressive voice. I was able to lure hundreds of people unto the tents. But I always got away before the show was over. I was afraid they might lynch me for telling too many lies about the shoddy shows they had paid to see.
>
> The agents and managers who came to see our nightly show seemed oblivious to the talent I felt I possessed so I moved on to the Academy of Music where I earned a role in *Black Crook*. I was Casper, the village boy, and had one line. I had to grab the hero of the play, and say "Come with me Rudolph." I rehearsed the line a million times but blew it on the opening night saying, "Come with me Casper." Nester Lennon, star of the show as Rudolph, answered me in no uncertain terms. "I will come with you Casper," he said. "But you are fired. Please leave the stage."

A veteran actor-producer in the audience was shocked at the public firing. He went back stage and immediately offered to hire Churchill as a member of his touring repertory company.

For two years Berton Churchill appeared in a variety of plays ranging from *The Sidewalks of New York* to *Hamlet*.

"It was an incredible experience," he recalled in 1930.

> The company was fourteen strong when we began the tour, but people kept quitting and at times we had only six people to perform ten parts in a play. But we muddled through and from that day to this I have never missed a line. I can read a play and perform it immediately. On more than one occasion that is exactly what happened. I remember coming off stage at a small theatre in Madison, Wisconsin, to find the company manager standing there with a costume, a wig and a moustache into which I had to change and be back on stage as a completely different character in less than a minute. Somebody had left the company in the middle of the show. But I knew every line in the play so it really was easy.

Another touring company snapped him up on his return to New York City. "I became a pompous villain in the national touring production of the Broadway hit, *The Fatal Wedding*," he said. "When the producer, Sam Harris, saw my performance he came round backstage and told me I was better than the actor who had appeared in the show on Broadway. He actually gave me a four dollar a week raise. I think they had heard of my union activities and figured this was the best way to keep me quiet."

While appearing in Boston near the end of the play's run, he was introduced to Edward F. Albee, who invited him to join the Albee Summer Stock Company, which played every year from April to September in Providence, Rhode Island. Unless the success of one of his plays on Broadway made the trip to Rhode Island impossible, he returned to work with Albee's company each summer for twenty years. Although he was earning big money as a major star on Broadway he always returned to Edward Albee and worked for several weeks at minimum scale pay. "I owed Albee for much of my success on Broadway. It was my way of repaying his confidence in me."

Toronto-born Berton Churchill predicted in 1938 that Ronald Reagan would one day be president of the United States. Reagan never forgot, and in 1980 he invited Mary Churchill, Berton's daughter, to his inauguration ceremony in Washington. He also gave her a cheque she never cashed.

It was from the mayor of the city of Providence, Rhode Island, that Berton Churchill received the only award given to him in his entire career on stage and in films. Mayor Joseph H. Gainer presented him with an official scroll emblazoned with the gold seal of the city, ribbons of blue and white, and an inscription that read as follows:

> Whereas the Albee Stock Company has come to be regarded by our entire citizenship as one of the community's most cherished institutions, and;

Whereas, since 1903, you have been associated with this institution and as one of the company's most able, renowned and popular members and have contributed largely to its success, and;

Whereas the City of Providence views with pride the manner in which, by sheer force of character, ability and hard work you have risen in your profession so that today you have taken rank with the foremost actors of America;

We the citizens of the Citizens of Province congratulate you on the success which you have already attained and wish you even greater and more substantial triumphs in the future.

So why would Berton Churchill lock this prestigious award away in a cupboard, refusing to let anyone other than his family see it?

The City of Providence had spelled his name wrong. On the citation he was not Berton Churchill, but Burton Churchill.

Churchill appeared in more than a dozen touring companies, and his scrapbook of reviews in the cities from coast to coast grew fat with great notices.

"But I wanted to be back in New York, " he told the *Times*. "I knew how tough it was to live on the pittance managements gave to supporting actors, and wanted to help get the theatrical union, Actors Equity, off the ground."

In 1908 Berton Churchill made his New York debut:

I was thirty-two. No spring chicken, but I was ready and well experienced when William Faversham, a renowned actor, who later became successful in Hollywood, playing the star role in Cecil B. De Mille's first movie, *The Squaw Man,* sought me out in my small apartment to tell me he had a role for me in his new play, *The World And His Wife* in which he was to star at Daly's Theatre.

The role of Severo gave me my first major recognition. Suddenly agents and managers started dropping by after the show to take me out to supper. The money William Faversham gave me was more than I ever dreamed I would make, but I still couldn't forget how small were the salaries being paid to other bit part actors in the production.

That same year, with William Faversham as his best man, Berton Churchill married Harriet Gardner, a girl he had met in his high school days in Newark.

For the next ten years Churchill was never out of work. He and his wife moved to a spacious apartment with three bedrooms, and in every play in which he appeared he took in as boarders, at no cost to the actors, as many as possible of the show's bit part players.

Over the next decade he appeared in four more Faversham productions, watching his name on the theatre posters getting larger and larger in every play.

Once a slim leading man, Berton Churchill aged gracefully, putting on, as the *New York Mirror* said, "weight and talent so perfectly balanced. The lean, wiry Berton Churchill has developed into a suave, imposing, dignified man of the world."

Roles for which Churchill was not available were described by agents as needing a "Berton Churchill type, a grouchy but dignified business man."

By 1918, Equity, for which he worked tirelessly, had grown in strength and there were threats of a nation-wide strike that was expected to close every professional theatre. "One thing I have never understood is why I, so vocal about the union, was never blacklisted before the strike started," he recalled. "I remember particularly the superb entertainer Marie Dressler, who couldn't get work in the New York theatre because she had the courage to stand up to managements on behalf of the poorly paid chorus girls. She was blacklisted for several years. It was disgraceful."

In the 1919 "Revolt of the Actors," as the newspapers called the strike that crippled live entertainment across the United States, Berton Churchill was one of the most vocal critics of the New York theatre managements.

He was a major leader of the strike, official treasurer of the strike funds, and was quickly elected second vice-president of the new union. As a result, for two years New York managements refused to hire him. He described it thus:

> Fortunately I had been earning good money for several years and my wife, Harriet, and our daughter, Mary, were never short of funds and were able to continue to live in a nice apartment. I went out with a few touring shows that had out-of-town managements and when we reached Los Angeles I got my first view of the silent film industry.
>
> I had lots of offers to appear in the silent films and actually did appear in one film, *Tongues of Flame,* in 1924. But silent movies gave me no satisfaction so I headed back to New York. To have no audience in a film studio was quite unnerving.

Finally one management company broke the blacklisting. Samuel H. Harris, who had raved about his work in the touring company of *The Fatal Wedding*, offered, in 1925, to give him the title role in his new Broadway play, *Alias The Deacon.*

The play was a huge hit, and overnight other managements forgot their animosity to the man who had made sure everyone on stage was compensated with a good salary, and scripts were piled high in his living room.

"I recall having more than twenty scripts offered to me at one time." he said. "Fortunately Harriet was an excellent judge of the quality of the scripts and I had to read only two or three out of every ten that came my way, the ones she approved."

Churhill's entire life changed after a visit in 1929 to a movie theatre in New York that was playing the first of the sound films to come out of Hollywood.

"It was as though a light went on in my brain," he said. "I went home and told Harriet and Mary that we were moving to California and I was going to work in the movies."

It was mid-winter in New York, and Harriet and Mary had no doubts about making a move to sunny California.

"I had few contacts in Hollywood," he said in 1936, "but on arrival I called William Faversham, then a successful film actor and he passed the word around to producers that I was in town. Within days I was working. In the remaining month of 1929 and through 1930 I appeared in more than twenty films."

Some of the films were memorable ... but some were not! "It didn't take me long to realise that most directors, straight from the silent era, had really no idea how to handle actors who spoke," he said. "I found any suggestions I made about dialogue, movements on the set, lighting, even camera angles, were willingly accepted by the company and the director. I was never pushy but never hesitated to improve any film I felt needed to be improved."

Asked why he never became a director, he said, "Why would I want the hard work of being a director when my life was so easy and satisfying as an actor."

In 1932 he appeared in the film *False Faces* with former cowboy star Ken Maynard, a major success in the silent film era who was now finding it difficult to get work. "We watched him drinking on the set and Harriet and I decided to try to help him. We took him, and his wife, into our home in Hollywood and after two years, we had got him off the drink and able to get some quite nice roles in the western talkies," Churchill recalled. "But we couldn't control him after he left us and by this year [1936] he had again become an alcoholic." Maynard lived until 1973, dying alone and friendless in a small trailer on the back lot of one of the studios. People like Clark Gable and Ronald Reagan supplied him with regular meals, but his drinking couldn't be stopped.

Bette Davis, with whom Churchill appeared in *Cabin In The Cotton* in 1932, fell in love with him. "I was only twenty-four when I appeared with Berton," she said in a story printed in 1956.

He was in his mid-fifties, old enough to be my father, but he was in such control of his life that I desperately wanted this man to be in control of my life. He was so calm and cool about every move he made. I tried to attract his attention by slinking around in the least clothing I dared to wear without being arrested for indecency. He is one of the few men I have ever accepted advice from willingly.

Harriet, his wife, who was a delightful person, often accompanied him to the studio and was quite aware of what I was trying to do. She chided me gently and it soon became obvious to me that their marriage was unbreakable and so I gave up my prowling before the shooting ended.

Will Rogers, who played with Churchill in *Judge Priest* in 1934, became a personal friend. He said this to *Film Weekly*: "Berton taught me how to retain my dignity without losing my sense of humour. I couldn't have taught him anything, he was the complete actor. A great man and a wonderful friend."

When, only twelve months later, Will Rogers and aviator Wiley Post died in a plane crash near Oklahoma City, Berton Churchill wrote and read the eulogy at the funeral. "I am here because the good Lord decided to spare my life," he said. "Will and Wiley offered to take me along on their final flight. I had to decline because of film commitments, so I will use what years I have left to honour the memory of these two great men."

Churchill founded the Will Rogers and Wiley Post Memorial Fund, giving one third of every cent he made to the fund. When the United States entered the Second World War, the fund was taken over by the government of the state of California and the money was used to train young pilots still in high school.

Shirley Temple, with whom he appeared in *Dimples,* loved Churchill. "He was so charming, not as severe as he always looked and he liked to share jokes with me on the set. I was very young but I recognized him as a kindly gentleman and a fine actor."

Asked in 1938 by a film magazine what he considered his greatest achievement was as an actor, he responded quickly:

> That's easy. When the actors all went on strike across the United States before Actors Equity was established, I was sent as the union representative to Chicago where a problem had arisen. George C. Tyler, a producer who was not a member of the Producing Managers Association, announced that he planned to open a non-union play at the Blackstone Theatre in Chicago. He proposed using actors and musicians who were not members of any union. Stopping that production from being staged was my greatest success. It cost me fifty dollars but I convinced the railway workers to lose the truck containing his scenery and costumes. They buried it somewhere on a spur line in the Chicago railyards and it was never found so his strike-breaking show never opened.
>
> A few days later Actors Equity demands were accepted by managements, and salaries they offered were in line with what the small part players and chorus singers and dancers deserved. If Tyler's show had been allowed to open I believe the strike would have collapsed and we would have lost.

Also in 1938, when he was playing a role in *Wide Open Faces* starring Joe E. Brown and Jane Wyman, he became friendly with a regular visitor to the set. The young actor, Ronald Reagan, was just beginning his rise to fame. He was there to visit actress Jane Wyman, whom he later married.

When asked in 1979, on the eve of the United States presidential elections, if he was confident of winning, Ronald Reagan told the *Hollywood Reporter* that he had no doubts at all. "Berton Churchill told me so forty-two years ago," he said. "His acting was so impressive that I felt strongly about his future in the motion picture industry and told him he would be a star in his own right very soon."

According to Reagan, Churchill replied, "My friend I am not star material, I like what I am now. I'll bet you'll be president of the United States before I ever become a star."

"It was the first time I had ever heard such a startling suggestion," said Reagan. "Was I actually thinking of being president all those years ago? Maybe it set my mind moving forward in that seemingly impossible direction. I'll never know now!"

After *Stagecoach* in 1939, John Wayne asked that Berton Churchill be given a good role in all his future films. "I feel a calmness when he is around," he said. "We are good friends and I hope will be all our lives."

A film encyclopedia lists one hundred films in which Berton Churchill played a role. His daughter, Mary, who kept an accurate account of every film in which he appeared, claimed there were at least another one hundred that were never listed because his name was not on the posters or in the film reviews.

"I took any role offered me if I liked it," he said in 1939. "I shocked my agent and directors on many occasions by turning down parts, good as they might be, in films I didn't think would be successful."

In 1940, in New York, he told the *New York Times* that not every time was he correct in his judgement. "I recall being offered the part of the wizard that Frank Morgan made so memorable in the Judy Garland film, *The Wizard of Oz*. I told the director, Victor Fleming, that I couldn't see Frank Baum's book making a successful film. Of course I had never heard the song, 'Over The Rainbow,' or had met Judy Garland at that time."

In the summer of 1940 he told his booking agent not to get him any more work in Hollywood. He had made ten films that year, including *The Way of All Flesh* and the screen version of *Alias The Deacon*, which had started his stage career in New York.

"I've been feeling rather tired recently," he said. He went on:

> Perhaps I should take a little vacation. A friend, Sam
> Harris, who gave me my first real break in the theatre
> after I was blacklisted following the strike that estab-

lished Actors Equity, called me the other day and asked
if I would like to return to the New York stage.

He sent me the script of the new George Kaufman-
Moss Hart play, *George Washington Slept Here* and I
loved it. I think I'll go back to New York where there are
live audiences, where everything started for me.

He left Harriet and Mary in Hollywood. They said New York in
October would be cold, and they preferred the Los Angeles sunshine.
Berton Churchill went by train to New York, took a suite of rooms at the
Hotel Lincoln, and settled in for rehearsals at the Lyceum Theatre. He
called home every day to report on progress of the production.

Mary recalled a year later that he began saying in 1940 that perhaps
he was, at sixty-four, getting too old for the hard work that had made
him a success as an actor. "I don't have the energy I should have," he
said, "but this is a great play and everything will be fine once we get
through the long rehearsals."

When he didn't report to the Lyceum Theatre on the morning of
October 10, 1940, and failed to answer telephone calls, a messenger from
the Hotel Lincoln front desk went upstairs to see if there was a problem.

He found Berton Churchill lying unconscious on the bedroom
floor. Rushed to the Medical Arts Centre Hospital, on West 57th Street,
he was pronounced dead on arrival. An autopsy discovered a serious
kidney ailment that must have been giving him the tiredness about
which he had spoken.

His body was flown back to California for a ceremony at the Wee
Kirk o' the Heather in Forest Lawn Memorial Park, where he was
later buried.

The Los Angeles newspaper printed a story on the day of his funeral from Harold Peary, known to millions of North American radio fans
in the late 1930s as The Great Gildersleeve. "I would like to pay a special
tribute to Berton Churchill at this sad time," he said. "With his permission and approval, I based my 'Great Gildersleeve' character on the
pompous and pretentious characters Mr. Churchill portrayed so well in
the theatres and on screen. There will never be another actor the equal
of Berton Churchill!"

Berton Churchill, had he still been living, would have cheered at a decision that followed by Actors Equity, which had he helped found in 1913. When Sam Harris, producer of the play, asked Equity for permission to forego paying salaries to any of the cast for two weeks because of Churchill's death, they refused. Irish actor Dudley Digges came in to replace Churchill, and while he was learning his role, the cast was paid full Equity salaries.

A program printed in readiness for the New York opening at the Lyceum Theatre was scrapped. But somehow a copy slipped out containing Berton Churchill's name and photograph on the cover. It was sold a few years back for two thousand dollars at a theatrical auction.

In 1980, forty years after Berton Churchill died, his daughter, Mary Churchill, received a surprise invitation from Ronald Reagan to attend his inauguration as President of the United States. With the letter was a clipping from the *Hollywood Reporter,* several months earlier, containing the story of her father's comment to him on the set of *Wide Open Faces* in 1938.

She told this story to her local paper after attending the inauguration ceremony in Washington. "He also sent me a cheque for fifty dollars in payment of his bet with my father fifty-two years earlier. But it will never cost him a cent. I will never cash the cheque. I'll keep it as a memento of Ronald Reagan the actor and Ronald Reagan the President of the United States. And, of course, my father!" she said. "President Reagan sought me out from the thousands who attended the inauguration. He said he wished dad could have been there in person. Said he was probably one of Hollywood's finest actors of all time. I was so overwhelmed I just wept, but I had my wits about me enough to keep as a souvenir the handkerchief he gave me to dry my eyes."

Fifi D'Orsay

Hollywood ballyhooed her in the 1930s as the "Bombshell from Paris." Despite the studio press releases, Fifi D'Orsay never set foot on French soil.

The nearest she got to France was owning two first-class plane tickets to Paris given to her in 1953, when Ralph Edwards selected her to appear on his popular flashback TV show, *This Is Your Life*. Often reducing her to tears of joy as he reintroduced into her life many of the people who had helped make her into a major Hollywood star in the 1930s, he told her that it would be wrong for one nicknamed the "Bombshell from Paris" never to see that city. So he gave her two first-class return air tickets from Los Angeles to Paris.

She told a reporter ten years later that the tickets were a generous gesture by Ralph Edwards:

> But he forgot to ask if I had the money to pay for a hotel, taxis and food in the French capital. So I never got there. If he hadn't sent a studio car to take me from my apartment to his TV studio I couldn't have got there either. I was flat broke.
>
> So, very reluctantly, I took the tickets back to the airline for a cash refund, jumped in my old car and drove to Las Vegas where I applauded wildly in the casino theatre where the Follies Bergere stars were performing. There I dreamed a little of the Paris I would never see. That is the nearest I ever got to Paris or France.

New York theatre publicists, and later the Hollywood studio publicists, used their imaginations to create a totally false background for Fifi D'Orsay. Newspaper clippings contain so many contradictions that the only hope was to visit D'Orsay in her New York apartment in 1972, when she was appearing on Broadway in the musical *Follies,* to ask if she would like to tell the truth about her birth, life, and success, setting the record straight once and for all.

"I was born on April 16, 1904, not 1907, 1908, or 1909 as some stories say, in Montreal, Canada," she said. "My real name was Marie-Rose Angelina Yvonne Lussier. Some people along the way added d'Sablon to my surname but where they got that I do not know. It was never a name in my family." She continued, "My father, Henri, worked for the post office as a letter carrier in the suburbs of Montreal. My mother, Blanche, worked in a milliners shop in the city. She designed and made hats and made more money than my father. This didn't help keep the peace in our house."

Asked if the stories that said she had six, eight, ten, or thirteen siblings were true, she laughed:

> You think I remember that now. I really don't know but there were a lot of us. When I went into show business in New York most of them disowned me. I was the black sheep of the family. I remember only one sister. Her married name is Alice Angloo. She lives in Pompano Beach, Florida.
>
> You must remember that there was no birth control in Roman Catholic Canada and since my father wanted to get his own back on my mother for earning too much money he just kept getting her pregnant. Perhaps there were eight or nine. I don't remember. Apart from Alice they are probably all dead by now.

Yvonne Lussier seemed destined for a career in a business office. "I was educated at the Sacred Heart Convent in Montreal. There I learned to type, do shorthand, and keep account books," she said. "Also I learned to speak English, without losing my French accent. So anyone who tells you I put on this accent as an actress is telling you lies. I love my accent and hope I will die with it on lips."

Fifi D'Orsay, still Yvonne Lussier, saved every penny she earned. "I slipped into the theatres where people sang and danced and before I was fifteen, I knew that was where I was going to be one day. My mother knew but didn't dare tell my father."

Lussier left a note at home in 1920 saying she was going to New York to seek fame and fortune:

> I had already chosen the name Fifi D'Orsay and told them to watch the newspapers for stories of my success

under that name. I'll tell you now where the name D'Orsay came from, not out of thin air, it was the trade name of a perfume I loved.

Later as I grew successful I always kept the perfume on my dressing room table. I told friends the company had named it after me. That was one more lie I am happy to correct now.

In New York the theatres and clubs wouldn't hire her because they said at sixteen she was too young to appear in clubs where they served liquor.

"I really had no talent to offer except a cheeky personality and rather good looks, if I say it myself, but I couldn't dance or deliver lines properly," she recalled. "I became a secretary in a theatrical office and looked enviously for two years at the actors and actresses who came in to sign contracts. I was Fifi D'Orsay then and a lot of people told me it was a perfect stage name. When they asked where I came from I said Paris, France. Remember my French was equally as good as my English."

Realizing that she must gain the poise and confidence shown by the successful performers with whom she came in contact every day, she spent every spare cent she could on singing, acting, and dancing lessons. "I hadn't been at the evening school more than two weeks when in walked a man named Gallagher. He was rather loudly dressed, but it was obvious he was in some form of show business by the easy way he talked to everyone."

She soon found out that Gallagher was half of a renowned vaudeville comedy double act, Gallagher and Sheen. "He was in the inner office talking with my drama coach for some time, then he opened the door and beckoned to me," she remembered.

"Come in my dear," said Mr. Gallagher. I went inside and made myself all bubbly and I was later told by my drama coach, sounded very phoney. My boss said Mr. Gallagher wanted a young girl to appear with his act and thought I would be perfect. "Yes, yes, please," I said, and next morning reported to Mr. Gallagher at a rehearsal hall on 42nd Street in New York.

He was very patient with me, helped me to project my lines so that they would reach the back of the theatre, then Mr. Sheen came in. Between us we rehearsed a comedy scene I was to perform with them that night in a New York nightclub. They were both very nice people and told me I would be paid thirty dollars a week, all my train fares, room and board, with *The Greenwich Village Follies* that was starting a national tour on Monday just three days ahead.

The Greenwich Village Follies was to be the touring version of the successful Broadway show in which Gallagher and Sheen had starred for almost a year.

Fifi D'Orsay, known as the "Bombshell from Paris", was Montreal-born and knew enough French to help her carry out her deception for years.

"When we opened in Boston I was very scared, but I must have done alright because at the final curtain I got a lot of applause," D'Orsay recalled. "One of the dancers in the chorus, Jenny Walton, took me under her wing and helped me learn a few simple dance steps. Within a couple of weeks I was tap dancing along with the rest in the finale."

Fifi D'Orsay earned her first rave review in Omaha, Nebraska. It read:

> Gallagher and Sheen are always funny, but this review-er would like to put the spotlight on a young lady from Paris, Fifi D'Orsay, who bubbled her way through the evening. Whether it was doing comedy skits, dancing with the chorus, or singing in a sensuous husky voice, she gave the audience a name to remember. I believe one day she will be the star of her own touring revue.

"Mr. Gallagher, who was the boss, read the review and instead of being annoyed or jealous, as I feared, patted me you know where and said my salary would be increased to fifty dollars a week and I was to get a spot of my own," she said. "It was Mr. Gallagher who created the 'Bombshell from Paris' name and it was printed on the posters and in theatre programs under my name."

D'Orsay recalled, "I must tell you now, because I am sure you have heard all the horror stories about young girls being picked on by the stars of a show, but none of that happened to me. Mr. Gallagher and Mr. Sheen were perfect gentlemen at all times. I was so grateful for that. I might have been a sitting duck had I started my career with less respectful people."

After *The Greenwich Village Follies* ended its tour, Gallagher and Sheen wrote a new musical, *In Dutch*. "I am not sure how being a Parisian Bombshell fitted in with the title *In Dutch*, but they hired me at eighty dollars a week, plus all expenses when out of New York, and put my name on the posters almost as big as their own," D'Orsay said.

The show was not a great success, and the company returned to New York after only four months on the road. D'Orsay recalled:

There Mr. Gallagher introduced me to a guy named Herman Timberg. Herman had written material for a lot of top vaudeville acts, and told me the comedian, Herman Berrens, was looking for a female partner. Mr. Gallagher told him Fifi D'Orsay would not work for less than one hundred dollars a week and guaranteed same size billing on the show posters as Mr. Berrens.

I went over to a rehearsal studio, met Mr. Berrens, and read the lines of a comedy spot Herman Timberg had written for us. I will never forget his comment at the end of the skit. "Herman," he said, "now the bloody skit is really funny."

Gallagher, who had accompanied her to the audition, chimed in. "You know Herman," he said, "Fifi will not work for less than one hundred and twenty dollars a week, with accommodation on tour in respectable hotels where the food is good, and she must travel first class on the trains and never be called on to carry her own suitcases."

"He agreed without a murmur," she said. "And he kept his word. I had never reached so close to heaven before. His wife travelled with us to look after costumes and train and hotel bookings. They stayed in the best hotels and I was always asked to stay in the same hotel wherever we appeared."

The act that went on a vaudeville tour was called Berrens and Fifi. Famed songwriter Jimmy McHugh wrote a special song for her, "Everything Is Hotsy Totsy Now." "That song expressed my feeling to perfection and every night I got a lot of applause, sometimes even standing ovations at the end of my performance," she said. "Looking back now I must admit that applause was more for the very short skirt I wore and the legs I displayed, which although I say it myself, without any blushing, were very delectable."

Fifi D'Orsay's success with Herman Berrens was short-lived. After only eight weeks on the road Berrens had a heart attack and was hospitalized.

I have never told this before because it was a sad time. Herman and his wife Marie had become good friends. So I was determined to carry on alone. Somehow, with the help of Herman Timberg, who came down to Baltimore immediately he heard of Herman Berrens' heart attack, I worked up an act as a singer and dancer who told jokes. From day one it was a success.

I remember one night cutting three inches off my skirt that was already short because I was still unsure whether the whistles and applause came for my act or for those legs that one critic called "the most beautiful under-pinnings in vaudeville."

Booking agents came to see her act and loved what they saw.

"I played every good theatre in the United States, and finally, in 1928, got the booking every act longed for, at the Palace Theatre, New York," she recalled. The Palace date opened doors that eventually led her to Hollywood. "Will Rogers came round backstage to meet me one night," she remembered.

"You are quite wonderful," said Rogers. "But let me give you a bit of advice from an old vaudevillian. Make those skirts five or six inches longer than they are now. If they still applaud and whistle it's your act they love not just those gorgeous legs."

D'Orsay continued:

From day one he had only one name for me, Froggy. I took it as a compliment, not an insult. Next morning I went out to a theatrical costume house in the city and bought a much longer dress. I waited on pins and needles for the end of my act. Would they still applaud when my legs were not so very prominent. Well they did. The applause and whistles were louder than ever. I made sure they saw more than the new dress allowed, I swirled around a few times and unless they were blind they saw everything I had to offer.

Rogers, who spent much of his time while in New York visiting the Palace Theatre, went round back stage again that night. "Now you've got it," he said. "Always leave a little to the imagination! Now you know they love you, but don't overdo it, those legs should never be completely hidden."

Rogers told Fifi D'Orsay that she should consider visiting Hollywood.

"I think there is a future out there for you, Froggy," he said. "Sound films will soon be all the rage and your voice, looks, and delightful Parisian accent will be a big attraction in the musical films they are planning."

D'Orsay recalled, "I still had six weeks on my vaudeville contract to complete, and was earning three hundred dollars a week. I had saved quite a lot of money and carried it around in a small suitcase. That was one suitcase I never let anyone but me carry."

In Pittsburgh she was top of the bill in one of the last big vaudeville houses in the country when she received an unexpected invitation. "When I got to the theatre there was a telegram waiting for me. It was from the Fox studios in Hollywood. It told me simply that Will Rogers was about to make a film called *They Had To See Paris,* and had told the studio that he wanted me in the film."

Two weeks more in vaudeville and Fifi D'Orsay was on her way to Hollywood. "I travelled first class all the way. Expensive but what I had become used to in vaudeville. My expensive tastes have been a problem all my life, but it was fun while it lasted."

After a screen test at the Fox Studios, at which she sang another Jimmy McHugh song, "My Man," she was called into the office and asked to sign a seven-year contract that would pay her four hundred dollars a week.

D'Orsay remembered:

> This was another stage of heaven in my life. Four hundred dollars and no train fares to pay sounded very good. The studio helped me find a nice apartment close to the studio. I left behind in New York a good man, Freddy Berrens, the brother of my former vaudeville partner, Herman Berrens. We had planned to marry later that year. Instead of a marriage contract I had a picture contract. I think I broke Freddy's heart but he told me to choose between him and the movies and I chose the movies.

Will Rogers was the star of *They Had To See Paris*. Fifi D'Orsay's role was not a big one, but her singing, dancing, bubbly, flirtatious French girl made her a star overnight. "I saw a lot of Will Rogers during the filming," she said. "He was much older than me and I want you to know that it was not Will who took advantage of Froggy, it was Froggy who took advantage of Will. I just fell head over heels in love with him."

Will Rogers guided her through her first year in Hollywood. "He read every script I was offered and turned down several that would not have helped my career. He had a lot of power at the Fox studio and they seemed to agree with whatever he said."

In the first year of her contract she made one other film. Victor McLaglen and Polly Moran were the stars of *Hot For Paris*, but it was Fifi D'Orsay who got all the rave reviews. New posters for the theatres showing the film were sent along to replace the initial printing. In the new posters Fifi D'Orsay's name was in type the same size as the two other stars.

In 1930 her fan mail was estimated, in a press release from the Fox studio, to exceed three thousand letters a week.

"That's not true," she later said. She explained:

> Maybe one hundred, two hundred, now and then three hundred letters were sent to me. They were coming in from all over the world. The studios always multiplied everything by ten because it sounded better. According to them I was being paid four thousand dollars a week. But I don't think anyone was getting any more fan mail than I did. Fox wanted to take all the mail, open it and reply to it. They had a secretarial department that did nothing but answer mail that arrived at the studio.
>
> I told them I was just as good a typist as anyone they had at the studio and I would answer my own mail. It didn't go down too well with the chiefs at Fox because they wanted to know what sort of things fans were writing about. They would have provided all the photographs and paid the postage on the letters if they handled the mail. When I said "no" they sent me a bill

for the photographs and told me to buy my own paper and stamps. But I did answer every letter myself. I bought a new typewriter and soon got back up to sixty words a minute. And I gave Fox a detailed accounting at the end of every month telling them what the fans liked, and I always added on the end of the list that fifty or forty or thirty men wanted me to marry them.

After a couple of months they hauled me in to the stills department and sat me in the middle of a huge stack of letters. They were all addressed to me. Someone must have been very busy writing all the envelopes. But they forgot to put stamps on the envelopes and when the picture was released a few weeks later with a story saying, "Fifi D'Orsay gets more fan mail than any other star at the Fox studio. Each week she gets more than three thousand letters and about two hundred of those contain proposals of marriage."

One intelligent columnist who ran the story and picture in a Chicago newspaper, said, "But how did the letters reach the studio. There are no stamps on the envelope, did all her letters arrive by hand?"

D'Orsay thought the film *Those Three French Girls*, made in 1930, showed that the publicity men at Fox went too far overboard in their press releases:

One read, "Three of the most succulent exports from Gay Paree will be starring in the latest Fox movie, *Three French Girls*." They said Fifi D'Orsay was from Paris, Yola D'Avril was from Marseilles, and Sandra Revel was from Monaco. They actually believed Monaco was in France. In fact none of us had ever left the United States. At least I could speak French, having been born in Montreal, Canada, but Yola was from Detroit and Sandra from Brooklyn. I had to teach them to use the proper French accent when they talked. I know now

that I should have asked for more money for that duty,
but at the time I knew no better.

In 1931 she made three films, *Mr. Lemon of Orange*, *Women of all
Nations*, and *Young As You Feel*. All were box-office successes. All
enhanced her growing reputation in Hollywood.

In *Young As You Feel* her co-star was again Will Rogers. "We had kept
in touch after the first film I made," she said. "When he was asked to do
a series of personal appearances in San Francisco, Dallas, Houston,
Oklahoma and Chicago, he would only agree when I was permitted to
go on the tour with him. Of course I lived with him, why not! It saved
the cost of my room!"

(Left to right) Yola D'Avril, Fifi D'Orsay, and Sandra Revel in *Those Three
French Girls*. Not one of the French girls ever set foot in France.

In 1932 she made what she always believed was the biggest mistake of her life. "Fox was paying me four hundred a week and I received an offer from RKO to make personal appearances at all their theatres for three thousand dollars a week plus all expenses." The contract was to escalate by five hundred dollars a week for the run of the tour, the length of which would depend of the success of her performance.

The tour was a major success. "When it ended after five weeks I was earning five thousand a week," she said. "All this money poured in my lap was like manna from heaven. I went to Fox and asked for a new contract for the four years I still had on my old one. I demanded at least two thousand dollars a week."

The studio lawyers told her the request was way out of line, but if she felt she could get that kind of money elsewhere they would agree to tear up the contract. "I told them to tear it up and I left Fox on very bad terms. It was thirty years before I drove through the front gates of the Fox studio again."

The announcement that she was free from the Fox contract brought her offers from six different studios. "But the offers were not for long-term contracts. They wanted me for single pictures. Although the money was good, more than two thousand dollars a week, when you took away all the down time between pictures I was making less than I got at Fox over fifty-two weeks. It was a stupid blunder, one I've regretted all my life."

In 1932 she made a film at Monogram Studio called *The Girl From Calgary.* "Why they couldn't have made the title *The Girl From Montreal,* I'll never know," she said. "I tried to convince them that a French accent would be more believable in Montreal than in Calgary, this is the reply I got in a letter from Phil Whitman the director: 'Dear Fifi,' he wrote. 'I don't think Calgary will be out of place for a Frenchwoman. After all, it isn't very far from Paris, is it!'"

In 1933 she was signed by Warner Brothers to appear in *The Life Of Jimmy Dolan.* "My co-stars were Douglas Fairbanks Jr. and Loretta Young," she recalled.

> I was the bubbly girl who tried to destroy their marriage. I succeeded on screen until the good girl, Loretta Young, won the hero, but off-screen it was a different

story. My romance with Doug Fairbanks lasted long after the film ended.

Even Mickey Rooney, then about thirteen, tried to come on to me in my dressing room. I've often wondered how Judy Garland survived working with him when he was a few years older. Was she really the impregnable virgin as they say?

Fifi D'Orsay's first marriage was to Maurice Hill, a wealthy real estate man in Los Angeles. "It wasn't a success. I tried hard to be faithful to him while we were married, but had to get a divorce in 1939 because there were too many other men distracting my determination to be faithful," she recalled. "I was not then and am not now cut out to be a wife. I loved being the other woman on and off screen. When we were divorced Maurice actually tried to get the judge to award him alimony. Would you believe that was the sort of man I thought I loved?"

D'Orsay continued, "While we were married I remained comparatively faithful; but after the divorce, oo-la-la. Suddenly I realized I wasn't getting star billing any more. It was then I changed my birth date from 1904 to 1907 then 1908 and 1909. I began to think my life was nearly over. So I chopped off years at every studio. Nobody seemed to notice and if they did notice, I don't think they cared."

Between 1933 and 1937 Fifi D'Orsay made only seven films. "The money was still good but my fan mail dropped. I was lucky if I got a hundred letters a week. This is when I should have been saving money but I didn't," she said. "I had to be seen in all the right places but in 1935 Will Rogers died in a plane crash and my world fell apart. I had no one else to turn to. If I made four thousand a week I spent five thousand."

In 1936, Fifi D'Orsay, realizing her film career was almost over, accepted an RKO theatres offer to appear live on stage in cities from coast to coast. "I was to do a twenty-minute act before the feature film. They provided a fine orchestra in each theatre but I don't think they broke even paying me four thousand dollars a week so they cut the tour short after ten weeks and gave me ten thousand dollars to stop me suing them."

Was she, by 1936 no longer the easy person to work with that she had once been? "Yes, I was snippy, I contradicted directors, told off the cameramen if I thought they were not shooting me from the right angle, in fact I became the number one bitch in the film industry," she admitted. "After I made *Three Legionnaires* at General Studios, quite a second rate studio, I was told by the director Hamilton MacFadden that I had better save my money I wasn't likely to get any more work."

McFadden was right. It was not until 1943 that she received another film offer.

"I played in a lot of nightclubs and the audiences, who remembered me from my films five years earlier, loved me. I had kept my figure as I have to this day and my personality got me through," she said. "Really I could never sing, hardly dance at all. It was just me they liked, I was still five foot four, one hundred twenty-five pounds, just as I am today. I have never had to worry about my weight. I can eat what I like and I never get fat."

In 1941 she received a request from the USO, the organization that provided shows to the American troops before they went overseas, to do a twelve-week tour along with a comedian and a small band. "I cut three inches off my shortest dress and said 'When do I start.'"

The twelve weeks was extended by the USO to twelve months. "I didn't make much money but I made a lot of soldiers ready to go to war with smiles on their faces."

Newspapers across the United States printed stories of her appearances. "I didn't even have to hire a publicist. The photographers were there every night. Since by then my birth date had been advanced to 1909 I was still only thirty-two and still attractive, especially to service men who had left home many months earlier."

Back in Hollywood she found herself once again in demand at the film studios. "I wasn't the star but the money was good, for a while I actually managed to save a little."

At the PRC Studio she made *Submarine Base* with John Litel, *Nabonga* with Buster Crabbe, *Delinquent Daughters* with June Carlson, and *Dixie Jamboree* with Frances Langford and Eddie Quillan. "They were all B pictures. These had become very popular with theatre circuits. They played the A feature, the big one, first, then the B picture, then the

A feature again. This meant that audiences could come early, see both films and get home early, or come in later and still see both films."

The fan mail started to arrive again for Fifi D'Orsay. "A lot of the letters were from soldiers I had entertained in 1941. They hadn't forgotten my live show and I got more proposals of marriage during the war years than ever before," she remembered. "I once seriously considered moving to Utah where the Mormons live. I liked their idea of polygamy. But I discovered it only meant men could have lots of wives. Women couldn't have a dozen husbands so I abandoned that idea."

Through her friend Frances Langford, who was a major singing star in the 1940s, Fifi D'Orsay got a lot of club work in the Los Angeles area.

> But for three years I got no more film work. I kept moving from apartment to apartment, each seedier than the previous one. I left a trail of unpaid room rentals and other bills, but they finally caught up with me and repossessed my last fur coat. It was worth eight thousand dollars and it was taken away because I owed a four hundred dollar telephone bill. I was supposed to get the balance between the bill and the coat value but a year later I only got eleven hundred dollars. It was sold at an auction for fifteen hundred dollars. I bet if they'd told the people attending the auction that it once belonged to Fifi D'Orsay it would have brought a much higher price.

Her final film, *The Gangster,* made in 1947, gave her a role that made the forty-three-year-old Fifi D'Orsay try to be twenty again:

> It was a good film starring Barry Sullivan, Belita, and Akim Tamiroff. I wasn't even named on the posters. When the film was wrapped up the director Gordon Wiles gave me the soundest advice I'd received in my entire life. "Fifi," he said. "I love the way you act but isn't it time you woke up to the fact that you are, at forty-three, forty-two or whatever is the truth, no longer able to play the bubbly young French girls that made you so

popular. Television is coming Fifi, start playing more mature roles, you are a great actor and there should be lots of work for you."

In 1950 she received an unexpected call from the man she had wanted to marry ten years earlier, Freddy Berrens:

> He said the Palace Theatre in New York was going to reopen and he thought he could get me booked there as the star attraction. Of course I squealed with delight, and on June 6, 1950, I returned to the theatre where I had once shared the top billing with Herman Berrens. The reviews were not bad. One writer said, "Fifi D'Orsay is dishing up memories of a wonderful era." Another said, "She sells her performance on her personality alone and it is a very bewitching personality."
>
> The year before I had married again. Peter La Ricos wanted to be my manager and my husband, but I kept getting calls from the Catholic Church telling me we were living in sin because they didn't recognize my first divorce, so in 1952 when Peter hadn't done a stroke of work since he married me I got my second divorce. Still, that didn't make the church happy unless I would attend confession and admit to living in sin. That was the day I left the church.

When actress Carmen Miranda came to Hollywood in the 1940s she was called the "Brazilian Bombshell."

"She was very much like me except she carried bananas on her head," said D'Orsay.

> One magazine called her the Equatorian Fifi D'Orsay. I liked that, even though I didn't know then and still don't know what Equatorian means. I met Carmen and we became good friends. She didn't know what Equatorian meant either.

When she played in *Copacabana* she was supposed
to be a French entertainer. We both had a good laugh
about that. She still had bananas on her head and in
France people don't walk around with bananas on their
heads. But she demanded that her character be called
Fifi. "That's specially for you, Fifi," she said.

In 1958, while singing at the El Rancho Hotel in Sacramento,
California, she met a Gospel singer named Mary Carson.

She was always smiling, always happy, and I asked her,
since she was about my age, how she managed it. "I
found God," she said. So I too decided to find God.
Mary gave me a book called *My Daily Bread* written by
a Jesuit priest named Tony Paone. I read it every night
before I go to sleep and no matter what the day has
been like I have a peaceful night's sleep. I told a
Catholic priest who continued to demand that I attend
confession that I had found my inner peace with Tony
Paone. I think he believed this Tony Paone, who I never
met, was having an affair with me. Thank God for Tony.
The Catholic priest never came back again.

It was in 1958 that Fifi D'Orsay decided to accept the fact that she
was now fifty-four years old. "Through Mary Carson I was invited to
speak to women's clubs. My hour-long seminars, followed by question
and answer sessions lasting sometimes two hours, were based on the
theme, 'I'm Glad I'm Not Young Any More,'" she said.

In 1960, on her income tax return, she admitted to earning more
than seventy thousand dollars. "I may have forgotten a few thousand,"
she said. "But God would forgive me for I had opened a lot of eyes to the
fact that getting old is no disgrace."

In 1964, on her sixtieth birthday, she received a phone call from actor
Dean Martin. "I have finally found you," said Martin. "I'm making a film
with Paul Newman, Shirley MacLaine, Robert Mitchum, Gene Kelly, Bob

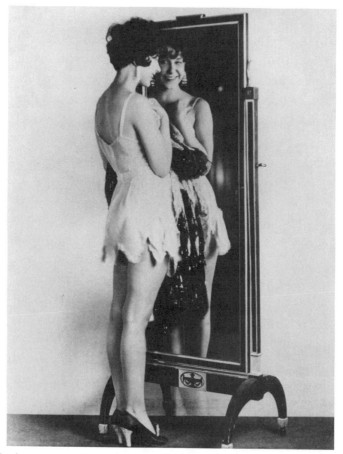

Fifi D'Orsay made more than $10 million in her Hollywood career but spent $12 million. At one time she owned thirteen expensive fur coats. She thought her career had ended until a phone call from Dean Martin put her back in the spotlight.

Cummings, and Dick Van Dyke, called *What A Way To Go.* There's a good part in it for you. Meet me at the Fox studios tomorrow at noon, we'll have lunch and see if we can't convince Lee Thompson to hire you."

"I didn't even know Dean Martin," she said.

> I had many faults but I never was one of the drinking crowd. But I met him there, and had lunch with all the cast. Mr. Thompson agreed with Dean Martin, and he hired me. I was to be a French baroness and had a nice

scene with Paul Newman and Shirley MacLaine. I got $20,000 for one day's work. On the day of filming Fox studios gave a party in my honour in the commissary. A big cake that read, 'Welcome home Fifi, you've been away far too long.' It had been thirty years since I had walked out of Fox in a huff. I wept a little, but when I saw the film I knew my small role was the finest performance of my career.

Director Michael Anderson gave her a nice role in *Wild and Wonderful* that same year with Tony Curtis and Christine Kaufman.

Norman Jewison gave her a role in *The Art Of Love*, which starred Dick Van Dyke and James Garner. "I never did find out for sure but I believe Dick Van Dyke, who I met when we were both in *What A Way To Go*, got me that part."

Fifi D'Orsay continued her lecture tours, and her fee rose from $2,000 a lecture to $5,000. "They even rented copies of the films I made in the thirties and booked a night in the local theatre to show the film and then listen afterwards to my speech. It was probably the best time of my life."

What A Way To Go opened other doors. "I found television producers had lots of roles, not big ones, for professionals as experienced as me," she said.

Most of the parts went by unnoticed, but she estimated she had appeared in about twenty different shows. "I could have had many more but in 1969 another film came along."

Assignment To Kill at Warners was her final film. "Director Sheldon Reynolds called me to say he would like me in his movie," she said. "The stars were Patrick O'Neal, John Gielgud, and Eric Portman. It wasn't a big role but it paid well."

In 1970, producer Harold Prince attended one of the lectures. "I was a little embarrassed because I was the only man in the house, but when I saw Fifi as she was at that time in her career I knew I had to get her into my new musical, *Follies*, which was just about to start rehearsals in Boston prior to going into the Winter Garden Theatre in New York," he said. "I talked to her and said, 'Miss D'Orsay, I don't know how I'm going to do it but I want you in my new show that starts rehearsals in one week.'"

Harold Prince called the composer of *Follies*, told him about Fifi D'Orsay, and requested that an extra song be written specially for her.

The song written for her turned out to be the hit of the show. "I am Solange LaFitte," she said. "'Ah Paree' is perfect for a fifty-year-old star aging gracefully. So what if I am sixty-six, nobody seems to care and my song stops the show every night. I'm wearing short skirts again and people say hello to me in the streets of New York. Thanks to Harold Prince I am a star again."

When the show opened in Boston, Fifi was distressed to see her name was not on the posters. "We were too late to change them after you agreed to appear," said Prince. "But if you are the success I think you are going to be I promise it will be there tomorrow."

On opening night Fifi D'Orsay stopped the show and received a standing ovation. The next morning when she arrived at the theatre for more rehearsals she found Harold Prince had kept his word. A strip pasted across every poster read, "Special Star Guest, Fifi D'Orsay."

Success in *Follies* brought her invitations to appear on the Johnny Carson Show. "We chatted and I sang my song from *Follies*," she said. "Mr. Carson got so many letters that he asked me back four more times. Four times I was also a guest on the Mike Douglas Show."

Her greatest satisfaction came from the letters she received after the TV shows and at the theatre. "They come not only from people my age but from youngsters in their teens," she said. "One letter summed it up so nicely, 'You are a real star,' wrote a teenager. 'I shall use you as an example in my life.' I answered him personally, as I do all my new fans, there is my typewriter on the table. I can still do about fifty words a minute without making any, well, perhaps a few, mistakes."

She was in tears on the *Today Show* when interviewer Barbara Walters told her she was an inspiration to all those who think getting old is the end of their lives.

Towards the end of the musical's successful run on Broadway, she received a visit from a man she had never met. He sang in her dressing room, "Fairy Tales Can Come True If You're Young At Heart." It was Frank Sinatra. "He said he would dedicate the song to me whenever he sang it in future. He held on to me until I stopped crying."

Feeling tired at the end of the Broadway run of *Follies* she decided a medical check-up might be a good idea before accepting any of the offers she was receiving.

The diagnosis was cancer. Medical bills soon took all the money she had saved, and when she had nothing left, friends say Frank Sinatra paid her bills and arranged for her to enter the Motion Picture and Television Country Hospital in Woodland Hills, California.

There she went into seclusion, refusing to see anyone. Elliot Goodman, the nursing supervisor at the hospital, said she lost her voice shortly after entering the hospital and that gorgeous French accent was stilled forever.

On December 4, 1983, the hospital announced her death at the age of seventy-nine. She asked for cremation "so that the evil inside me will never be allowed to spread anywhere else." Her wish was granted.

Few remember her name today, but several of the films from the thirties are now available today on VHS and DVD. Many are still shown on late-night television. It is easy to see, from her bubbly personality, why more than seventy years ago, she stole film after film from the biggest stars in the industry. Barbara Walters, asked in 2002 if she remembered Fifi D'Orsay, said, "Of course I remember her. It's a pity there aren't people like her around today. She was a delightful person. Very talented."

Yvonne De Carlo

Yvonne De Carlo is the perfect example of a major Hollywood star who did not become an overnight success.

When it finally happened, in 1945, after she had played the title role in *Salome, Where She Danced,* newspapers from coast to coast in the United States ballyhooed her as the girl who became a star in her first film.

They, and the studio's publicity men, conveniently forgot the twenty-one other films in which she had appeared from 1941 to 1945. They forgot because in only two of those films, some of them major box-office successes, did she even have her name on the final film fade-out credits. In 1943 in *Deerslayer,* the credits said Wah-Tah — Yvonne De Carlo. In *True To Life,* made that same year, those watching the screen closely read Girl — Yvonne de Carlo.

In all the others she was not named on the screen, and film scripts gave no name but things like chorus girl, showgirl, handmaiden, bathing girl, native girl, student, Lona's companion, office girl, and hatcheck girl.

Not one of the stars who appeared in these films saw anything unusual in her beauty or talents to suggest she might have a future in the film industry. Not one director or producer picked her out for future stardom.

Many years later Alan Ladd, the star of *This Gun For Hire*, filmed in 1942, claimed he pointed Yvonne de Carlo out to director Frank Tuttle as being "a girl to watch. She deserves better that just being a showgirl." But he added, "Tuttle wasn't impressed so I said no more."

Bob Hope and Bing Crosby couldn't even remember her in their film *Road To Morocco*. Hope was quite honest in 1962 when asked what he thought of her performance in the film. "Gee, was she in *Morocco*. I can't believe I didn't spot that luscious creature." Crosby, that same year, said, "Wasn't that the film my wife was on the set every day? I don't think I even noticed [Dorothy] Lamour in that film."

Dorothy Lamour said in 1954:

> Paramount had signed her to a small contract. It didn't
> pay her much money but she got extra roles in a lot of
> films. I was told by Bing Crosby that she was being

groomed for my role in the *Road* stories. I guess I had been getting a bit temperamental at the time and they were ready to dump me and put Yvonne in future films if I didn't behave better. Fortunately for me, unfortunately for her, I listened to what my agent told me and became meek and mild and continued to appear in all future *Road* films.

It was left to producer Walter Wanger, in 1942, to give her the break she needed. There are so many different stories about this "discovery" that her own simple explanation in her book, *Yvonne,* must surely be accepted as correct.

She claims to have been sitting in the waiting room at Universal Studio hoping to see Bob Speers, the studio's casting director, when Walter Wanger, the renowned producer, walked in and spotted her. He told Speers he was astonished to see someone who looked so much like his wife, actress Joan Bennett, and he wanted to consider her for the lead in *Salome, Where She Danced,* which he was then preparing for production.

Other stories suggest Universal had sent out a publicity release asking anyone in North America who wished to nominate a girl for the title role to send along a picture of their choice. Among the 21,348 suggestions received, said this story, was one from a group of Royal Canadian Air Force flyers in Saskatoon, Saskatchewan. They are said to have submitted a photograph of Yvonne De Carlo that they had received from Paramount the previous year when they asked for a pinup picture. It was, said Paramount, one of twenty thousand publicity shots they had sent out a year earlier when she was working on their lot as a contract artist.

Yvonne De Carlo later did have a picture taken with one of "the flyers from Canada," but this was presumably taken to convince people that the contest had not been fixed from day one. The picture, of herself with Lieutenant Kenneth Ross Mackenzie of the RCAF, is not too credible because in 1942 the RCAF didn't have lieutenants. The lowest commissioned rank was pilot officer. It is also implausible to think that a bunch of RCAF flyers would, unless they were blind, have sent back to Hollywood a glamorous picture they had requested only a year earlier.

Add to this the fact that the Kenneth Ross Mackenzie in the picture was her cousin, the son of her Aunt Connie, and you have all the ingredients for a good publicity stunt. It was so good that even hard-boiled columnist Hedda Hopper fell for it and used the tale and the picture in the story she sent worldwide.

But Yvonne De Carlo did make the Walter Wanger film *Salome, Where She Danced,* and she did become, in the eyes of the news media, "an overnight sensation."

It was Wanger, or his publicists, who decided to give her the title "The Most Beautiful Girl in the World." The news media picked up the title and spread it worldwide with glamorous pictures the studio supplied.

Was she really "The Most Beautiful Girl in the World"? She didn't think so in a 1945 article written by Michael Sheridan and printed in *Collier's Magazine.* "I'm not," she said. "The most beautiful girl in the world would be a blend of five women, Linda Darnell, Hedy Lamarr, Merle Oberon, Madame Chiang Kai-shek and Lady Louis Mountbatten."

Yvonne De Carlo's life began in Vancouver, British Columbia, Canada, on September 1, 1922. She was twenty-one when she finally reached stardom in Hollywood. But her search for success had started in Vancouver, eighteen years earlier, when she was only three.

She was born Margaret Yvonne Middleton. Her father had deserted the family before she was three, so her mother went back to her maiden name, De Carlo. Over the years many people, including actor Robert Taylor, claimed to have suggested the De Carlo name to her as being better than Middleton. But her mother's birth certificate proved that he, and others who wanted to cash in on her success, were opportunists who made up their stories.

Marie De Carlo worked as a waitress after her husband walked out and left her penniless. She told reporters in 1943 that she had always dreamed of being in show business herself and because that was not possible "I moved heaven and earth to make sure my daughter would have the opportunities that had been denied to me."

Yvonne De Carlo was named "The Most Beautiful Girl in the World" by producer Walter Wanger.

Yvonne De Carlo told *Today Magazine* in 1982 that at three she began studying the basics of dance with June Roper at the Vancouver School of Dance.

For some years Marie and Yvonne De Carlo lived at the home of Marie's parents, Margaret and Michel De Carlo, at 1728 Comox Street in Vancouver. "I enjoyed everything there but the vegetables," she said in 1946. "Yellow squash, turnips and carrots I hated then and hate now. But my grandparents were so very good to both my mother and me that to complain about the vegetables would have seemed very unreasonable."

At seven she had her first taste of success. One of her schoolteachers asked the class to write a poem. It had to start with "As I was walking down the street." All the entries were then sent in to a contest being run by the *Vancouver Sun*. "I was astonished and delighted to learn from my teacher that my poem, 'A Little Boy' was the contest winner," she told the *Los Angeles Examiner* in 1946. "I received five dollars which meant as much to me at that moment as if I had won the Nobel Peace Prize."

Before she was ten, De Carlo had composed many short plays, most of which she staged in her grandparents home. "I did my own version of Charles Dickens' *A Christmas Carol* and all the neighbours came to see it," she said. "That may have been not because the play was good but because my friends, their children, were also in the play."

At eleven De Carlo took a first look at Hollywood. A year earlier her mother had headed to California and left her with her Aunt Connie and her cousin Ken. "We heard little from Marie and when Connie suggested all of us should drive down to see how she was doing I was very happy," she said.

Connie, Yvonne, and Ken soon returned to Vancouver, depressed by the run-down rooms in which Marie was living. She promised they would all be reunited very soon. They were, but it wasn't in California as Yvonne had hoped. "She came back to Vancouver and told me she still believed California was the place of opportunity but that it wasn't yet time for us to stay there."

When she was fifteen, De Carlo received the news from her mother that they were going to try to conquer California again. At that young age she had already won a job dancing in the Palomar Club in Vancouver. "I did impressions of Eleanor Powell and Ruby Keeler dancing and Mae West being Mae West," she said.

In Hollywood, Marie and Yvonne De Carlo visited the offices of every casting agent and talent scout they could find, but after a few months, when no work materialized, disheartened and disappointed they again returned to Vancouver.

When Yvonne De Carlo was eighteen she graduated from King Edward High School in Vancouver. She had appeared in several plays with the Vancouver Little Theatre, achieved success as a dancer in local productions, and her voice had brought her solos with the St. Paul's Anglican Church choir in the city.

Marie announced it was now time for her and Yvonne to try once more to find fame and fortune in Hollywood.

This time her trip to Hollywood was not a failure. Within weeks of their arrival she found a job singing and dancing in the chorus at the Florentine Gardens, one of the most popular nightclubs in Hollywood during the 1940s.

She didn't even have to audition for Nils Thor Granlund, owner of the Florentine Gardens, known to everyone in show business in New York and Hollywood simply by his initials, NTG. Her mother had entered her in a beauty contest at Venice Beach, near Los Angeles. She won the contest, using dancing as her talent. NTG was one of the judges. "Would you like to join the chorus at the Florentine Gardens," he said.

It was as simple as that, if we believe the story Perry Lieber, publicity chief at RKO Studios, sent out in a press release in 1946.

According to De Carlo's book, there was no beauty contest. She says Marie took her to the Florentine Gardens after they had walked out on an Earl Carroll audition for dancers for his spectacular night club, at which Yvonne had refused to parade topless in front of Carroll, something he demanded of all the hopeful dancers (who would, if accepted, wear very skimpy costumes on stage).

At the Florentine Gardens they met choreographer Dave Gould. He promised that NTG would see her if they arrived back at the club around eight o'clock that night. "Wear red," said Gould. "NTG likes red!"

In a bright red short dress she danced to "Tea For Two," accompanied by the pianist from the Paul Whiteman Orchestra, then appearing at the club. The club audience liked what they saw and gave her considerable applause for her unrehearsed solo. NTG hired her on the spot. She learned the chorus routines in one day and was a member of the chorus the following night.

Take your pick. They are both good stories!

The Florentine Gardens was one of the places where top actors, producers, and directors spent their out-of-studio hours. But apparently not one of the thousands who visited the club visualized Yvonne De Carlo as the star she was to become only three years later.

By 1941 De Carlo had found an agent. Jack Pomeroy said years later, "I believed she had something to offer, but right then I wasn't sure what." He convinced her to go back to Earl Carroll's nightclub for another audition.

This time she was ready for the Earl Carroll inspection. "I was a bit embarrassed but ready for the chest examination," she said. "He gave me a quickie look and said I was hired."

But it was to make movies that she had come to Hollywood. Earl Carroll's club paid the bills for food and a place to sleep, and for that she was grateful. But Carroll had a strict rule that his girls must refuse any opportunities given them by photographers to pose for magazines and newspapers. He insisted that they not work or appear in public elsewhere unless he gave permission.

When Jack Pomeroy called to tell Yvonne that there was a small part in the Alan Ladd movie *This Gun For Hire* at Paramount Studios that he could get for her, she decided to ignore Earl Carroll's rules.

She headed to the Paramount Studio and was tested for the part. She had only one line, "Cigarettes, sir?," but she had broken into the film industry. After her debut was filmed she asked permission to stay around all day to watch Ladd and his co-star Veronica Lake at work. She stayed so long that she had to rush straight back to the nightclub just in time to change into her costume for the opening act. Unfortunately, Earl Carroll saw her entering the club. He spotted the film makeup still on her face.

"That's motion picture makeup," he said. "You have violated your contract with me. You're fired!"

Marie tried to convince Earl Carroll to take Yvonne back. When he refused she threatened to tell the newspapers that he had hired an underage dancer in his club. In those days anyone under twenty-one was not permitted to work in licensed premises. Carroll didn't like the threats, and the next day Jack Pomeroy told her that she'd be lucky if she ever got any more work in Hollywood. Carroll had blackballed her all over town.

But Marie was determined. She contacted a friend at the Motion Picture Relief Fund, and he helped pull the necessary strings to get the age restriction lifted. Thanks to Marie De Carlo the age was lowered to eighteen.

Yvonne returned to NTG at the Florentine Gardens and told him her sad story. NTG smiled and offered her her chorus line job back.

Paramount also came through with a six-month contract thanks to the efforts of Jack Pomeroy. It paid only sixty dollars a week but got her inside the studio every day.

On October 19, 1942, Paramount announced to the *Hollywood Reporter* that they had signed six young actresses to three-year contracts. Among the names was Yvonne De Carlo. At the end of three years the girls would be receiving five hundred dollars a week, said the press release.

After signing De Carlo, Paramount immediately loaned her out to Monogram Pictures, where she played, in *Rhythm Parade,* a Florentine Gardens dancer. She found out later than NTG had requested that she be in the film to give her confidence that she had a future in the movies.

The studio used her in screen tests with so many handsome young hopeful actors that she once told the *Hollywood Citizen-News* that it was impossible to distinguish one face from another.

But the studio also introduced her to some of the most important stars in Hollywood. The introductions didn't get her work, but did get her lots of dates.

When she told band leader Artie Shaw, then getting over his divorce from Lana Turner, that she wanted to be a singer, he told her that it took a lot of work to become a successful singer. He suggested she get out of nightclubs. He even offered to pay her a month's salary if she would find a drama and vocal coach and use the money enhancing those talents.

Red Skelton invited her out to dinner but called up to cancel just before he was to meet her. He said he wasn't being fair to Georgia Davis, his girlfriend at the time. A year later Skelton married Davis and both lived happily ever after.

Singer Rudy Vallee, then at the peak of his Hollywood career, took her out dancing and dining and said he wanted to further her career. Those dates stopped when Yvonne made it clear that she too wanted to further her career but not to further her personal relationship with Vallee.

People like James Stewart asked friends for her telephone number. He took her out dancing and dining, but when she declined to invite him into her small apartment he never called again. "I didn't have the guts to tell him my mother was inside snoring away on one of the two beds in our only bedroom," she said.

Yvonne De Carlo became so adept at finding ways to sidestep the many invitations she received to spend time in the bedrooms of the stars that she became known as "Hollywood's only virgin."

Director Sam Wood gave her a small part in *For Whom The Bell Tolls,* a major success for Gary Cooper and Ingrid Bergman. After watching Cooper and Vera Zorina play a scene, only to see Ingrid Bergman taking over Zorina's role next day, she realized for the first time the small value of long-term contracts in the film industry.

After two years at Paramount Yvonne De Carlo asked for her release from the three-year contract. Paramount showed how much faith they had in her future by agreeing to let her go immediately.

Her rounds of the studio casting departments took her to Universal, where Walter Wanger spotted her and gave her the lead in *Salome, Where She Danced.*

"I was delighted with the role," she said, "and very excited at playing with a fellow Canadian, Rod Cameron, from Alberta. Hollywood was full of Canadians at that time."

Yvonne De Carlo didn't forget Universal, and when shooting of *Salome* was over and she became an "overnight star," she accepted a five-year contract with the studio. "I wanted to thank Universal for the way they had handled me in *Salome,*" she said. "I was convinced that my new-found fame would be safe in their hands."

Her faith was not misplaced. Universal starred her in *Frontier Gal,* and then in *Song of Scheherazade.* Neither were huge box-office successes, but moviegoers loved her performance and her fan mail continued to mount at Universal. One review read, "After *Salome, Where She Danced,* one might have expected Universal Pictures to find better vehicles for this extremely attractive young star. Audiences love Yvonne De Carlo even though the films they are giving her are not worthy of her immense talents."

Her faith in Universal was beginning to fade, but *Brute Force,* with a superb cast including Hume Cronyn and Burt Lancaster, helped her accept others like *Slave Girl, Black Bart, Casbah*, and *River Lady*, which did nothing to satisfy her growing legion of fans.

According to a 1946 Universal publicity handout, Yvonne De Carlo "speaks fluent French, loves reading Shakespeare, Greek mythology and any books available about theatre and film." It continued, "Her hobby is collecting records, especially of symphonies and operas."

The same press release decided to take two years off her actual age, twenty-four. The studio changed her birth date from 1922 to 1924.

In 1969, shown the release while appearing in Toronto at the Royal Alexandra Theatre in the Abe Burrows' play *Cactus Flower*, she laughed. "They made up anything in those days. Rarely did we get the chance to read or approve press releases, no matter how important we were. All they wanted was publicity in the papers," she said. "If the stories were printed and were complimentary they were happy. We were supposed to grin and bear it. The biggest problem was keeping up with the things they invented so we didn't put our foot in it when we were next being interviewed for a story."

Her interest in opera was apparently accurate, unless Hedda Hopper fell for the studio publicist's imagination. In one of her columns that was syndicated worldwide to more than a thousand newspapers, she said Yvonne De Carlo's voice tutor, operatic tenor Miklos Rozza, said he was almost ready to present her to the Metropolitan Opera in New York.

De Carlo enhanced that statement by producing pictures of her latest boyfriend, Jerome Hines. "He is the leading basso at the Metropolitan," she said. "We sing duets from *Don Giovanni* together."

Whatever happened to Hines or her hopes to sing opera we don't know. No more was heard of this ambition.

When she played in *Frontier Gal* she refused the offer by the director and producer to provide her with a double to do all the riding. "I did every scene myself," she proudly told newsmen.

Between films she had joined a Los Angeles riding club and continued the sport she had been introduced to by her Aunt Connie in Vancouver many years earlier. She became so efficient that she won trophies with her horse, King, in rodeos and horse shows in many parts of the United States.

Yvonne De Carlo with her husband, Bob Morgan. Morgan, a stuntman in films, later lost a leg in an accident and their marriage ended in divorce.

"Most of the people watching never realized who I was," she said. "It was wonderful to be among people who were interested in my riding, not my acting, singing, or dancing."

In 1948 Burt Lancaster co-starred with her in *Criss Cross.* It was intended to be a B picture, playing second on theatre programs to the main feature, but initial reports back from showings in selected theatres were so good it was moved up to be the main feature.

De Carlo, determined to remain in the spotlight, spent a great deal of her earnings studying voice, diction, drama, and dancing.

In 1951 she flew to England to appear in *Hotel Sahara* with Peter Ustinov. "A brilliant actor," she told the *London Daily Mail.* "He never muffs a line."

She returned to England and Ireland to make an Allied Artists feature, *Tonight's The Night*. There she worked with an English cast including David Niven and George Cole. Having enjoyed the filming experience she returned a year later for the official opening of the film in Dublin, Ireland.

"I'm beginning to believe I will go anywhere in the world if it takes me somewhere I have never been before," she said.

In 1953 she accepted another offer to film in England, this time to make *The Captain's Paradise*. "I admired actor Alec Guiness so much that the chance to work with him made the long journey well worth while," she said. Guiness told the *London Daily Express* that he was "amazed that Yvonne was such a fine actress. In this film, perhaps for the first time, she is being allowed to show her ability to handle comedy lines and situations with ease and great competence."

Allan Dwan directed her that same year in *Passion*. "We used to get together for talks about Canada," she said. "Allan, Raymond Burr, and John Qualen were all Canadians."

In 1955 she accepted a role in *Shotgun*, to be filmed in Sedona, Arizona. It was not a major feature, and with Yvonne De Carlo at the peak of her career, many wondered why she agreed to be in the film. She responded, "When they told me Sterling Hayden would be my co-star I had no hesitation in saying yes! I'd met him once before and worshipped him for many years, so how could I say no?"

Sterling Hayden was a much-decorated marine from the Second World War, and De Carlo found out that he was no longer the light-hearted actor she had met casually five years earlier. "The war had changed him," she said. "When I invited him to join me for dinner in town he declined. He said he was going through a divorce and had to be very careful where he was seen."

So it was not Sterling Hayden who remained in her mind after the film was complete. It was Bob Morgan, one of Hollywood's best stunt men, who had been hired to do the dangerous shots that the producers felt were too dangerous for Hayden.

"As a horsewoman," she said, "I admired his horsemanship. But Bob was married with one child and I had no intention of causing that marriage to break up."

They met a few times for dinner in Hollywood, but De Carlo stopped seeing him because she feared the attraction between them was getting too strong.

Earlier that year Marie and Yvonne De Carlo had moved into a house on five and a half acres in the hills above Hollywood on Coldwater Canyon Drive. "It was the first really beautiful home we had owned," she said. "I built stables for my horses and rode around the grounds every day, totally relaxed because there was nobody looking over my shoulder."

Her career continued to grow, and De Carlo remembered:

> I had made a picture at MGM entitled *Sombrero* which Cecil B. DeMille saw. He told me that he wanted me for the role of Sephora, the wife of Moses, in *The Ten Commandments*. He was about to leave for Egypt where the film was made in 1955. Unfortunately I had already signed to make *Magic Fire* in Germany. It was a Republic feature to be directed by William Dieterle so reluctantly I had to decline his offer. But I told him that when the film in Germany was complete not to be surprised to see me in Egypt.
>
> He made no promises and looked very surprised when I arrived in Cairo. We had wrapped up the German film very quickly and I was in Cairo before *The Ten Commandments* had started shooting. A few days after I arrived he told me the role of Sephora was still mine if I wanted it. Of course I accepted. Working with Mr. De Mille was a learning experience that I will never forget.

Studio records show she was paid $25,000 for the part that helped establish her as a first-class actress who could handle any kind of role. It was a superb role unlike anything else she had done up to that time, and critics lauded her acting in a film that is today still considered a classic.

"It wasn't until I was in Egypt to work with De Mille that I saw Bob Morgan again. He was working on the film. This time we seemed immediately attracted to each other." She learned that Morgan's wife had died tragically at only thirty-three and he was left with a young daughter, Bari, to care for. The De Carlo-Morgan romance continued back in Hollywood, and they were married in the Episcopal Church in Reno on November 21, 1955.

When *The Ten Commandments* was released in 1956 it became one of the box-office bonanzas of all time. De Carlo accepted without hesitation an invitation to be the guest of honour at the premiere of the film in Buenos Aires.

She had been working hard to perfect a nightclub act that would allow her to make the personal appearances that she enjoyed so much. So she decided to add a little icing to the cake. She translated her entire nightclub act into Spanish and introduced it to South America in Buenos Aires. It earned rave reviews and much enthusiasm for the Hollywood actress who had taken the trouble to present the show in the language of the country, something that had never been done before.

Back in Hollywood she starred in more than a dozen feature films that were box-office successes.

In 1957 she was teamed with Clark Gable at Warner Brothers. "I played the part of a girl sold to a slave trader, Gable. He was totally professional both on and off the set. I enjoyed working with him. The film was a great success."

Gable said, "I admired her determination to give the role everything it demanded. Wish I could have made more films with her."

In 1958 she flew to Italy to make *The Sword And The Cross*. For months before making the trip she hired a language coach, and by the time she left for Rome she could speak fluent Italian. "I enjoyed the idea of working in different countries and it was quite an experience working with an Italian company, made much easier because I was able to follow all the conversations on the set."

Having enjoyed the success of her Spanish performance in Argentina, she decided to enlarge the show from a solo act to a complete production. In 1959 she put the show into rehearsals and decided to open it in July at the Chaudiere Club in Ottawa. "It was chaos from beginning to end," she recalled in her autobiography. "Costumes didn't fit and we had to cut the best comedy number from the show."

Even though the production drew capacity crowds wherever it played, including the famed Cocoanut Grove in Los Angeles, it was not a financial success. "I had spent $47,027.13," she said, "but grossed only $53,500."

It was also the beginning of the end of her marriage to Bob Morgan. The differences between them grew more stormy during a nightclub tour she did in South America in 1961. De Carlo was ill most of the time and claimed she got little or no sympathy from her husband.

In 1962 she made her summer musical theatre debut at the Papermill Playhouse in Milburn, New Jersey. The show, *Destry Rides Again*, was a huge success that she later repeated at the Dallas State Fair theatre.

Shortly after returning back home she received a shocking phone call. The voice identified himself as Bob Morgan's buddy, stuntman Chuck Hayward. He was calling from the set of *How The West Was Won* being filmed in Arizona.

His message told her that Bob had had a serious accident jumping from a train. "He's in bad shape," said Hayward. "You'd better get here as fast as you can."

On arrival in Phoenix the next morning she was rushed to the Good Samaritan Hospital, where Morgan was in the intensive care unit.

The next day, Bari, Morgan's daughter from his first marriage, arrived at the hospital. His mother arrived the day after. "She is one of the bravest women I have ever met," De Carlo told the Phoenix newspaper. "She has kept us all together without shedding a tear or complaining about anything."

The final blow came when De Carlo realized that her husband had lost one of his legs. "If I had been thinking about divorce," she said, "all thoughts disappeared at that moment. Bob had been earning good money but now it would be up to me to keep the family together."

When, in 1971, Vivian Blaine was completing her run on Broadway as the lead in the Carl Reiner hit comedy *Enter Laughing*, De Carlo was asked if she would take over the role as star for the North American tour that was to follow when the show closed on Broadway. She got an added unexpected bonus, the opportunity to play the role of the vamp, Angela, for one week before it left the city.

Vivian wanted out, and Carl Reiner urged Yvonne to take over the final week of the show in New York.

Yvonne De Carlo hid her beauty under layers of makeup to become a
major TV star in *The Munsters*. From left: Butch Patrick, De Carlo, Fred
Gwynne, Beverly Owen, and Al Lewis.

When, some years later, she returned to star in a New York musical,
press agents conveniently forgot *Enter Laughing* and told the world the
new show would be her debut on the Broadway stage.

For six years De Carlo tended to her husband's injuries, trying to help
him recover the confidence he needed to get back into society. But the
medical bills continued to mount, and the Morgans had to mortgage
their Coldwater Canyon home to get the cash to keep solvent.

Finally it became apparent to both of them that the marriage must
end. Their two sons, Bruce and Michael, decided to stay with their

mother. The divorce was a quiet one. They agreed to split all their assets equally, and the divorce was soon final.

She told her agent to accept any jobs that were offered in nightclubs or movies, no matter how small the film or club, if they paid money.

Film roles were getting harder to find, so when in 1963 she was offered the chance to be tested for the role of Lily Munster in *The Munsters*, a television comedy series due to be aired in 1964, she jumped at the chance. "We needed the money and I was prepared to take anything offered."

For the first time in many years she had to audition for the role along with other performers known and unknown. Happily, a few days later, she was told she had the part.

The Munsters went on the air on September 23, 1964. From day one it was a great success. She didn't complain when she had to arrive at Universal Studios, where the show was filmed, at six o'clock in the morning, as her makeup took almost three hours to apply.

Overnight Yvonne De Carlo, at forty-two, was once again hailed as a star. Newspapers and magazines asked for interviews. Every talk show host in the United States asked her to be a guest. Soon the De Carlo bank balance was back in the black.

"I even customized my Jaguar with coffin handles, spiderweb hubcaps, and the Munster family crest on the doors," she recalled in 1969.

De Carlo never dreamed that a role in which her face was painted white and her beauty hidden under tons of makeup would perhaps be the role she will still be remembered for fifty years from now.

Nobody seems to know today why the show was cancelled after only two seasons. It was still high in the ratings, although it had been challenged by *Bewitched* and *The Addams Family*, shows that their producers agreed had only been put on television because of the success of *The Munsters*.

With the demise of the television show, De Carlo accepted the offer to make a full-length film, *Munster, Go Home*. It was successful, but producers were slow to offer her roles in other feature films. Everyone, they said, thought of her now not as the glamorous Yvonne De Carlo of the forties but as the 150-year-old Lily Munster, who had brought her more fan mail than ever before in her long career.

She started accepting roles in summer stock musicals and prepared a nightclub act in which she danced, sang, and did light comedy. Both were great successes.

Donald O'Connor asked her to co-star with him in *Little Me*, a musical comedy that was to play for five weeks at Harrah's Club in Lake Tahoe and another five at the Sahara Hotel in Las Vegas.

One of her biggest successes at this time in her career was the starring role in the stage production of *Hello Dolly*. The musical provided her with five months of work in major U.S. cities.

In 1969 she was teamed with actor John Vivyan in *Cactus Flower*. The play was a big success, drawing full houses everywhere it played.

A meeting in New York with Ruth Webb, a theatrical agent, gave her the opportunity to really make her mark on the Broadway stage. Harold Prince was producing the Stephen Sondheim and Michael Bennett musical *Follies*. Prince turned her down for the lead role, but Sondheim liked her audition so much that he wrote in a role, Carlotta, especially for her. Alexis Smith had won the lead role, Dorothy Collins another principal role. "All of us Canadians," De Carlo proudly told the New York press.

The song Stephen Sondheim wrote for her, "I'm Still Here," turned out to be one of the biggest hits of the show that played for more than a year in the huge Winter Garden Theatre. The lyrics to the song introduced her as a former showgirl who became a film star and then went on to become a television personality. She told a *Newsweek* reporter that doing the song was easy. "It was my life," she said.

Night after night "I'm Still Here" stopped the show. Yvonne De Carlo, in what everyone called her Broadway debut, earned many standing ovations during the run of the show. Once again the major talk show hosts clamoured for her presence.

In addition to her role as Lily Munster, De Carlo accepted many other roles on TV shows. Memorable are her part as a doctor in *Death Valley Days*, her part as Helen Haldeman in *The Virginian*, her role as Imogene Delphinia, also in *The Virginian*, and her part as Miss Springer in a 1984 episode of *Murder, She Wrote*.

Often she still accepts small roles in films, and in 1981 she played her final lead as Lily Munster in *The Munster's Revenge.*

Her two sons play an important role in her life. Bruce, the oldest son, is now a film director. Michael is not in show business but has been very successful out of the spotlight.

Is there any part she regrets taking? She told *People* magazine in 1987 that perhaps her biggest mistake was accepting the role of a "rumpled landlady" in a Canadian-made film, *A Masterpiece of Murder*, starring Bob Hope, made in her hometown of Vancouver. It was made for TV in the Masterpiece Movie series. "I'm not ready yet for old sweaters and safety pins. It was a mistake to take a role that didn't even have one tinge of glamour."

Offers continue to arrive for her to appear in TV series or films, and she still receives a great deal of fan mail every day at her ranch home in Solvang, California.

Her autobiography, *Yvonne*, published by St. Martin's Press, New York, in 1987, became a best-seller. Written with Doug Warren, it is one of the most readable and satisfying autobiographies ever published. It will give you many wonderful hours reading her remarkable success story that still hasn't reached its ending.

Walter Huston

In a remarkable career in vaudeville, on Broadway in comedies, dramas, and musical plays, and in Hollywood as an acclaimed character actor, Walter Huston received many honours, and achieved one record that likely will never be eclipsed.

In 1948, in the film *The Treasure of the Sierra Madre*, in which he played a gold prospector, he won an Oscar for Best Supporting Actor. What makes it unique is the fact that, for the same film, his son John Huston also won an Oscar as Best Director.

It is the only time in Oscar history that a father and son have won Oscars in the same year. Though other fathers and sons have since been nominated, they have not yet taken home Oscars in the same year, and none were nominated for work on the same film.

An even more delightful epilogue to his career is the fact that Walter Huston's most enduring success came not in vaudeville, not on Broadway, not in Hollywood, but in a field of entertainment that he had never tested before, the recording industry. Even more amazing is that this worldwide success came after his death.

On Broadway in *Knickerbocker Holiday* in 1938, Walter Huston acted, danced, and sang. A recording was made on the stage of one song from the show. "The September Song" didn't have much impact at the time, but when it was used in the 1950 film *September Affair*, not released until months after Walter Huston's death, an enterprising record producer issued it as a 78-rpm vinyl record. It became a national and international hit, reaching the number-one spot on best-seller charts in twenty-two different countries.

The record company reported receiving over thirty thousand letters asking Walter Huston for his autograph in the two years that followed his death. "We sent out photographs, but of course Walter was not able to sign them," said Jonathon Walker.

Copies of the original 78-rpm recording of the song by Huston, in mint condition, have sold for more than $20,000 at memorabilia auctions in recent years, but today a remastered version of the song can be purchased on at least two different CDs for less than fifteen dollars.

Walter Huston was born Walter Houghston in Toronto, Ontario, on April 6, 1884. He was the son of two immigrants to Canada; his mother, Elizabeth McGibbon, was from Scotland, and his father, Robert Houghston, was from Ireland. His hard-working father, with an engineering degree from Dublin University, prospered in Canada, and at the time of Walter's birth he owned a flourishing construction company.

Robert Houghston, who had dabbled in electricity from the day it was created, believed electricity was the key to solving all the world's problems. At a very early age Walter Houghston and his two sisters and brother were all told by their father that their future lay in electrical engineering. "Prepare yourself for a successful future with this thought in mind," he said.

While he was still at Lansdowne Street School in Toronto, Walter worked nights in the hardware section of a local department store. He spent the money he made from this work at the Shaw School of Acting in downtown Toronto.

"I knew when I was only twelve that my future would not be in electrical engineering but the world of entertainment," he said in 1943. "To this day I recall waking from a very satisfying dream that I was singing on the stage of a large theatre and the audience was standing up cheering me. That dream changed my life. Every day on my walk to work after school I had passed the Shaw School of Acting, but the day after the dream was different. I walked into the school and asked to be enrolled."

His stage debut came when he was just sixteeen. In 1902, he joined a local stock company that travelled around North America. "My first play was *In Convict Stripes*. I had only four lines but I was determined to make them the most important four lines in the play," he said. "That really wasn't hard, the acting quality among the players was abysmal."

When the company folded after a sheriff seized all the costumes and sets to pay a few of the debts owed by the producer, Houghston decided to head for New York. "I suppose I could have got the train fare from my parents," he said, "but decided I had to do this on my own if I was to gain any respect from them about my belief that I was, or could be, an actor." He continued:

I jumped aboard a freight train in Buffalo that had labels on the doors saying it was destined for New York. It was a very rocky trip. Unlike the real hoboes who took blankets with them I had to lie on the hard steel floor of the truck. But I got there with nothing worse than an achy back, more than forty dollars in my pocket, enough to eat and pay for a room for a few weeks. But my first job was to take a bath. I think I must have been the most odorous actor in the city that morning in New York.

His arrival in New York coincided with Broadway actor Richard Mansfield's search for young people to appear in his play *Julius Caesar*. Walter Houghston, cleaned up and in his best suit, was waiting in line at the theatre two hours before the auditions started, hoping to be selected by Mansfield. "He listened while I recited a few lines and snorted not too politely," said Houghston. "'I can use you as an extra, no lines,' Mansfield said. At five dollars a week that was close to Paradise."

He recalled, "When nothing substantial followed *Julius Caesar*, I headed back to Toronto, this time paying my coach ticket with my last seven dollars, and told my parents I would be willing to attend the University of Toronto, studying, at my father's request, electrical engineering. I became almost as enthused as he was about the future of electrical power and graduated top of my class."

In 1905, his father used his considerable influence to push him into a job in St. Louis with the Universal Light and Power Company.

"It wasn't the best time of my life and it wasn't my worst," he said in 1943. "I found I knew much more about electricity than anyone else on the power company's payroll. I might have made something of myself if I had stayed with the company. Through the company I met my first wife, Rhea Gore, who was a journalist, and settled down to making a good home for the son we brought into this world." Their son, John, later became an important and successful film director in Hollywood.

The marriage to Rhea Gore lasted only four years. "Rhea wanted me to be a domestic engineer," he said. "My father wanted me to be an electrical engineer, and I wanted to be where electricity was being used as I thought it should be used, lighting the faces of actors in theatres around North America."

The divorce was finalized in February 1909. "It was not an angry divorce and we agreed to remain on friendly terms for the sake of John," he said in 1943.

In May of 1909 he met Bayonne Whipple, a young actress who was struggling to get a start in the professional live theatre.

"It was her unusual name that first drew me to her," he said. "But it was her wonderful sense of humour that convinced me to ask her if she would like to be my partner in a vaudeville act. I had no idea what the act would do but with her humour and my acting talents I thought we might achieve something."

Late in 1909 the act was ready for vaudeville. An audition with a touring manager brought the duo a twenty-week contract.

"I decided that to make sure that Bayonne didn't desert me if the act was any good I had better marry her," Houghston said. "Her first demand was that I change my name to Huston since it fit on the posters better. With a name like Whipple why should I demand her to change. It was the perfect name for vaudeville."

For fifteen years, from 1909 to 1924, Whipple and Huston travelled around North America, appearing at first in small theatres where "the pay allowed us to eat frugally and live in small boarding houses where there were often more cockroaches than guests," Huston recalled. "We sang, danced, did comedy skits, and managements soon found out that we could do the time on stage of three acts, so they hired us so they wouldn't have to pay the salaries of the two acts we replaced."

The vaudeville act of Whipple and Huston soon came to the attention of the major vaudeville theatre circuit bookers. "Within a year we had moved up to the best theatres in the nation which meant good hotels and the best the local restaurants had to offer. We actually travelled first-class from town to town by railroad. This was paradise as I had imagined it to be," Huston recalled. "On the Keith-Orpheum circuit we earned more than fifteen hundred dollars a week, an immense sum in the early 1920s."

The act kept going until vaudeville started to wane in the early 1930s. Sound films from Hollywood started drawing the big crowds. Vaudeville theatres were almost empty.

In New York a theatrical agent came round back stage. "You are a fine actor," said David Goldblum. "I want you to attend an audition tomorrow for a new play scheduled to open in two months on Broadway. You are too good an actor to be working in vaudeville."

"David Goldblum changed my life completely," said Huston.

> I found the part he had sent me to audition for wasn't just a supporting role but the lead, the title role in *Mr. Pitt*.
>
> One good thing about my Toronto University education, I had learned to read pages at a single glance and when they asked me to read several pages as Mr. Pitt, I was able to throw away the script and do the part entirely from memory.
>
> There was a silence when I finished and I was ready to leave the theatre when a ripple of applause broke out, in seconds all the other audition hopefuls, theatre management and casting people were also applauding.

Walter Huston said at that moment his mind flashed back to the dream that had convinced him to become an actor. "This was very close to being a wonderful standing ovation."

Huston bowed to the play's director, and said, "I hope you will call me and I won't have to call you," paraphrasing the oldest line in the industry.

"Neither of us will need to call. You have the job Mr. Huston. You will be starring on Broadway one month from now," said the director.

"Every day at rehearsals I waited for some newspaper man or photographer to come up to me and say, 'We'd like to do a story about you Mr. Huston,' but it never happened," Huston recalled. "There were a few small items in the New York papers saying the play was about to open, but if I was mentioned by name I must have missed it. I had all my great reviews from vaudeville sitting in an envelope I kept on stage, but nobody asked to see them."

Walter Huston had the unique ability to bring to life the characters he
played in Hollywood films. Actor Gary Cooper said Huston never
became a star because audiences didn't realize the brilliant actor whose
work they enjoyed so much in one film was the same actor they had
applauded only a few weeks before in a completely different role.

The morning after *Mr. Pitt* opened it was a different story.

"A New Star Is Born," said one headline on the theatre pages.
Another said "Walter Huston Is Mr. Pitt."

"I actually got that standing ovation I had dreamed about the day the
play opened," said Huston. "Newspapers lined up to do stories about the
vaudeville star who had grabbed the legitimate theatre by its ears and
come up smiling. I was concentrating entirely on my role and didn't have
time to wonder why David Goldblum hadn't been around to see me."

Late that same year Walter Huston was accosted in the street by a man who introduced himself as playwright Eugene O'Neill. Huston remembered:

> I had never seen O'Neill or even his picture, so I asked as politely as possible for some form of identification if the conversation was to continue. He grabbed two people passing by and asked point blank, "Who am I?" One lady said, "I think you are Mr. O'Neill the playwright."
>
> "Is that enough," he said, "or do I have to waste time getting whole population of New York together to identify me."
>
> I was so astonished and fascinated by this man's outgoing personality, I decided it really must be O'Neill.

The playwright dragged Huston into a nearby restaurant, and ordered two black coffees. Huston recalled the incident:

> "Now," he said "will you listen to what I have to say?" I laughed and said of course.
>
> "Well I have a play called *Desire Under The Elms* which will open later this year and I want you as the star. How does that grab you Mr. Huston?"
>
> "Give me the script and call my agent, Mr. Goldblum. He will discuss everything with you."
>
> "Goldblum," said O'Neill. "You've been far too busy getting standing ovations in *Mr. Pitt* to have read anything but your excellent reviews. Mr. David Goldblum, your agent, died two days after your play opened. He had a heart attack and went immediately."
>
> I too almost had a heart attack and died on the spot. This man who gave me a remarkable start as a straight actor had died and I didn't even know about it!

Walter Huston spent the next few days day searching for relatives of David Goldblum, but couldn't find any. "I had wondered why he hadn't been around for his ten percent of my salary, and each week had put aside the correct amount in an account separate from my own. After failing to find any family member who deserved the money I gave it to a charity in his name."

Desire Under The Elms was another triumph for Walter Huston. After the opening performance Eugene O'Neill brought backstage a handwritten note, scribbled on the show program. It read, "I, Eugene O'Neill give Mr. Walter Huston permission to appear in any of my plays in any form without the producer having to consult me for approval. This approval will stay in force until the day he or I die."

Huston was to remember this some years later when a radio drama producer wanted him to star in a Eugene O'Neill play. "Mr. O'Neill says if we want his play we must hire you," said the producer.

After *Desire Under The Elms* Huston received several offers from Hollywood. "I ventured out to California to see what the movies were all about," he said. "I made two silent films, *Gentlemen Of The Press* and *The Lady Lies*, but having no sound and no audience convinced me that Broadway was still the best place to be."

Walter Huston's Broadway triumphs were a major factor in the breakup of his marriage to Bayonne Whipple.

> She was very jealous of the fact that I was suddenly important in the legitimate theatre where, before our vaudeville success, she too had hoped to succeed.
>
> We were living in a beautiful apartment only a stone's throw away from most of the theatres. Our friends were growing in number, among them many famed Broadway actors and actresses, and she felt she was being pushed aside.
>
> She tried hard to get roles on Broadway, but the wisecracking character she had created in vaudeville was the only character she knew. Vaudeville had

destroyed a fine actress. I got her several auditions
but one producer told me that whatever she read it
was always in her raucous vaudeville style.

In 1929 Bayonne Whipple asked for a divorce. "I had no choice but
to agree," he said. "She had moved out of the apartment and was associating with some rather unsavoury characters."

What happened to Bayonne Whipple? "I'm afraid I must confess
that I don't know," said Huston. "I gave her a substantial money settle-
ment, much more than she would have got if we had fought over our
assets in court. She just went away and I never heard from her again."

Walter Huston's star on Broadway continued to rise.

"You must remember I was a good looking six-foot-tall leading man
in those days," he said in 1943, "not the gruff and grizzled old actor you
are talking to today."

He played in *Kongo*, *The Barker*, *Elmer The Great*, and *Knickerbocker
Holiday*, the musical show that brought him unexpected fame and a new
audience a year after his death.

"My favourite play was *Dodsworth*," he said. "I didn't realize it at the
time, although I loved the play, that I would one day repeat my
Broadway success in the Hollywood film of the same title."

In 1926 Walter Huston went to court in defence of an actress whose play
had been closed down by the New York censors.

Her play, *Sex*, was closed along with another, *The Captive*, starring
Basil Rathbone and Helen Menken. The publicity brought a film contract for Basil Rathbone.

But *Sex* was considered so lewd as to make it liable for prosecution
under the city's indecency bylaws. It was considered to be so bad that its
twenty-six-year-old star was taken to court.

When Walter Huston heard this he tried to round up other
Broadway stars to support the young actress in court. He recalled:

But none of them wanted the possible bad publicity
that they expected would come from an appearance in

court to support a play denounced by the morality squad. I contacted the actress, told her I believed in freedom of speech and would attend her trial to say so. She had no money to pay a lawyer so gladly accepted my offer to pay her legal fees.

I went alone to the hearings to hear the judge find the young actress guilty of indecency. I stood up and told the court if she was to be fined, I would pay the fine, if she was to go to jail, I would serve the sentence in her place. I told the court I felt that freedom of speech was enshrined in our Constitution.

The judge thanked me and said where he was planning to send the actress would not be a place in which I could substitute for her.

He said "freedom of speech and freedom of actions were two different things," and that it was on the actions that he had found her guilty.

I asked the judge if he had seen the play and he said "no."

"Then how can you find her guilty without seeing her perform?" I asked.

"I find her guilty on the strength of the evidence before me," said the judge. "Supposing I was asked to decide whether a man was under the influence of alcohol when he was involved in an accident, would you say I would have to have witnessed the accident to make my decision?"

I looked him straight in the eyes and said he had made his point. I actually saw a glimmer of a smile on his face.

But he sentenced her to ten days in the women's workhouse on Welfare Island where all the ladies without visible means of support were incarcerated.

The case and my intervention made all the newspapers. After the sentencing my lawyers said there was nothing more I could do about the case.

The happy ending to the story came two years later when the young actress was given a film contract in Hollywood. It was the beginning of an illustrious, if somewhat daring, career for the lady who invited her audiences to "Come up and see me sometime." Mae West became a superstar in Hollywood, but she never forgot Walter Huston's generous gesture in paying her lawyers and offering to serve her sentence. But that story comes much later in Walter Huston's career.

In 1930 Walter Huston met the woman who was soon to become his third and last wife:

> Nan Sunderland was a very competent actress, and our paths crossed on many occasions. I saw her looking at me in a very peculiar way one day at a party given in my honour before I left for Hollywood, so I stared back at her. We both broke out laughing.
>
> "Are you thinking what I'm thinking?" she said.
>
> "I believe so," I replied.
>
> "Then let's have dinner together and see if our private lives have as much in common as have our lives in the theatre," she said.
>
> I agreed, and two days later we announced our engagement. Two months later we were married. It was the best move I ever made in my entire life. She seems to be able to know what I'm thinking, and I seem to be able to read her thoughts, so we never had any secrets and now, twelve years after we were married, we have never had a cross word.

Two of Walter and Nan's greatest friends were Dr. and Mrs. Loyal Davis. Edith Davis was known to theatregoers as actress Edith Luckett. Dr. Davis, a world-renowned neurosurgeon who later became president of the American College of Surgeons, lived in Chicago.

In 1936, at their home, Walter Huston met the thirteen-year-old daughter of Mrs. Luckett from a previous marriage. She had been legally adopted by Loyal Davis and spoke of him as her father.

Nancy Davis loved the theatre, enjoyed her mother's successes, and was ecstatic to meet the the man she from that day on called Uncle Walter, then the toast of Broadway.

Nancy Davis grew up, became an actress on Broadway and in Hollywood, and her only marriage was to a Hollywood actor who rose higher in the world than anyone ever dreamed possible. As Mrs. Ronald Reagan, wife of the President of the United States, she was delighted to talk about Uncle Walter. "I could talk about him for hours," she said. She continued:

> At times he was almost like a father to me. If I had any problem I always asked Uncle Walter for a solution. And always with his immense knowledge of humanity, he was able to give me an answer.
>
> I often wished he had been my teacher when I was in school. He was a great actor but what a wonderful teacher he would have made. He was considerate to everyone and never claimed he was too busy to spend time with whoever wanted to talk to him.

After Walter and Nan Huston moved to Hollywood late in 1930, his success as an actor brought him worldwide fame. Nan had decided to retire to make sure there was always someone to greet him when he arrived home after a long day's work.

He received rave reviews for his first Hollywood sound film role in *The Virginian*. Gary Cooper, who starred with him, said on many occasions to journalists that "Walter Huston is the reason I am still a big star today. He showed me how to change my rather insipid young leading man roles into the tough character I created in *The Virginian*. Victor Fleming, our director, had great respect for Walter and between us we changed my role completely."

In 1931 Huston accepted a challenge thrown down by Canadian-born evangelist Aimee Semple McPherson, who had built her own gospel temple in Los Angeles. Nightly she drew capacity crowds to hear her speak.

Huston had spoken out against the prohibition then in force in the

United States. The evangelist challenged him to debate prohibition with her. She was for it. He was against it.

The two combatants fought for nearly two hours. The evangelist produced figures to prove that prohibition was saving lives. Huston produced figures to show that liquor was available everywhere and there was more drunkeness with prohibition than without. "I had six friends in the temple," he said. "They applauded my side of the story. The other eighteen hundred supported Aimee. Guess who won?"

Perhaps his most memorable role was the title character in *Abraham Lincoln*. Huston recalled, "I was delighted to be the star of the first sound production directed by one of the greatest, if not the greatest directors of the silent movie era, D.W. Griffith. I was told he had asked for me and had first been turned down by the producers."

Walter Huston appeared in vaudeville, on Broadway in dramas, and in Hollywood in silent and sound films, winning an Oscar for his role in *The Treasure of the Sierra Madre*.

"I wouldn't have made the film if they had refused to give me Walter Huston as Lincoln," said Griffith.

Huston's *Abraham Lincoln* is today considered the finest role in his career, but the film itself was not a success.

"I can say now, thirteen years after the film was made that D.W. Griffith was not the same director he was in the silent era," said Huston. "He did not make the transition easily, and perhaps he will forgive me for saying that I created my role of Abraham Lincoln without his direction, often, I must admit, against his direction."

Una Merkel, a big star on Broadway in the thirties, made her sound film debut in *Abraham Lincoln*. She recalled the making of the movie at her home in California in 1962.

> I had made a couple of silent movies, one for Mr. Griffith, before returning to Broadway. When I heard he had asked for me in what looked like being a film people would talk about for ever, I came back to Hollywood.
>
> I don't recall any tension on the set. It was as though Mr. Griffith was ready to let his actors take over in many of the major scenes. Dear D.W., he was a star in silents, but he looked tired and often let us create the scenes ourselves. Walter Huston was, of course, an incredible actor. I still consider it was a privilege working with him.

Walter Huston and his wife rarely went to Hollywood parties. Walter explained in 1943, "At many of those parties there were people who neither of us admired. So we gave our own parties and selected our guests carefully."

As more and more stars became unavailable to their fans and the newspaper writers, Walter Huston became more accessible.

"I stopped my car at the studio gates every night if there were people waiting for autographs," he said. "Those people had made me a wealthy man and I really did enjoy signing autographs. I never just signed my name, always adding a personal line. If a young girl had nice eyes, I wrote that in her book. By the mid thirties most of the

Hollywood actors had taken their names out of the telephone book. Mine was never left out of the book and is still there today."

His wife, Nan, said, "Walter would talk for hours to fans. If he liked the way they sounded he would often invite them to our home, some to stay overnight. And as far as newspapers are concerned, I don't believe he ever turned down an interview request."

Joan Crawford, with whom Walter Huston appeared in *Rain*, called him "the most considerate man I ever met. Why was someone like this never around when I was free to marry."

Walter Huston was nominated four times for Oscars, but only won once. In 1936 he was nominated as Best Actor in *Dodsworth* but lost to Paul Muni. In 1941 he was cited for Best Actor in *All That Money Can Buy* but lost to Gary Cooper. In 1942 he was in the running for Best Supporting Actor in *Yankee Doodle Dandy* but lost to Van Heflin. In 1948 he finally won an Oscar. For *The Treasure of the Sierra Madre*, directed by his son, John Huston, he was called to the podium to receive the Best Supporting Actor award. Half an hour later John Huston received the Best Director Oscar for his work on the same film.

The talented actor Oscar Homolka, one of the losing nominees, said to the *Hollywood Citizen-News* after the ceremony that had he won he would have given the statuette to Walter Huston. "He is surely the greatest and most natural of all the fine character actors in Hollywood."

Nancy Davis, then in Hollywood starting her film career, recalled that in the late thirties, when the top salary for anyone in the film industry was around $75,000 for each film, "Uncle Walter was getting at least $80,000."

The Hustons were the first Hollywood couple to build a home at Lake Arrowhead in the mountains about fifty miles from Los Angeles.

"I visited often," said Nancy Davis.

> It was like a home away from home for me. The house had a swimming pool, a tennis court, and a fully equipped workshop where he made most of the chairs and tables that graced the lawns around the pool.

He had a treehouse called Crovenay House. A nameplate on the tree read, Alastair, duc de Crovenay. At first we thought it was some ancestor of Uncle Walter, but one day he let us in on a little secret when he had as his guest a rather bumptious expert on the wildlife that abounded in the area.

As some ducks flew across the skyline, Uncle Walter said to the expert, "Aren't those Crovenay ducks?" The know-it-all replied, "No not Crovenay, I know them well, they never come so far north."

After the know-it-all had left, Uncle Walter told us his secret. There was no Alastair, duc de Crovenay. He had created the name so he could bring down to earth people he believed didn't know nearly as much as they boasted.

Together we formed the Crovenay Society. I'll give you an example. We were listening to an expert on the growing of grass. This gentleman from Georgia talked of a new blue grass, much hardier than most other

Walter Huston is still remembered for his portrayal of Abraham Lincoln. Una Merkel played Mrs. Lincoln.

grasses. Walter asked him if the Crovenay grass from Georgia wasn't hardier than the new grass. The so-called expert replied: "I know the Crovenay well. It's good but it won't grow in many states."

That was another expert we crossed off our list.

Ty Cobb, the star baseballer, a great friend of Walter Huston, who loved the game of baseball, was inducted into the Crovenay Society. Some years ago he put this story in the Crovenay records:

> I asked a rather objectionable baseball scout to go and see a young player who had impressed me greatly. I told him Tom Crovenay was playing in some remote town in the north-east. The scout promised to check him out, and when I bumped into him some months later I asked about Tom Crovenay. "He was great in the field but he couldn't hit at all," said the scout. "He'll never make the majors."
>
> That is the only time in my long career that I went into our front office and demanded that someone be fired.

After *The Treasure of the Sierra Madre*, Walter Huston, then sixty-four, told his wife he was feeling rather tired and would take only the films that really appealed to him in future.

He only made three more films, *Summer Holiday* in 1947, *The Great Sinner* in 1949, and *The Furies* in February of 1950.

"Let's go to New York," he said to his wife. "Perhaps they have a play for me there. I love playing to people, not just a camera."

Nan and Walter Huston flew to New York. "I couldn't believe the reception we received," he told the *New York Times*.

> Within a few hours of arriving I had more than a dozen scripts sitting in my room at the hotel.
>
> Nan came with me because a good friend was quite ill and she wanted to help his wife during the illness.

The friend died the day we arrived so Nan will stay a few days here in New York helping her friend get over the loss of her husband.

I am going back to Los Angeles by plane. I'll take all the scripts with me and you can expect to see me back on Broadway later this year.

His return to Hollywood coincided with his birthday. Once back in his suite at the Beverly Hills Hotel, he discovered his son, John, had planned a special party in his honour. "Only a few guests, your real friends," said John.

April 6, Walter Huston's sixty-sixth birthday, saw him up early planning to take a walk in the grounds of the hotel. John accompanied him.

"I feel tired," said Walter. "I have a pain in my back, we'd better go back to the hotel."

"He was moving very slowly," recalled John Huston, "so I called a doctor immediately. When Dr. Verne Mason arrived he said he believed the pain might have been caused by a vascular aneurism or by a kidney stone. He was inclined to believe the latter." He continued, "My father wanted to get up to attend the birthday party, but I advised him to stay in bed. Presently he fell asleep, so I left to join the waiting guests. It was a sombre party and by ten o'clock the last guest had gone home."

John Huston made a quick phone call to Dr. Loyal Davis, then living in Arizona. He recalled:

> I explained the symptoms and he said he would be on the first plane in the morning. I called Nan in New York and she too said she would be on the first plane she could get to Los Angeles. Unhappily they both arrived too late.
>
> A little after one my father fell asleep. I continued to sit by the bed and about an hour later realized he was no longer breathing. I called the hotel doctor and he promised to come over immediately. My father had died peacefully. There was no struggle. I have never seen so quiet a death. He died as modestly as he had lived.

I am telling it this way so that the people who loved him will be reassured as to his last moments. His death will be harder on those of us left behind, I suspect, than it was on him.

His time had come so he just died.

When the story hit the world's newspapers next day, the funeral home named in the story received thousands of calls from unknowns and the biggest stars in Hollywood and on Broadway.

"They all wanted to pay tribute to my beloved father," said John Huston.

There was no church or funeral home that could accommodate the people who wished to attend his funeral. Charles Brackett, president of the Academy of Motion Picture Arts and Sciences, suggested to John Huston that the funeral service should be held in the Academy theatre. About two hundred seats were reserved for personal friends, many famous, many from outside the film industry, people who had been important in Walter Huston's life. Telegrams were sent to the two hundred, who were told the telegram would get them into the theatre through a side entrance.

Once the invited guests were seated, the rest of the theatre was opened to the crowds, estimated at more than one thousand people, milling around outside the church.

John Huston recalled a special incident:

> I went outside to see if any of our friends had perhaps been forgotten, and I spotted Barbara Stanwyck stand-ing at the back of the crowd weeping. I pushed my way through to her, grabbed her arm and took her into the theatre. We had to put a special chair in the front because all the seats were occupied. I told her I was sorry if somehow her name had been missed when we sent out the telegrams. She replied, "Oh no, I received the telegram but stupidly left it at home."

The famous people who paid tribute to Walter Huston are too numerous to list. Among them were Humphrey Bogart, Spencer Tracy,

John Garfield, Walter Brennan, Leo Carrillo, Jimmy Durante, Nancy Davis, Ronald Reagan, James Cagney, Mary Astor, and, of course, Barbara Stanwyck.

Spencer Tracy spoke the eulogy. "Professionally, he was the best," he said. "In private life he led an exemplary life, helping more people than this world will ever know. It is obvious from those here today that he had more friends than anyone else in this industry of ours."

One of the most moving moments of the ceremony came when a dignified woman in black, wearing no makeup, stepped out from among the uninvited guests, walked to the casket, and said, "Dear Walter if I could change places with you and serve your sentence in another life, I would do it willingly."

She broke down in tears, ran to the exit doors, and left the theatre. Few recognized Mae West. Even fewer had any idea what memories had brought her to the service. Not one newspaper reported the incident.

Ruby Keeler

"I was always in the right place at the right time!" This is how Ruby Keeler, the darling of moviegoers in the late 1930s, explained her remarkable success in life.

"I was a good dancer, a so-so actress and not at all a singer," she said. "Add those together and there is nothing to explain the fame I achieved back in 1933 in Hollywood. I was there, in the right place when they needed a hoofer for the film *42nd Street*. But my being in the right place at the right time started to happen long before 1933."

In 1973, she said, "If I could write my life story it would only be about the twenty-eight wonderful years of my life I spent with my husband, John Lowe, sadly he died in 1969. But nobody would read it! So why don't we go back to Halifax, Nova Scotia, where I was born on August 25, 1909."

Ethel Keeler was the second of six children born to Ralph and Elnora Keeler. After her birth they stayed only three years in Canada before heading south to New York City. She changed her name to Ruby when she was seven, "because it sounded more theatrical than Ethel."

"I had no memory of Canada until I went back a few years ago at the request of a television station," she said.

> My father was a truck driver in Halifax. He was doing quite well, but a friend who had moved to New York a few years earlier told him the same job paid twice as much in New York as it did in Halifax.
>
> My mother told me a few years later that we packed everything we could into about ten suitcases and cardboard boxes and before we left gave away all our furniture to friends. All of us fitted into the back of a small van and off we went to New York City.

Was the trip uneventful? "Yes," she said, "if you count two flat tires, a snowstorm in September, and sleeping, eating and living in the truck or by the side of the road uneventful. But we got there. My real memory of the trip is that I was always thirsty because mother wouldn't let any of us drink much because then we would have had to make too many bathroom stops along the way."

The Keeler family found a three-bedroom apartment that would accept children only hours after they arrived in New York. Two days later Ralph Keeler found work as a driver for the Knickerbocker Ice Company.

"When I was five mother enrolled me in the parochial school of St. Catherine of Siena, part of the Roman Catholic Parish in which we were living," Keeler recalled. "That was where I first learned to use my feet. They called it drill, but really the class, led by one of the teachers, Helen Guest, was a rhythmic exercise program that included simple tap dance steps."

By the time she had reached the age of ten she had improved on the early tap steps she had learned, and had performed as a solo tap dancer at a number of community concerts.

"A member of the parish was a professional dancer and he encouraged me to work with him until I had reached what he called 'a professional standard,'" Keeler said.

In 1923, at the urging of her first "dance" teacher, Helen Guest, her parents enrolled her in the Professional Children's School.

"I went back and forth every day in my father's ice truck. On hot days I used to sit on the ice to keep cool. Dad always dropped off a chunk of ice at the school so we could have cold water all day long."

Ruby Keeler was definitely in the right place when Broadway star George M. Cohan visited the school to see if he could find a young dancer able to keep up with his own superb toe tapping.

Cohan later told the New York World that "there were lots of good tappers at the school, it was the principal type of dancing taught in that era, but after I had watched a few of the school's routines I had no hesitation in selecting thirteen-year-old Ruby Keeler to appear in my new show, *The Rise of Rosie O'Reilly*."

"By the time I was fourteen I was so cocky that I passed by my photographs displayed outside the theatre as though they had been there for years," said Keeler.

> But George M. soon brought me down to earth and kept my head from getting too swollen. One of the teachers told him I had been boasting to some of the

other kids from the school about how good I was. He gave about twenty of the senior students tickets to see one of the afternoon shows and when I danced with him at that performance he showed how good he was by adding twice as many taps as usual to the routine. He didn't really show me up because there was nobody better than George M. but he whispered to me during the routine, "See kid, you aren't quite there yet." From that day on I stayed with my feet on the ground and never again boasted about my abilities.

At Cohan's suggestion, she had joined the Jack Blue School of Rhythm and Taps for six hours of tuition each week. "It didn't help my

Ruby Keeler, from Halifax, was only fourteen when she danced in Texas Guinan's nightclub in New York, which was frequented by gangsters. How she was allowed to be there is quite a story.

knowledge of history and geography," she said, "but it taught me a great deal about dancing."

When the Broadway show folded, Ruby Keeler was urged by Cohan to enter a contest being organized by impresario Nils Thor Granlund. Granlund was the man who booked the acts and dancers who performed at most of the top nightclubs in New York City.

"George M. took the trouble to come to the school I attended and show me how to achieve the twinkling taps only he could do," Keeler said. "He spent several days with me and when the day of the Granlund competition came around I was astonishing myself at how many taps I could get into a minute."

Granlund liked what he saw but was doubtful whether he could consider hiring a fourteen-year-old.

"He told me that at fourteen there was no way he could get permission for me to perform in clubs where most of the audience was usually drunk," Keeler said.

> It was the prohibition era, but apparently club patrons could get as much as they wanted if they would pay the price. Then George M. came in and did a brief dance with me. Mr. Granlund shrugged and said, "If I say you are eighteen nobody will know the difference. Nobody would ever believe a fourteen-year-old could dance like that." George M. told him that he would have to pay for a chaperone, perhaps one of the teachers from the Professional Children's School.
>
> One week later I was eighteen, they had added four years to my age, and I found myself standing on the stage of the El Fey Club, the nightclub frequented by gangsters and many other undesirable characters. It had made Texas Guinan, the entertainer who owned the club, into a wealthy woman. It was Texas who coined the phrase, "Give the little lady a big hand." I heard her shout it to the audience every night when I finished my act. The applause was great but some of the rather drunken roars of approval I heard as I stepped

out from the chorus to do my own special dance in the spotlight scared the life out of me.

Most of the chorus dancers, quite a lot older than me, went out into the audience and sat on the knees of the patrons pouring drinks down their throats. I learned later that they got extra money for each shot of illicit liquor they convinced the patrons to buy and drink.

Texas Guinan once said to me, "You'll be out of this vile atmosphere long before you have to sit on the customers' knees. Mark my words you are going to be a big star very soon."

She wouldn't let any of the customers talk to me. She was a much better chaperone than the teacher who was supposed to be watching me. I saw her night after night drinking with the club patrons.

But once again Ruby Keeler was in the right place at the right time. After two years with Texas Guinan she was introduced to producer Charles Dillingham, a visitor to the club.

"I remember him telling me that he hoped I wouldn't think he was a regular club patron," she said. "He told me George M. had told him to drop in and see me dance." She recalled:

"I want you for my new Broadway show, *Bye Bye Bonnie*," he said. "You won't be the star but I'll give you a specialty dance number that will open a few eyes. How soon can you get away from this place?"

Later that evening I spoke to Texas and told her about Mr. Dillingham. "I know all about that," said Texas. "Respectable men like that don't come here often. We cater to gangsters, bootleggers, drunks, and reprobates. When does he want you to start?"

"Soon as I can be free from my contract with you," I said.

She walked into her dressing room, beckoning me

to follow. She unlocked a safe inside a closet, rooted through a lot of papers, and handed one to me.

"That's your contract," she said. "Tear it up. You are free to leave the show tonight. You deserve better than these bums out front."

I remember hugging her and saying, "Thanks Texas."

"Don't thank me," she said, "Texas Guinan doesn't do anything without a reason. One of these days I'll be coming to you for a favour. I hope at that time you'll remember what I did for you tonight."

Did Texas Guinan ever ask for the favour to be returned?

"Yes," said Keeler. "About eight years later, only a few months before she died in 1933. I was able to help her. It wasn't money, just something she needed to be sure would be done after her death. I will never tell our secret, but I remember now that it satisfied me more than anything else I've done in my entire life. Texas Guinan may have been a tough cookie but I'm sure more people than me know she had a heart of gold."

Ruby Keeler's "Tampico Tap" number in Charles Dillingham's *Bye Bye Bonnie* took her out of the chorus and into her first Broadway spotlight.

"I got my first reviews for that solo dance. Audiences liked what I did, and critics were not hesitant to say the number actually stopped the show," she said. "I couldn't believe I was only sixteen and already a showstopper on Broadway. I might have got very big-headed at that time in my life but George M. who saw the show, and Texas Guinan, who slipped in the theatre to see my one number, brought me down to earth with the same comment, 'You've got a lot to learn yet baby!'"

When *Bye Bye Bonnie* closed after a six-month run, Charles Dillingham put her immediately into his new show, *Lucky.*

"It was an unfortunate title," she said. "It only lasted four nights. The critics praised me but panned the show unmercifully."

Charles Dillingham didn't give up because of one failure.

"He signed me for the run of the show in *The Sidewalks Of New York*. It was still 1926 and two weeks after my seventeenth birthday I was appearing in my third Broadway show. *Sidewalks* was a big success, running almost a year. I still have the reviews," she said. "Remembering that

I had been officially eighteen when I worked with Texas Guinan, the newspapers now referred to me as the 'nineteen-year-old dancer who has taken New York by storm.' It was several years later, when I made *42nd Street* in Hollywood, that I demanded the studio publicists take me back four years to my real age. I had to produce my birth certificate from Nova Scotia before anyone would believe me."

One of her dance partners in *Sidewalks* was a young comedian named Lester Hope. He later went on to fame in Hollywood as Bob Hope.

In 1928 she was once again in the right place at the right time.

"Flo Ziegfeld, who had been quite ill, came to see *The Sidewalks of New York*," she said.

> I had hoped he would come around back stage to meet the cast but he didn't appear. We all learned next day that he had to be carried out of the theatre and taken by ambulance to hospital. Any hope of a *Ziegfeld Follies* contract seemed to have flown out of the window.
>
> But next night when I arrived at the theatre there was a huge bunch of red roses waiting for me with a card that read, "May I make you a star? If you are interested please call me." It was signed Florenz Ziegfeld.

Because of his illness the new Ziegfeld show, *Whoopee*, starring torch singer Ruth Etting and comedian Eddie Cantor, was delayed for several months.

Representatives of the Loew's theatre chain, who had seen her in all three Charles Dilllingham shows, asked if she would be available to do a twenty-minute solo tap dance spot in all their main theatres as a prelude to the opening of the first talking picture, *The Jazz Singer*, starring singer Al Jolson. She recalled:

> My agent said it was a good deal and in just a few weeks I went from New York to Los Angeles. At this point I want to tell the simple truth about my first meeting with

Al Jolson. He later came up with a lot of romantic situations, and the newspapers over the years embroidered those stories.

This is the truth. I got off the train in Los Angeles where I was to meet William Perlberg, the Loew's Theatre west coast agent. Perlberg was standing with a man I had never seen before. He introduced us. That is how I met Al Jolson. He was very complimentary, said he had seen me in *The Sidewalks Of New York* and wished me luck in the new Ziegfeld Show, *Whoopee*. The entire meeting lasted two minutes before he and the top people from Warner Brothers studio were called away to meet Fanny Brice, the star they had come to meet. Mr. Perlberg took me by car to the hotel where I was staying and then on to the Loew's theatre in Los Angeles.

That was it! Al claimed years later that he was immediately smitten by my friendly smile, and film studio publicists said I almost swooned at meeting the big star. None of that is true. I didn't have the slightest feeling for him, and I can't believe he had any for me at that moment. His mind was on publicity pictures with Fanny Brice.

After they were married, Jolson told Carolyn Somers Hoyt, a magazine writer, that he first saw Ruby when she was only fourteen. "She was dancing, as an eighteen-year-old, in Texas Guinan's club. I knew before I left the club that I would one day marry her."

Texas Guinan denied that Al Jolson had been in one of her clubs. "He was a prude," she said, "wouldn't have dreamed of associating with someone like me. He is not only prudish he is also a very accomplished liar."

Keeler remembered, "I went back to New York by train, stopping in Chicago to do a final show for Loew's. A few weeks later I was told that Mr. Ziegfeld was well enough to start rehearsals for *Whoopee*." She continued, "During rehearsals in Pittsburgh, one of our out-of-town stops before the scheduled New York opening, Al Jolson walked into the theatre and asked Ziegfeld if he might take Ruby Keeler out to supper. That

It's all too wonderful, and so I'll stick to words

In *Ready, Willing and Able*, Ruby Keeler danced with her partner, Lee Dixon, on a giant typewriter keyboard. Ruby said the dance, the creation of choreographer Busby Berkeley, was the highlight of her film career.

first evening he produced a ring from out of his pocket and asked me to marry him. I was shocked, perhaps a little flattered, for he was a big star, but I said 'no.'"

The next day at the theatre she found one hundred red roses waiting for her. The card read simply, "From Al."

"I was astounded," she said. "I'd never seen so many roses outside a florist's shop." The stage doorkeeper, who had obviously experienced similar incidents in the past, told her to take as many as she wanted and he would call the local hospital to collect the remainder for distribution around the wards.

"I kept twelve," she said. "Someone found a bowl to put them in and I took them into my dressing room. Guess who was waiting there? Al Jolson!"

Jolson and Keeler went out to supper the next two nights before he convinced her to marry him.

"Finally I said yes!" she said. "He was a very persuasive man and I couldn't see any other way of getting rid of him without marrying him."

Ruby Keeler, a Roman Catholic, and Al Jolson, a Jew, were married before a justice of the peace in Pittsburgh on September 21, 1928.

This was perhaps the one time she was in the wrong place at the wrong time. She and Jolson had a very short honeymoon in Pittsburgh before she returned to the *Whoopee* out-of-town performances.

"I got some very good notices in the three cities in which we played, but before we got to New York Al told Mr. Ziegfeld that he was taking me out of the show to go with him to Hollywood."

Ziegfeld said he was very unhappy at the decision. Eddie Cantor and Al Jolson were ready to have a fist fight when two stagehands pulled them apart.

"Leaving the show was a grave mistake," she said.

It should have alerted me to the fact that Al didn't like anyone to be in a bigger spotlight than himself. Mr. Ziegfeld was very kind to me. He told me my name was on the posters outside the New York theatre where *Whoopee* was due to open the next Monday, but that he would have it removed as quickly as possible. He shook my hand and told me he was sure one day we would be working together again. He was obviously annoyed with Al but with me he was kindness itself.

Whoopee was a great success. It introduced the song that remained associated with Eddie Cantor for the rest of his life, "Making Whoopee." It also put Ruby Keeler's name on the posters for the first time in a show in which she was not appearing.

"In many biographies you will read that I was one of the stars of *Whoopee* in New York," she said. "I've corrected writers about this many times over the years but they don't seem to pay attention. Apart from the tryout weeks on the road I never was in *Whoopee*. Mr. Ziegfeld did send me one of the New York posters bearing my name, but that is as near as I got to Broadway with Mr. Ziegfeld at that time."

Ruby and Al travelled aboard the New York to Los Angeles train in a suite that occupied an entire coach. "There were people to look after us every minute of the way," she recalled.

> I told Al that I hoped for a little peace and quietness when we reached California, but he only laughed and said, "Mrs. Jolson will never be alone. She is now the wife of the greatest entertainer in show business."
>
> He owned a beautiful home surrounded by gardens. There were enough bedrooms to house an entire football team. I loved the immediate attention that came with my every word. I was convinced that my career as a dancer was over and I was destined to be just Mrs. Al Jolson for the rest of my life.

After her divorce from Jolson, Keeler refused to talk about him or what the differences were that caused the breakup of their marriage.

"I want to make it clear," she told newsmen, "that he never was abusive toward me, and any stories written about that are totally false."

A year after their wedding, Jolson received a letter from Flo Ziegfeld urging that a talent such as Ruby Keeler's should not be hidden in California when audiences were still waiting to see her in New York.

Incredibly, since Al Jolson had always liked to be the only star in his household, he told Ruby that he was sending her by train, first class, to New York where she was to be the star of the new Ziegfeld musical, *Show Girl.*

"I never did know how much money I was receiving for my appearance in New York," she said. "Soon after my marriage I had signed a legal document giving him power of attorney over any business matters in which I might become involved."

When, fifteen years later, Jolson approved the scripts for *The Jolson Story* and *Jolson Sings Again*, he insisted on adding in a scene where he stood up in the audience and sang the song that Ruby Keeler was singing on stage when she almost fainted.

In 1971 Keeler pooh-poohed the story. "I have never fainted on stage in my life. Al certainly did stand up and sing the song in the audience on one occasion but it was simply to let people know he was there, and perhaps to let the audience know who was the boss in our family."

Despite excellent reviews of her two solo appearances in *Show Girl*, Ruby Keeler left the show before it ended its New York run. Ziegfeld said he had agreed to release Ruby because Al Jolson had told him she was expecting a baby.

Whether she thought this was the case or whether Jolson simply wanted her out of the spotlight that he wanted exclusively for himself will never be known now. When asked the question, Ruby Keeler said simply, "And what is the next question?"

When Al Jolson was still at the peak of his career, he was approached by Jack Warner, whose Warner Brothers Studio had made him a major star in the first talking film, *The Jazz Singer*.

Warner said he told Jolson it was a shame that Ruby Keeler's talents should be hidden from the public. "I said he could be on the film set every day if he wished to make sure the director did nothing to embarrass the Jolson name."

"That appealed to his vanity," said Warner. "I had him hooked but he didn't know how I was going to cut the line."

Once the contract was signed for Ruby Keeler to star in *42nd Street*, and a start date agreed on, Warner presented Jolson with a script he felt could enhance Jolson's own career.

"I told him he hadn't made a film since 1930 and that his fan mail had dropped to almost zero," said Warner. "I told him this new film, *Hallelujah, I'm a Bum*, would put him right back on top again. The only problem was a minor one. It had to be filmed at the same time as *42nd Street*. I promised that I would personally supervise the shooting of Ruby's film and that her maid could be with her at all times when she was working."

Warner then told the director of *Hallelujah* to take and retake as many scenes as he needed to keep Jolson busy. "I used a lot of tricks to keep him off Ruby's set," said Warner. "It worked and the film is still considered a classic, often shown on television, often in prime time."

The new Jolson film did little to enhance his career, but *42nd Street* made Ruby Keeler into an overnight sensation.

Busby Berkeley, who created all the dance numbers for the film, told the *New York Times* that he had been able to create new and previously untried routines "because Miss Keeler was able to dance better than any woman I had ever seen. Her twinkling feet made it possible for me to achieve a miracle with her talent."

Asked what she thought was her best number in *42nd Street*, she said, "The simplicity of the 'Shuffle Off To Buffalo' number made it my favourite. If I had allowed Busby to make it into the big production number he wanted it might have spoiled the show. This sudden contrast to the big production numbers made it to me the most important moment in the film."

The *Los Angeles Times* spoiled the glory that descended on Ruby when the film was released. Their reviewer said, "Ruby Keeler's hesitant, clear speech and demurely fresh appearance make her a far more effective and appealing personality to the industry than her husband, Al Jolson, in spite of his importance as a revolutionary tradition."

According to Ruby Keeler's maid, Lena Sanders, who stayed with her for more than twenty years, it was this review that started destroying the marriage. "When he read it, Mr. Jolson yelled so loudly that he could have been heard outside. He said nobody had a better personality than he did and he would sue the paper for suggesting that his wife was now a bigger star than he was," she said. "He stormed out of the house and walked around the grounds for more than an hour, mumbling and at times shouting to himself. Poor Mrs. Jolson was in tears."

If Jolson ever did sue the *Times* it is not on record in the legal department history of the paper.

"It was never the same after that," said Lena Sanders. "He didn't ever shout at her again, perhaps because the son they had adopted when Mrs. Jolson couldn't get pregnant, had heard the first tirade and clung to Mrs. J, hiding his head."

Jolson even suggested to Ruby on one occasion that she and her co-star in *42nd Street*, Dick Powell, were having an affair.

"I had never spoken back to Mr. Jolson before that moment but I had to say something," recalled Sanders. "I said 'Mr. Jolson, Mrs. Jolson is never out of my sight from the moment she leaves this house until she arrives home every night. What you are suggesting is ridiculous.' Mr. Jolson turned beet red but didn't say a word. He turned and walked out of the room and we heard him tell the housekeeper that he wanted his bed made up in the guest bedroom from now on. They never slept together after that night."

The huge success of *42nd Street* convinced Warner to team her up again with Dick Powell in *Gold Diggers of 1933*. Again the audiences packed theatres worldwide to see Ruby Keeler.

Later that same year, Keeler was teamed with James Cagney in *Footlight Parade*. "Mr. Cagney was quite a dancer," she said. "I'd always thought of him as just another tough guy without much class, but he danced extremely well and was a dignified, rather quiet man off the set."

Cagney remembered Keeler as "a doll who never raised her voice, never got tired when scenes had to be reshot, and was considerate of everyone on the set. I remember her one day signing about fifty autograph books which one of the electricians had brought in from the kids in his son's school. She looked in the front of each book and used the name there to personalize each autograph. A doll, a real doll."

By 1935 Ruby Keeler's fame was at its peak. Jack Warner said the studio had hired four secretaries to handle her fan mail, but that "Ruby insists on reading every letter and dictating and signing the letters herself. She signs every photograph herself, and refused to let us make it easier for her by allowing the four autograph writers we had on the payroll to sign even one picture."

Jack Warner, many years later, said:

> It was then I began to wonder about her marriage to Jolson. She stayed late many nights reading and signing letters that I began to wonder if she didn't want to go home.
>
> One day, Jolson walked into my office. He pushed the door open and sat down in the chair opposite my desk.
>
> "I have a brilliant idea," said Jolson. "I want you to team me, the greatest entertainer in the world, with my

wife, Ruby, probably the best dancer in Hollywood, in a song and dance show. It will be box-office magic. Get me some scripts and I'll decide which one we will do."

He got up and walked out of the office slamming the door behind him. There was obviously no point in arguing with him, so I called my writers in, gave them a few hints, and sent them back to work.

A month later Jolson arrived back in Warner's office. "He came alone, didn't bring Ruby, it was as though he thought of her as an insignificant part of any film he was to make. I gave him one script and told him bluntly, 'This is it. This is it or nothing.'" Warner recalled. "Three days later he returned, the script had changes on every page. 'We'll do it,' said Jolson. 'With these changes we have a winner.' He slammed the script on my desk and walked out, as he got to the door he said, 'We'll both be ready in two weeks.'"

Go Into Your Dance was promoted heavily by Warners before it opened. Jolson opened his home to the studio photographers, who shot hundreds of pictures of himself and Ruby in romantic poses.

Filming went smoothly. Director Bobby Connally said:

It was the easiest film I ever made. Both Al and Ruby were fully co-operative. They were always smiling and made friends with even the lowliest members of the crew. Jolson got everyone together one day before we wrapped shooting and said he had hired two buses that would be at the studio when we had completed the last shot. The buses, he said, would take them to his home for a party that would last as long as the last person was on his or her feet. It was the wrap party to end all parties. Most of the crew had never tasted caviar but that night there was more than enough for everyone.

Patsy Kelly, a featured performer in the film, remembered things a little differently some years later.

They were co-operative but I noticed them looking at each other as if each was daring the other to blow up. They had separate dressing rooms on the set and neither said a word to the other as they went into the rooms at the end of a day or for costume changes. The film was a success because its story that told of a young dancer who helps an older entertainer, whose popularity was fading, to make a successful comeback. I wondered many times if this was almost a film about their own lives. Al loved it because the finale saw him a big star again and Ruby standing in the background happy at his success.

"I wasn't beautiful, couldn't really sing, and my acting was so-so," said Ruby Keeler after her Hollywood career ended. "It was my dancing that made me a star."

The Jolsons made personal appearances at major theatres from coast to coast to promote the film. They were mobbed wherever they appeared. In Chicago a newspaper gossip writer said, "The smiles they give each other look much too forced. Is there a snake in their Garden of Eden? The audiences wanted to get near these two big stars but I wonder if the two stars really wanted to be so close to each other."

Jack Warner told the *Los Angeles Times* that although *Go Into Your Dance* did nothing to hurt Ruby Keeler's career and certainly put Al Jolson back on top again, Keeler visited him in his office a few weeks after the film was released.

"If Al wants us to team up again for another film," she said, "I want you to tell him that it would not be good for either of us."

There is no record that Jolson ever did make such a request, and for the rest of their careers they worked alone.

In 1935 and 1936 Ruby Keeler made two more movies at Warner Brothers. Both saw her co-starred with Dick Powell, the team that had been so successful in *42nd Street*. Critics weren't too kind to either of the films. Ruby Keeler told a New York newspaperman, "Perhaps people are getting tired of people tapping their way through life and out of every difficulty. Perhaps audiences are getting tired of these films which have no relationship to reality."

Her final film at Warners, *Ready, Willing and Able* in 1937, was not one of her best, but it is still remembered today for the dance she did with Lee Dixon on the keys of a giant typewriter. "I always think of that scene as being the most enjoyable and original in my career," she said in 1972. "I couldn't watch many of my old films today but I could watch that scene over and over again."

In 1937 Jack Warner told Al Jolson that he was not renewing his contract. "We had watched his career slide, not because of bad films, but because that enthusiasm he once showed in everything he did had gone. The spark had gone."

Ruby Keeler still had one year left on her contract at Warners. "Jolson asked to buy out her contract for that year. I agreed," said Jack Warner. "They obviously were not without money. He paid $50,000 to get Ruby out of her contract. But I remember when the check came it was signed by Ruby, not Al."

A year later, with no offers of work for Ruby, and only two small parts given to Al, they announced their separation. A year later Ruby filed for divorce.

Ruby Keeler made one picture for RKO studios in 1938, but *Mother Carey's Chickens* surprised and disappointed her fans. Her straight dramatic role, in a non-musical, didn't draw the crowds as RKO had hoped, and it was the final time they offered her work.

In 1939 she made her last film. Columbia cast her in the lead role of *Sweetheart of the Campus*. Once again she and the film didn't draw the crowds. Years later she said, "It was the worst film of my career."

With her divorce from Al Jolson becoming final in December 1940, Ruby Keeler announced her official retirement from show business.

A year later she married John Lowe, a prominent California broker whom she had met only a few months earlier.

Her only comment to the news media was this simple statement: "I always hoped for a marriage in which both my husband and I would have no competitive conflict. I believe I have found it this time."

John Lowe taught her how to relax and how to play golf. "It took a while but I started to get quite good on the golf course," she said.

But Keeler didn't completely retire. "With John's approval I accepted a few television dates. It was quite early in the TV era and I found my experience in films gave me an edge over newcomers to the industry," she said.

> I played a few roles where my name was used in publicity, but more often than not I played a minor role in which my name never appeared in the credits. I believed I must have made about thirty spots like that before comedian Jerry Lewis came up to me one day at the television studio.
>
> "Want to go back into the movies?" said Jerry.
>
> "No," I said.

"Want to do a guest spot on my television show, perhaps dance and sing a little? he said.

"I might," I said. "What do you have in mind?"

I reminded him this was 1963, and I was fifty-two! What could I do that the current TV audiences might enjoy?

"You can dance with me, share a joke or two, and astound the audience with how fit and beautiful you still are," he said.

I talked it over with John and he said, "Give it a whirl if you like. I'll be in the studio audience to give you support."

The spot with Jerry Lewis brought thousands of letters from fans she thought would have forgotten her long ago.

One critic, in the *Los Angeles Times* said, "She took my heart back thirty years to the days when films were entertaining. Give us more of Ruby, please Jerry."

She declined the invitation by Jerry Lewis to drop in any time she wished on the show. "Now I am retired," she told Lewis in a letter. "But I thank you for letting me relive those days when I really was a star."

Jerry Lewis read the letter on his next show. "But Ruby dear," he said "You are still a star in my heart and always will be." The TV studio audience did something they had never done before: they rose to their feet, cheering and applauding.

In 1969 John Lowe died after a heart attack. "I felt my life had ended," Keeler said a year later, "but good friends came around and refused to let me get depressed. I was a grandmother and our four children were with me any time I needed support. At sixty I could still play a fair round of golf, I entertained at home, with few if any of my guests being in show business. John had told Jerry Lewis that he was welcome in our home any time and he did drop by on many occasions."

The Lowes had moved to a beautiful home in Rancho Mirage, one hundred miles away from Hollywood. It had been almost thirty years since she had left the Columbia studio for the last time; she now went to very few stage shows in Los Angeles and rarely watched television. She said:

I thought I was completely forgotten when one day a strange little man rang the door bell. My maid opened the door to a man who introduced himself as Harry Rigby. I have never been shy about inviting strangers into my home, and when Julie, my maid, gave me this man's business card, I told her to bring him in.

"I'm going to revive the 1925 Broadway musical, *No, No, Nanette*," said Harry Rigby. "I want you to play the role of Sue, not the principal role, but one which I believe you can make into a show stopper. Can you still dance Mrs. Lowe?"

At that moment he sold me on the idea. Calling me Mrs. Lowe added dignity to this rather insignificant man who was so in earnest about *No, No, Nanette* that I couldn't believe one so young would appreciate the beauty of such a show.

Once he had convinced me that this wasn't going to be a parody of the show I had seen many times and loved, I told him I was prepared to think about it.

"You do still tap, don't you, Mrs. Lowe," he said.

I stood up and gave, without the benefit of tap shoes, a pretty fair move or two on the tiles of the fireplace. "Now you must give me time to think about your offer."

"Wouldn't it be better," said Rigby, "if I waited while you read the script. I have it in my briefcase. Then, if you think the idea is a good one we could sit down so I could answer all the questions I know you are going to ask?"

Rigby gave Ruby Keeler the script that was about to change her life forever.

"Mr. Rigby said he would walk around the grounds of the house and my maid could call him when I had read the part," Keeler recalled. "I was convinced when I read the brief note he had attached to the script. It said that Busby Berkeley, who had made me a star in *42nd Street*, was being hired as consultant to the dance director, Donald Sadler."

On January 19, 1971, *No, No, Nanette* had its first night at the 46th

Street Theatre in New York City. It was still drawing capacity audiences when it closed because Ruby Keeler said she was exhausted. The final curtain fell on October 28, 1972.

Keeler's role in *No, No, Nanette* was that of the wife of a Bible sales-man upset by his quite innocent involvement with three young girls.

"I knew my dialogue two days after Mr. Rigby came to see me," she said. "Unconsciously I had wanted one last fling in live theatre. This was my one final chance to show I wasn't a has-been from forty years earlier. Believe it or not I was still a size eight!"

The two numbers in which she was featured, "I Want To Be Happy" and "Take A Little One Step," brought audiences to their feet every night.

"I had always kept fit but I never realized that I could still do taps like I did on that stage," she said. "Somehow I doubled the number of taps I did at rehearsals and even the rest of the cast broke with tradition and applauded what I achieved."

Patsy Kelly, who had appeared with Ruby in *Go Into Your Dance*, the one film she made with Al Jolson, was one of the show's stars.

"I was in tears night after night," she said. "It gave me a new lease on life. Ruby and I became close friends."

After *No, No, Nanette*, Ruby Keeler allowed her hair to go to its natural silver. She returned to Rancho Mirage and her many non-professional friends.

"I had succeeded beyond my wildest dreams," she told Patsy Kelly. "Now I will forget show business and concentrate my life on my children and grandchildren."

On November 23, 1974, while visiting her daughter in Grand Falls, Montana, she was rushed to hospital and operated on for an aneurism on the brain. It was months before she was seen in public again.

She remained in seclusion until her death was announced on February 28, 1993, at her home. Her doctor, supported by her five children, including Al, the son she and Al Jolson had adopted, said that she had "quietly and bravely battled cancer for several years."

"Her five children and fourteen grandchildren were at her bedside when she died," said John Lowe, Jr. "It was a peaceful end of a life in which she loved her family much more than her remarkable fame, as we can all attest."

David Manners

When the American Dracula Society announced its first meeting in 1966, David Manners, the one surviving star of the 1931 blockbuster film *Dracula*, was invited to attend. From his mansion in Pacific Palisades, California, overlooking the ocean, Manners sent his regrets.

For the next thirty years the society renewed its invitation annually. Anxious to have him at their convention, they asked him to name his own price for a personal appearance. Manners continued to decline the invitation.

On many occasions society members tried to visit Manners in his beautiful home. His butler always told them, "Mr. Manners is not well enough to see anyone today."

It is fortunate that the large treed and landscaped lawn area behind his home was not visible to his would-be guests from the driveway, since, more often than not, David Manners, very fit and well, would be behind the high walls practising his golf shots, at his desk tapping away on a typewriter to complete one of the seven books he wrote, or working on one of the many striking paintings that he completed every year.

The Dracula Society's records show that among the people who signed in for the annual get-together for each of those thirty years was a founding member named Duan Acklom.

Apparently no one connected the elderly Duan Acklom to David Manners because, at sixty-four, when he first attended, his handsome looks had faded and Duan Acklom looked just what he was, an elderly but prosperous retiree.

"I loved to see the enthusiasm the society members paid to my 1931 film," said Manners in 1996, "but I felt it would destroy the illusion if they saw me as I was then, an old man."

That same year Manners attended his final Dracula Society meeting. His health was failing, and a nurse travelled with him. A Los Angeles newspaper reporter wrote that Duan Acklom, the society's oldest member at ninety-four, had never missed a meeting in the thirty years of the society's existence. The reporter told his readers that Acklom declined to have his photograph taken. "I am too old for such nonsense," he said. Incredibly, still no one realized Duan Acklom was David Manners.

David Manners was born Rauff de Ryther Duan Acklom in Halifax, Nova Scotia, on April 30, 1902. His father, George Acklom, ran Harrow House, a boys' school on Tower Road in Halifax. It was a prestigious school that specialized in providing the quality education its students would need to enter one of England's major universities like Oxford or Cambridge. The family was quite wealthy, and his mother, Lillian, never had to work. They lived in a beautiful home five minutes away from the school.

When the *Titanic* hit an iceberg and sank in 1912, the Ackloms were among the first on the dock in Halifax to welcome survivors brought to shore from the disaster. "We had three very frightened people as our guests for several days before they were considered fit enough to travel to their homes in New York State," said Duan Acklom. "I had nightmares for weeks after hearing their stories and tales from others who came to visit."

Duan Acklom was an outstanding scholar, fluent in both English and French. In September of 1917, when he was only fifteen, he entered what should have been his final year at Harrow House before heading for college.

Fate intervened on the morning of December 6. He recalled:

> Classes began at 9:30 and I was just about ready to leave the house shortly after nine when I heard an incredible explosion and found myself being hurled across the living room to crash into the wall by the fireplace. I remember nothing else until I heard mother saying, "He's still alive, we must get him to hospital." I had no idea what had happened but I could see my parents were both alive. I learned later that mother was in the kitchen and father was in the bathroom. Like me, both were hurled against the nearest wall, but neither was badly hurt. The living room was the longest room in the house and I was hurled more than thirty feet.
>
> I came in and out of consciousness and later that day was taken to an emergency hospital set up in father's Harrow House School and there treated for a broken arm.
>
> None of us knew what had happened but saw hundreds of houses flattened to the ground, fires burning

in the ruins of many, and the sky was dark with some of the most unpleasant acrid smoke swirling about.

Several days later the truth about the explosion that almost obliterated large areas of Halifax was printed in local newspapers. A munitions ship and a war relief ship had collided in the channel narrows only two miles from our home and school. The Great Halifax Explosion, as it is still called today, killed more than two thousand people, many of them our friends and my school chums.

Incredibly Harrow House was almost undamaged, and four weeks later, after a very sombre Christmas vacation, the school doors reopened for another semester. Like many other students I lost almost a year because of my injuries and the shock that followed and it was 1919 before I finally graduated.

Although the World War in Europe was over, Acklom decided he would stay in Canada for his education. "It was frightening to think that there would be other desolate sights like Halifax over in England," he said.

"I've had asthma ever since that terrible day in 1917," Acklom said in 1996. "I'm convinced it came from the filthy smoke that hung in the air over Halifax for weeks after the explosion. Although nobody in our family was hurt, our house was badly damaged. We considered ourselves very lucky to be alive."

In 1919 Acklom enrolled at the University of Toronto, planning to earn a degree in forestry engineering. "I was convinced that protection of Canada's forests held the key to the pollution that was gathering everywhere, from garbage dumps, uncontrolled fires, and the dumping of hazardous waste. I feared for our future."

But membership in a college drama group, which presented plays at Toronto's Hart House Theatre, changed his mind and gave him the unexpected enthusiasm that whetted his appetite for acting.

When the play's producer, Bertram Forsyth, told him his lengthy name was too difficult to be remembered and far too long to be printed on posters, he adopted Manners, his mother's maiden name. In 1996 he said the name David came out of thin air. "If there was a reason then I've forgotten it now," he said.

In February of 1923 he received a call from actor-manager Basil Sydney in New York. "I have a touring company leaving here in three weeks. We shall be travelling from coast to coast in the United States. We need a young leading man. Bertram Forsyth tells me you have immense talent so I would like you to join our company next week for rehearsals," Sydney said. "The company pays all travelling expenses, hotels and meals on tour, and all costumes other than normal day and evening wear. In addition I could offer you thirty-five dollars a week, would this be acceptable."

"I was on the train to New York next morning," recalled Manners. He went on:

> It was a great experience. Mr. Sydney was a tireless producer, director, manager and actor. In less than a year I played leads and small roles in more than ten plays that ranged from potboilers to comedy and the classics.
>
> I should have graduated from Toronto University in May of 1923 with my degree in forest management but when I quit school to join the New York company I never did receive my diploma.
>
> When we returned to New York Mr. Sydney introduced me to Helen Hayes, the queen of Broadway at that time. She in turn introduced me to her producer, and one week after arriving in the city I was rehearsing for the Broadway version of a role I had played on tour, the lead in *He Who Gets Slapped* at the Booth Theatre. It was so successful that Helen Hayes, who came to see the play, immediately hired me to be her co-star in *Dancing Mothers*, at the Maxine Elliott Theatre, one of the big hits of the 1924 season. It lasted nine months with the theatre full every night. If Helen Hayes had not wanted to go into another play we might have gone on for another nine months.

Other successes followed. "I was never out of work more than a month in the six years I stayed in New York," he recalled.

In 1978 Helen Hayes, in an article printed in the *New York World*, said that one night after a cast meeting at the beginning of the play's run, she was accosted outside the stage door by a drunken man. "He punched me in the face," she said. "Fortunately for me David Manners came out of the stage door and saw the incident. He attacked the drunk and in two quick blows knocked him to the ground. We left him there, I think he was unconscious, and David helped me to my car just around the corner, and once I was safely inside he strolled away as though nothing had happened."

On hearing this, Manners smiled. "Did I indeed? Remember I was young and foolish in those days. I was quite a boxer in my teens so what she said was probably accurate. I would hate to contradict Miss Hayes since her comment was so complimentary."

Douglass Montgomery (left), Claude Rains (centre), and David Manners in Universal Pictures major film *The Mystery of Edwin Drood*. Manners and Montgomery were both from Canada.

A young British stage director, James Whale, in New York from London in 1925 to discuss the possibility of his British stage hit being produced on Broadway, saw Manners in *Dancing Mothers* and invited him to play the role of Raleigh in *Journey's End*, should the production become reality.

In 1956 Whale recalled his first encounter with Manners in New York. "He was an incredibly charming young man," he said. "I could see stardom in his every move. David read the script and accepted the role. I was to pay him $100 a week." But production of the New York version of *Journey's End* was delayed until 1928.

"When I wanted him for the role of Raleigh he was tied up under contract to another manager so I had to find a substitute for the part," said Whale. "Two years later, when sound films were all the rage, I was invited to Hollywood to make a film of *Journey's End*. I immediately contacted David and asked if he would be interested in a trip to Hollywood. I offered him a three-month contract."

Manners remembered the invitation clearly. "I was rather glad to get out of the pollution of New York, my asthma was acting up at times and I felt that California, touted as paradise by everyone I knew, would be perfect for my problem," he recalled. "The five-hundred-dollar-a-week guarantee was more than most people could ever hope to make on Broadway and Jimmy Whale offered me a first-class train ticket to California, with all expenses en route paid. In Hollywood he even found me a very pleasant apartment close to the studio. Again his company paid the rent."

Journey's End was a big hit in the early days of sound films, and the handsome looks of David Manners, with his soft but expressive voice, brought him offers from several producers. When the film was released, his fan mail from all over world started coming in. "I was getting at least three hundred letters a week shortly after the film was released and had to hire a secretary to help me answer the deluge. On weekends my secretary, Joan Hartford, and I often worked fifteen hours a day trying to answer each letter individually," he said. "Joan and I became quite inseparable, and she moved in with me in the apartment. At that time such things were rarely done, certainly not openly as we did, but it seemed natural to both of us. I have often wished over the years that we had married. Never since have I found a woman who matched her integrity. But I waited too long and she finally married someone else."

The years 1931 and 1932 gave David Manners memorable roles that are still talked about today, seventy years after the three most important films in his career were made.

In 1931 he co-starred with Bela Lugosi and Helen Chandler in *Dracula*. In 1932 he received top billing over Boris Karloff in *The Mummy*, and the same year he co-starred with Bela Lugosi in *The Death Kiss*. Today these three horror films are still in demand on videocassettes and DVDs. In 2000, a new fan club for David Manners was formed. Its president, twenty-three-year-old Marty Crandall, said membership quickly reached fifteen hundred. In 2003 it is still flourishing.

By 1935 David Manners had his first official fan club, which boasted more than eighty thousand members. He employed four full-time secretaries, but always claimed he found time to personally sign every letter they typed. He wrote and produced a twelve-page newsletter four times a year for his fans. "Before I officially retired in 1936 we were printing and mailing more than 100,000 copies of each copy of the newsletter," he recalled in 1996.

In 1932 and 1935 his name was listed as one of the top ten box-office stars in North America and England.

Before he died in 1957, James Whale, who became a major director in Hollywood's sound era after his success with *Journey's End* in 1930, recorded in a magazine story that "David Manners, a young Canadian with no experience in films, was an outstanding personality in my first American film, *Journey's End*. He even eclipsed the great John Barrymore who I had expected to steal every scene in the movie."

David Manners' co-stars in other features between 1930 and 1936 were the top leading ladies of the era: Loretta Young, Katharine Hepburn, Barbara Stanwyck, Joan Blondell, Una Merkel, Ann Dvorak, Claudette Colbert, Constance Bennett, Carole Lombard, Myrna Loy, and Heather Angel.

Constance Bennett was reputed to be difficult to work with, but found Manners an exception. "My film with David Manners is one of the

few movies I enjoyed making," she said. "I had become so used to leading men and directors pushing me around that I was startled with
David's quite gentle approach to the women on the set. He also quietly
and effectively subdued the director when he started getting abusive with
me. I don't remember the film but I will never forget David Manners."

Loretta Young, who made six films with Manners, and who was
almost as completely a recluse as Manners, refused to be interviewed
for more than twenty years. But a message to her, through a friend,
brought an instant phone call and an invitation to lunch in 1960
when she was told the questions would not be about her but about
David Manners.

"He hadn't an ounce of difficulty or obstinacy in him," she said.
"Every girl in town wanted to work with him. He was the dream actor,
handsome, charming and totally genuine. He was very competent, never
flustered, always knew his lines and was always ready to help newcomers to the film industry."

Young and her sister, actress Sally Blane, used to double-date
Manners and another young actor, Edward Flanagan, who was just
beginning to get roles in the booming film industry.

"Mother was very particular about every date we had," said Young.
"David and Edward were the only two she let Sally and I go out with
unchaperoned. They were both nice guys, just the opposite of the wild
set you so often associate with Hollywood. It should be told that, at
David's suggestion, Edward Flanagan changed his name and later
became very well known as actor Dennis O'Keefe."

A busy Lucille Ball didn't hesitate when asked to recall David
Manners. "I'll give you all the time in the world to talk about the dear,
charming young man. I still have a thing for him after all these years,"
she said in 1984.

> I had a very small part as a dancer in *Roman Scandals*
> in 1933 which starred Eddie Cantor, Ruth Etting and
> David. David wasn't in the one scene in which I
> appeared, but he was always on the set to watch every
> scene shot. At the end of my one day on the film he
> walked across to me and invited me to supper.

Now I'd met a few stars like that in Hollywood, but I figured I knew how to take care of myself and I sure needed a good meal, so I said I'd go.

He took me to a really swanky restaurant and we went dancing afterwards. He was mobbed everywhere, but he always had time for his fans. The reason why I spend so much time with my fans today is because David showed me on that special date it was the right thing to do. All the time he kept telling me I had style and personality and I would get somewhere if I persevered. Now I'd heard that line so many times before and it always ended the same old way, so I got ready for the $64,000 question so I could hit him straight between the eyes.

But the question never came. Not once did he hint that he would like to take me home to see his boudoir. He drove me to the front door of the apartment block where I lived, gave me a very dignified goodnight kiss, and wished me luck.

Next day he called me to say he had made an appointment for me with his agent who later arranged screen tests at three different studios. That's how my career began. All because of the wonderful David Manners. We never did have another date, but I saw him around the studios several times and we sometimes had lunch together.

I must be honest and tell you that had he later invited me to see his boudoir when I was becoming famous I would have accepted.

Edward G. Robinson, the tough guy of the movies, was already a star at Warner Brother First National studio when David Manners arrived on contract in 1930. In 1970, he said:

I must tell you an amusing memory of David that I don't think has ever been told before. We were attending the premiere of *Sweet Mama* in which he starred with Alice White. She had been a very important star and this was to be her last film so everyone who anyone was attending the opening night. I got out of my car just ahead of David when a rowdy broke through the security lines and came at me. "Let's see how tough you really are, Robinson," he said. He swung and hit me in the ribs and I cringed back. I'm not really so tough as the movies make me out to be. David, just behind me, grabbed the rowdy, floored him with one punch and security officers took over. I went over to David and thanked him. His knuckles were bleeding, but he just wrapped a handkerchief around them and together we went into the theatre. The crowds outside were cheering. He was a charming man but I'm not sure how I would have fared had I been in line for one of his punches.

Katharine Hepburn made her Hollywood debut in 1932 in *Bill of Divorcement*. In 1977 she recalled her first day on the set:

I was so much in awe of David, he was a huge star then, that I was actually trembling awaiting my cues. On the first day of shooting we were talking, David, myself, and the wonderful director George Cukor. I was finding it impossible to look either of these important men directly in the eye and I found myself looking down at David's highly polished shoes. Anything to take my mind off these two important people. Suddenly I saw a speck of dust on the shoes so I knelt down at David's feet and started polishing the shoes with the hem of my skirt.

I'll never forget Cukor's roar and David's laugh. Cukor informed me that David's shoes might be worth ten dollars but my skirt was worth hundreds. He told me he would polish his shoes on my rear end — but he didn't say it so politely — if I ever did such a thing again.

David sensed my situation and if he hadn't put his arm around me I think I would have shrivelled into the ground. He was a perfect gentleman at all times, just a dear to work with and a totally professional and polished actor. He was so talented it is very sad he abandoned Hollywood in the late thirties.

Zita Johann, who starred with David and Boris Karloff in *The Mummy*, was living in retirement in West Nyack, New Jersey, in 1977, where she was operating a successful kindergarten, when she recalled her special memories of Manners:

> Few people know that David and I had worked together years before *The Mummy* in 1932. He and I were two members of the Basil Sydney touring company. We became very close during our travels from coast to coast. I was only seventeen and David rescued me more than once from members of the troupe who had evil designs on me.
>
> I remember him hitting one over-amorous actor, who I shall not name since he became quite famous on Broadway in later years, and knocked several of his teeth out. Basil Sydney had to wire to New York for a replacement actor but he told David that his actions were laudable and the actor was well out of line.
>
> I last saw David in 1945. My fame from films like *The Mummy* had faded and I had moved back to New York to take what parts I could get on Broadway. But there was little interest in me until a producer called from out of the blue to ask if I would like to star in George Bernard's Shaw's *The Devil's Disciple*. He said he still had to find a co-star who would not ask for too much money to get the project off the ground. I immediately thought of David. I'd heard he was back in Pacific Palisades but it took me nearly a week to get his private telephone number.

David was reluctant at first, but said he loved Shaw's play and would let me know in a day or two. Next day he called me back and said he would do the play and would work for Equity scale, that's the minimum, it was around $200 a week at that time. Peanuts compared to the money he had earned in Hollywood.

I got back to the New York producer with the good news, thinking the publicity saying that two of *The Mummy* stars would be appearing in the play would bring in people to the theatres, but was shocked to hear that I was too late, he couldn't get backing and had cancelled the tour.

I called David and told him the bad news. He said he was very sorry and hoped something would come along for me. Next day I received $1,000 wired to me by Western Union. There was no sender listed but I knew it was David.

Three days later the producer called me again and said he'd been able to get the financing and the play could go ahead.

Once again I called David and he accepted the role immediately. He was so wonderful, insisting that I be given star billing. When I saw the posters during rehearsal I was astonished. They read: Zita Johann, Hollywood Star, and listed films like *Luxury Liner*, *The Man Who Dared*, and, of course, *The Mummy*. Then came the rest of the cast and right at the bottom it read, Guest Star, David Manners. Just that, nothing more.

Of course we were packed every night. They really came to see David, not me, but we did give them a first class production.

At the end of the eight-month tour the producer said he had made a lot of money and he planned to share $25,000 with the cast. He gave me $10,000 and the other kids had the rest.

That $10,000 allowed me to start this kindergarten which I have been operating successfully now for 32 years.

Many years after 1945 I bumped into the producer of *The Devil's Disciple*. By then he had become very successful presenting plays on Broadway. We reminisced for a while and quickly came around to talking about how wonderful David Manners was.

He told me that David had called him, knowing he was trying to break in as a producer, when the first version of *The Devil's Disciple* fell thorough. He said David himself put up all the money to finance the play and didn't take out one cent for himself, not even travelling expenses. He said David just wanted to help me.

David Manners and Zita Johann in *The Mummy*, a Universal film made in the 1930s in Hollywood. Johann now operates a kindergarten in New Jersey.

I called David in California and told him what I had discovered. Do you know what he said? "Did I really? I forget!" Most unassuming, never looking for thanks, that is David through and through.

In 1946, following the success of *The Devil's Disciple*, David received a host of new offers from Hollywood producers. He turned them all down. But he did accept an offer from an old friend, who had fallen on hard times, to star in a Broadway play providing the run was limited to a maximum of six months. Again he agreed to work for Equity minimum pay to help his friend.

"I didn't like the idea but he was a friend in need so I said yes," Manners recalled in 1996. "The play only lasted a few months. It really wasn't very good, but a young actor named Marlon Brando played a small role that was impressive."

Brando ignored several letters, and even a request from his sister failed to have him return calls, but when finally cornered in an airport at Los Angeles, he had this to say about David Manners.

"Remember him?" said Brando.

> Of course I remember him. David Manners spent hours coaching me in my small role. He allowed me to steal the one scene I played with him by telling me how to do it. When the play ended he paid my fare to Hollywood, introduced me to his former agent, and opened doors that probably would never have been opened to me. You asked me if I remembered David Manners. It would have been better if you had asked if I felt I owed anything to David Manners. The answer then would have been simple. I owe my entire career to David Manners. I don't know where he is today, but I will never forget his generosity and professionalism. If you know where he is give me his telephone number. He was a great actor.

Years later David Manners told friends that Brando called him from out of the blue. "He later came to see me on several occasions and we talked theatre. His final visit was just before he was heading to Australia, or somewhere down there," Manners recalled. "The first time he called on the phone he asked me if I was running out of cash and needed any financial help. But he laughed when he saw my house and butler. 'Maybe I should touch you up for a few bucks,' he said."

When in 1936 David Manners abandoned Hollywood, never to return to try to recapture the fame and glory that he had so rightly earned, he left gossip columnists to speculate on his sudden departure.

"I always refused to tell anyone why I left Hollywood," he said in 1986, "but I always vowed, after in Halifax incident in 1917, that throughout my life I would never complain to anyone about my injuries or ailments." He explained, "Really my departure was quite simple. My asthma had returned. It came back with the smog that was quickly taking over many areas around Los Angeles. The gossip columnists tried to concoct different reasons for my departure, so I let them create their own illusions."

Investments in land and buildings in Hollywood and Beverly Hills had made David Manners a rich man. The year 1936 was a good one for property sellers, and he quietly unloaded his investments and made huge profits.

For several years he lived on the thousand-acre Yucca Loma Rancho in Apple Valley, on the edge of the Mohave Desert in California. "I did all the things I'd wanted to do," he said. "I wrote three novels, rode my horses for miles, created more than one hundred paintings, and every day milked the cows myself."

Publishers accepted his first three novels, and one, *Under Running Laughter*, became a best-seller. A few of his paintings he sent to an art gallery owner in Santa Monica sold quickly. He subsequently wrote and published four more books.

"I didn't want to return to Hollywood, but I needed to be nearer to the action, so I built this beautiful house on the cliffs overlooking the water at Pacific Palisades, hired three people to look after me, bought the art gallery in Santa Monica under my real name, and settled down to a new life where I could be both anonymous and successful," he said.

"Few moments, even fewer people, were memorable enough for me to want to remember Hollywood."

During the Second World War he opened the doors of his home to servicemen and women visiting California. Rejected from military service because of his recurring asthma, he decided to make give visitors to Hollywood the time of their lives. He purchased a bus to bring the military men and women to parties in his home from the hospitality centres in Hollywood. He recalled:

> I have several guest books with more than two thousand signatures of soldiers, sailors, marines and airmen who came perhaps for a meal or perhaps to stay several days. The other day I spotted the name Johnny Carson in one book and asked a friend to check if it was the Johnny Carson who had been one of the servicemen in the area on the date in the book.
>
> Two days later Carson called me and said he remembered his visit well. "I and thousands of others will never forget your hospitality," he said. He was astounded when he knew of my past as an actor, said he never thought to connect me with the film industry. Wanted me to appear on his program but I looked at myself in the mirror and reluctantly declined the invitation.

Studio publicists wrote many stories over the years suggesting that David Manners did graduate from the University of Toronto and became, among other things, the foreman of a logging gang in Ontario who once fought, barehanded, a bear that had strayed into the lumber camp. Another suggested that he was apprenticed to an antique dealer in New York before becoming an actor and was considered to be an expert on antique furniture. Other stories said he moved to New York when his parents decided to close their Halifax school and buy a house close to the big city.

"All were rubbish," he said. "They seemed to write whatever they felt like writing and the fans gobbled it up. As long as it was not detrimental I never argued."

In his Pacific Palisades home he proudly displayed a sixteen foot by eight foot wall chart that displayed his family's ancestry. He explained how he could trace his family back to William the Conqueror, winner of the Battle of Hastings in 1066 in England. Among the other famous names on the huge document were Lady Diana Cooper and the Duke of Rutland. The Acklom bloodlines also included Arthur Conan Doyle, the renowned author.

Over the years, quietly, without seeking any recognition, Manners financed many small theatre groups in California. Through a network of the young people he invited to his home he was kept informed of actors in need of help, and through a bank in Santa Monica these actors received sufficient money to help them through difficult periods of their lives. He also paid medical bills for many people in the film industry. This information came from a doctor resident at St. John's Hospital in Santa Monica.

As Duan Acklom he was active until his eighties in anti-drug crusades. He paid thousands of dollars to help rehabilitate performers who had become addicted to drugs.

At eighty he worked tirelessly in the two-acre property around his mansion. "I love flowers and green grass and the leaves that come down in the fall," he said. "Did you notice that all the trees on my property are maples. I loved the change in colours of their leaves in the fall in my teens in Canada and I still look forward each year to their brilliant foliage in California."

In 1992, David Manners told a very weird story about an incident while they were making *Dracula*:

> We received a lot of warnings that Dracula was not a subject that we should trifle with, and because there were a lot of unexplained delays in production, accidents and problems on the set — scripts used to vanish mysteriously — a sort of legend grew up from somewhere that we should beware of thirteen — the reverse of the thirty-one in 1931. The stories were

printed in newspapers across North America but we laughed off the incidents as being the work of an over zealous publicity man.

Bela Lugosi was an odd sort of man. I believed he was using drugs, and somehow I was always a little scared of him. One day just before shooting ended he brought a mystic to the set and he and the mystic sprayed incense over the set and everyone in it. It was bizarre but we had got used to Lugosi by that time.

There was a fire in the projection room of the theatre on opening night and the projectionist was badly burned but *Dracula* was a huge success and it made a lot of us wealthy so why should we think there was any bad luck attached to the film.

After the film was finished the mystic somehow got our unlisted telephone numbers, probably from Lugosi, and called about a dozen of us. He warned Tod Browning, our director to beware of the figures one and three. He told the same tale to Dwight Frye, a distinguished actor in *Dracula*.

Both died in 1944, very unexpectedly, thirteen years after the film was completed.

Thirteen years later, in 1957, Bela Lugosi, who played Count Dracula, told a newspaper writer the legend was ridiculous and he was in fine health. A week later he was dead. Frances Dade, one of the company, died later that same year.

When 1970 came around a panicky Helen Chandler, leading lady in *Dracula* came to see me. She was quite a wreck and was drinking heavily. On May 1 she died with what doctors called a surprising heart attack. A month later Edward Van Sloan a great character actor in the film, also died. Herbert Munston, the last of the film's featured players, followed him in November.

In 1983 I was eighty-one and figured if there was a curse I'd beaten it.

It's now 1996 and if nothing happens this year to
me I think I'll live to be one hundred, perhaps even one
hundred thirteen.

But before the end of 1996 David Manners' health began to decline
rapidly. Doctors seemed unable to diagnose his problems, so that year
he sold his Pacific Palisades home and the art gallery in Santa Monica,
and moved into a retirement home near Santa Barbara in California.
Still wealthy, he was able to live in luxury to the end of his days. At
Christmas he sent cards to friends with a note on each. "So much for the
curse I've beaten the 13-year date once more."

He survived two more years before dying peacefully in his sleep on
December 23, 1998. Found in his pocket after he died was this brief
note: "Don't ever believe 13 is unlucky. I have survived five anniversaries
of 1931 but don't expect to be around much longer. Thanks to everyone
I have had a great life. Goodbye!"

David Manners and Ann Dvorak as they appeared in
Without Consent, a Warner picture.

Raymond Massey

When Raymond Massey received word in 1940 that he had been nominated for an Academy Award for his portrayal of Abraham Lincoln in the Warner Brothers film *Abe Lincoln in Illinois*, Jack Warner, head of the studio, was the first to call and congratulate him.

"Raymond Massey is one of the greatest actors on stage and screen today," said Warner to the news media. "He is not the kind of man you ever need ask a question. He seems to sense what someone is thinking before the words are spoken. He often answers my questions before I even ask them."

Over the years many people who acted with him commented on Massey's apparent ability to know what they were thinking.

When *Arsenic and Old Lace* was released in 1944, actor Peter Lorre also remarked on Massey's apparent mind-reading skills. "I recall on several occasions, when I was struggling to remember my lines, he would say to me, before I spoke a word, 'Not those words Peter, try again.'"

Massey said the suggestion that he could read minds was rubbish. "I have no such abilities," he said in 1950 to the *New York Times*. "Perhaps I get so wrapped up in the character I am playing that it becomes obvious to me what the person about to speak to me is going to say."

Katherine Cornell, one of Broadway's most renowned actresses, told a reporter, "Appearing with Raymond Massey is like being put in the glow of a summer sun. He has an aura that makes everyone around him feel completely at ease and the whole play is enhanced. I adore working with him."

Katherine Cornell and Raymond Massey first met on a farm in Cobourg, Ontario, when they were both teenagers. Cornell, visiting the farm from her home in Buffalo, New York, told Massey that she already knew she was going to be an actress and would one day be a major Broadway star. Massey told Cornell that acting was not in his future. "I want to be a writer," he said.

His family never intended him to be an actor. His parents hoped he would be interested in mechanical things to follow his father as head of the largest farm machinery company in North America, Massey-Harris (later to become Massey-Ferguson). The company was founded by his grandfather, Hart Massey, but Raymond disappointed his father with his lack of interest in the company.

Raymond Massey was born in Toronto on August 20, 1896. As a child he received his early education at Appleby School in Toronto, one of the finest private schools in Canada. He said much later in life that the "superb teachers there pointed me not toward farm machinery but in the direction of becoming a writer."

He recalled, "I disappointed them too, because on a visit to London my mother had taken me to the best theatres there and encouraged my enthusiasm for live theatre. I was only seven and there were no films then, only stage plays."

Tragically, only a week later his mother died from a ruptured appendix, and never was able to show him the London theatre scene the way she had hoped.

Upon graduating from Appleby School he attended the University of Toronto, where he found his enthusiasm for writing was overpowered by fellow students who convinced him to enrol in the university's drama classes.

After his father attended the Eugene O'Neill play *In The Zone*, presented by the students, he congratulated his son and told him, "If this is what you want for your future I will not object. You were memorable tonight."

When finished at Toronto, Massey went to Oxford University, but he failed to become enthused by the teaching at Balliol College and quit after only one year. "I had been able to see some remarkable live theatre in London and simply couldn't concentrate on the university course," he said.

In 1915 he volunteered to join the Canadian Army, then fighting in the First World War. Wounded twice and shell-shocked in France, he was sent home to Canada to recuperate. In March 1918, he was back in uniform with a brigade of Canadians who were shipped across the Atlantic to Siberia, where the unit was expected to fight alongside the Russians trying to overturn the Bolsheviks. He recalled:

> We were there for months doing nothing, getting more and more bored every day when General James

Elmsley, the unit's commander, called me to his tent. He said he heard I was somewhat of an actor and gave me fourteen days to put together an entertainment unit to help put some enthusiasm back into the men.

I recruited others who I felt had potential and in ten days we had written and rehearsed a two-hour show. We decided on a minstrel show because that sort of entertainment gave us opportunities to do just about everything.

We did fifteen different shows in less than a month and before we wore out our welcome the unit was ordered back to England and home to Canada.

Massey, at the urging of his father, returned to the family farm machinery business. "He gave me $25 a week and told me to learn the business from the lowest rung of the ladder. After six months I walked into the office and handed in my resignation."

Before making a final decision about his future he walked into the dressing room of renowned British actor John Drew, then appearing at the Royal Alexandra Theatre in Toronto.

"How do I become an actor," he asked Drew.

"You go to England and with that Canadian accent you should be able to find parts that are intended for Americans. Better tell them you are from the United States, they won't know the difference."

Massey had little money, but with the two hundred dollars he had saved he bought a passage on the smallest and oldest Cunard liner bound from Montreal to Liverpool, England. "I had no idea what the future would bring but I believed, even as my heart sank as we approached England, that somebody out there was looking for an actor like me."

As the liner steamed close to Liverpool he spotted a dingy old theatre on the end of a pier with a sign that read Winter Gardens, New Brighton. Three weeks later he was on stage in that theatre, but first he tried London.

He invented eighteen months in a Philadelphia repertory company, but it didn't impress managers or agents. "I told them I'd played Shaw and Ibsen, but it was a good job nobody asked which plays because I'd never seen any of them, much less appeared in them."

Just about at the end of his rope he tried the small Everyman Theatre in north London. By good luck he found the company was about to stage the one play, *In The Zone*, in which he had acted in Toronto. They needed an American to play the role of Jack, which he still remembered by heart. "I recited a few of the lines and was hired on the spot," he said. "We rehearsed for two days in the Everyman Theatre and left by train to open in Liverpool on the following Monday. I wasn't the least bit fazed that my debut was to be at the dingy old Winter Gardens Theatre in New Brighton just across the Mersey from Liverpool. When we got closer the building was older than I had imagined from the boat, but it was work and I was finally a professional actor."

For his professional debut Raymond Massey was paid three pounds a week, his train fare to Liverpool was paid, and he received one extra pound towards his food and lodgings while the company was away from London.

The Merseyside audience loved *In The Zone*, and the Everyman Theatre in London booked it for three weeks after its tryout in New Brighton.

All the London newspapers sent critics to cover the first night. "The *London Times* writer was especially kind. He congratulated me on a sterling performance and I accepted the praise without a blush but never told anyone that Charles Morgan, the critic, was a friend I had met at Oxford University."

Massey heard frequently from his older brother, Vincent, who remained in Canada but, like Raymond, never did go into the family business. "I remember well one letter saying he was doing well in the political arena, and that one day he planned to be the first Canadian-born Governor General of Canada," Massey recalled. "I laughed when I read it, but didn't laugh twenty years later when he was appointed to be the King's representative in Canada, the highest post in the colonies as they were at that time. I was able to attend the swearing-in ceremony when he ascended to that lofty post."

Having the success of *In The Zone* in his resume, Raymond Massey moved to the West End London theatre scene very quickly. An experience he always remembered was meeting George Bernard Shaw.

"In those days there were no directors in London theatre as there were in New York. Either the lead actor or the stage manager put the plays together," Massey said. Sir Lewis Casson, the famed actor and producer, gave him a small role in Shaw's *Saint Joan*. "It was an awe-inspiring experience," he recalled. "Shaw attended every rehearsal and if Casson tried to alter even one word it was vetoed by Shaw."

Saint Joan ran for a year in London. Before it closed he had been chosen to play a much more substantial role in a comedy, *Masses and Men*. "I met a beautiful young lady, Peggy Freemantle, while I was in *Saint Joan*," he said. "She was enthused by me more as an actor than a man, but I loved that and we got married before the play ended its run."

Massey recalled:

> Flushed with success George Carr, Allan Wade and I took over a long lease on the Everyman Theatre. We had no set policy, there was no sign of a new play being offered to us, so we decided to play revivals, including some of Shaw's earlier plays. For some generous reason I never understood, Shaw, who received fifteen percent royalty from all his plays, decided to let Everyman stage his plays for only five percent of the box-office take.

The trio's big break came when a play, *Mr. Pepys*, was chosen to move from the Everyman to London's West End Royalty Theatre.

In 1929, after Shaw had seen one of his plays at the Everyman, which Massey directed and appeared in, he sent to Massey one of his famed postcards that today bring thousands of dollars at theatre memorabilia auctions. Massey was so delighted with the words from Shaw that he had the card framed and it was in his dressing room for every play and film from then on. It was in the study of his Beverly Hills home when he died many years later.

Shaw's card read: "I have a considerable grudge against you for letting me slave over Saint Joan when you could have produced [directed] it as well as I or better. Why were those talents hidden? Producers [directors] are one in a million. Anyone can play La Hire or D'Estivet. Why didn't you tell me, confound you! George Bernard Shaw."

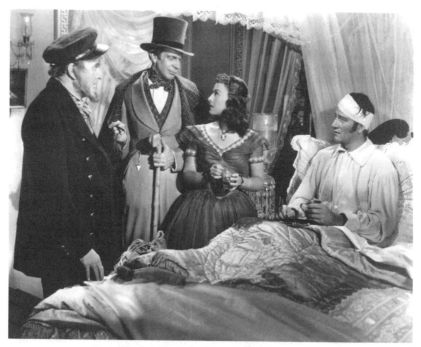

Raymond Massey with Paulette Goddard and
John Wayne in *Reap the Wild Wind*.

Massey later said, "At anytime in my life if I was in doubt about my talents I read the Shaw postcard again and my career was instantly renewed and refreshed."

In October 1924 his first son, Geoffrey Massey, was born at the Massey home in Kensington, near London. "Sadly the relationship between myself and my wife was deteriorating rapidly as I was spending so much time away from home at the theatre."

In 1926, when Raymond Massey's career was becoming more and more successful, every union in the British Isles decided to go on strike.

The General Strike paralyzed the country. "There were no trains, no buses, no mail services," he recalled. "Electric power ceased, coal mines were closed and since all these things contributed to theatre, the theatres were closed. I have always been in favour of unions, in fact I helped found the British actor's union that gave small role performers a decent wage, but this was not just a strike it was a thinly disguised revolution," he said.

Massey decided he could not join the strikers so he volunteered to drive one of the lorries that made efforts to distribute mail all over the country.

"We had some hair-raising experiences," he said. "The lorry I was driving was more than once almost overturned by strikers before police stepped in. But we got the mail through and that was the beginning of the end of the General Strike of 1926."

When the theatres reopened, Massey was deluged with offers to appear in plays and to direct them.

In 1927 he played for the first time before King George V of England. Sir Gerald du Maurier, who organized an annual production to raise money for the Actors Pension Fund, invited him to play a good role in *Bulldog Drummond*.

"If you are expecting to hear that the king rushed back stage to congratulate me on a magnificent performance you are going to be disappointed," he said. "Because the front of house spotlights were so brilliant I never even saw him. I was told later that he didn't really care for the theatre but attended this show once a year because it was a goodwill gesture from Buckingham Palace."

In the 1920s and early 1930s, when money became more plentiful, Massey took short sea trips back and forth between Southampton and New York. "I saw as many as ten shows in a week," he said. "Because my London success had reached New York before me I was often invited to attend rehearsals of shows soon to open on Broadway."

Back in London he was invited by Basil Dean, one of the greatest British producers/directors, to work in an American play by S.N. Behrman, *The Second Man*, with only four characters. "With Dean directing Noel Coward, Zena Dare, Ursula Jeans and myself the play drew much attention while it was in rehearsal. Sam Behrman arrived from the United States. The opening night at the Playhouse Theatre was a triumph. The play ran for five successful months," Massey said.

Basil Dean had already signed Massey to appear in his next play, *The Constant Nymph*, at the Garrick Theatre before *The Second Man* closed. The cast included Jean Forbes-Robertson and Cathleen Nesbitt and marked the stage debut of a young actress who later went on to major successes on stage and in Hollywood. Madeline Carroll and Raymond Massey remained friends for life after the success of the play.

One night, late in September 1929, Raymond Massey found a large envelope awaiting him at the theatre where he was directing a new Noel Coward play. "I could scarcely believe my eyes, the envelope bore the magical name of C.B. Cochran, the biggest name in British theatre at that time," he recalled. "It was the script of *The Silver Tassel*, the new play by Sean O'Casey. Charles Cochran wanted me to direct it!"

It was in *The Silver Tassel* that Barry Fitzgerald, later one of Hollywood's most memorable character actors — but until that time a semi-professional actor at the Abbey Theatre in Dublin — made his professional debut. Charles Laughton, with little experience, was also hired. Massey spotted a young lady in a London restaurant. He sent a note over to her table asking if she was an actress. The reply, "I'm not sure but I think I am," was signed Binnie Barnes. She too went on to fame in Hollywood after appearing in *The Silver Tassel*.

A young Welshman walked into the rehearsals and asked Massey if perhaps there might be a role he could play. "That afternoon I hired Emlyn Williams to make his stage debut," said Massey.

Despite this incredible cast the play closed after only twenty-six performances, and Raymond Massey found time to deal with the realization that his marriage of seven years was a failure. He moved out of the Kensington home into a small flat.

His next directing job was the London version of a Broadway play that had failed in New York. *The Sacred Flame*, as created by Massey, ran for more than a year in London.

His divorce final from Peggy, Raymond Massey promptly married actress Adrianne Allen on October 30, 1929, at the Westminster Registry Office in London. Massey's two witnesses were actors Herbert Marshall and Edna Best, friendships he would renew many years later in Hollywood.

The Masseys asked for and received custody of Massey's five-year-old son, Geoffrey. Two children were born from his marriage to his second wife. Both Daniel and Anna Massey emulated their parents and went on to considerable fame in the London theatre and in British films.

A telegram from Harold Harwood in New York invited Massey to make his debut on Broadway in November in the play *The Man In Possession*, the London production from which he had withdrawn in September after an eight-month run because of illness (later diagnosed as colitis, a little-known disease at that time). He suffered severe pains from colitis throughout his life but never missed a day on stage or on a film set throughout his entire career.

Because of the illness, afraid he might let the New York producer down, he declined the Broadway offer in favour of appearing in a new London play, *Topaze*, a satire on French politics.

"It was a disastrous choice. The enthusiastic audience prompted director Reginald Denham to demand that Alice Delysia and I take an unprecedented curtain call at the end of the first act," he recalled years later. "At the end of Act three we were lucky to take even one extra curtain. The audience loved Act one but hated Acts two and three. There were catcalls and boos at the final curtain. The show closed after only three performances."

With unexpected freedom and time on his hands, Raymond Massey accepted the invitation of Gerald du Maurier to visit a London film studio. Sound was still in its early stages, but Massey became enthusiastic about the new medium, which most established actors were ignoring.

After considerable thought, he accepted an invitation from du Maurier to play Sherlock Holmes in the film of *The Speckled Band*.

"It soon became apparent that du Maurier's interpretation of Holmes and mine were miles apart," he said. "Instead of the Holmes office and home he made the set almost futuristic. It was a travesty of Conan Doyle's classic."

But the Sherlock Holmes film introduced Massey to Angela Baddeley as the movie's heroine. She was later to receive much more fame as Mrs. Bridges in the television series *Upstairs, Downstairs*, still being shown on some small North American television networks.

He tried one more film the same year in the British studios, *The Face at the Window*, but again he was not enchanted with the results.

While on a search for a play to bring to London, Massey received a call from Noel Coward. "I have just turned down the role of Hamlet on Broadway," said Coward. "I have told the director and producer Norman Bel Geddes that you are the perfect actor for the part. You'll be hearing from him."

Bel Geddes did call. He explained his revolutionary version of the play to Massey. "Do you want to do my *Hamlet?*" he asked. "Yes," replied Massey, "I want to do your version of *Hamlet* as my debut on Broadway."

"You have the role," said Bel Geddes. "We will open in 1931, around November, mark it on your calendar."

Back in England Massey directed a revival of Somerset Maugham's *The Circle.* When it settled in for what looked like a long run he turned his mind to the plans for staging *Five Star Final,* a Broadway hit for which he had obtained the London production rights.

He approached producer Alec Rea to find the money needed to stage a play with twenty-six scenes. Rea agreed if Massey would read a new play by Ronald Jeans, *Lean Harvest.* Rea agreed to finance *Five Star Final,* now to be named *Late Night Final,* if Massey would direct and appear in it. In return, Massey also agreed to direct *Lean Harvest.*

Despite all these activities Raymond Massey also agreed to direct Vicki Baum's novel *Grand Hotel,* dramatized for the stage.

"I had four major plays running or in rehearsal. I was acting in one. During that period I was responsible for more than one hundred actors who I spread around sixty-eight different scenes," he said.

When all four shows were running in London at the same time, Massey handed over his role in *Late Night Final* to actor Godfrey Tearle.

While Massey was working eighteen hours a day, seven days a week, Norman Bel Geddes arrived in London from New York.

"I am ready to start casting *Hamlet,* he said.

"That was the only day in my life I worked for twenty four hours non-stop," recalled Massey.

Bel Geddes wanted an entirely British cast for *Hamlet.* "We interviewed over fifty of London's most competent actors," said Massey. "It seemed everyone wanted to do *Hamlet* on Broadway."

On November 21, 1931, Raymond Massey made his Broadway debut as Hamlet. The play ran for its four-week limited season schedule to full houses. On the final night producer Robert Sherwood came backstage. The eight words he spoke to Massey defined the path of Massey's future forever: "I would like you to play a young Abraham Lincoln," said Sherwood.

"Yes please," said Massey. But it was to be six years before Sherwood's dream became reality.

Massey's wife, Adrienne Allen, had opened on Broadway in *Cynara* just before *Hamlet* had its first night. Planned for an indefinite run, it looked as though it would be running for at least six months.

"Adrienne was so good that four major Hollywood studios offered her contracts," he said. "I directed all the tests, one for each studio, and she chose Paramount who offered her a two-picture a year deal, with options for five years."

Universal Pictures also offered Raymond Massey a two-year contract to direct and act, so the Masseys boarded the 20th Century, the fastest train to Los Angeles, full of hope that their careers were both heading in the right direction.

Years later Raymond Massey learned that Carl Laemmle, Jr., head of Universal Pictures, had not even known his studio had signed Massey until he was advised that the actor was waiting at the studio front gate asking permission to enter.

"I'll never forget his words," said Massey, "they turned out to be as hollow as so many other words spoken by agents, directors, producers in Hollywood."

Without having ever heard Massey's name before, Laemmle said, "We have great plans for you Raymond. You are an actor aren't you?"

Fortunately for Massey, Ernst Laemmle, Carl's cousin, came into his life on that first day at Universal. Ernst told Massey that he had lived in London for some years and knew his work well. "But this is Hollywood," he said. "I urge you to escape to the land of your achievements."

Working with William Wyler, one of Hollywood's finest directors, convinced Massey that he never wanted to be a writer or film director. "In theatre there was always collaboration between actor and director, in films there was none. The director was boss and he made all the decisions. I didn't care for that," he said.

Producer Walter Wanger had met Massey in London, and a chance meeting again at Universal got him an invitation to go with the Wangers for a weekend at the William Randolph Hearst Castle in San Simeon, in northern California. At Hearst's request, the weekend was extended to seven days.

The following week Raymond Massey made his Hollywood film debut in Universal's *The Old Dark House*. In the cast were Boris Karloff, Charles Laughton, and Ernest Thesiger, old friends from England, plus Americans Melvyn Douglas and Gloria Stuart. Massey recalled, "It was the first of the fifty Hollywood movies I would make. It turned out to be a good one. Or so I was told. Nobody ever showed it to me!"

Adrienne Allen was also finding success. Paramount gave her two excellent roles. But the lease on the house the Masseys rented in Hollywood was about to expire, so they headed back to Broadway. Nothing was happening there, so they continued eastward to London.

Raymond and Adrienne both accepted lead roles in London in a new play, *Never Come Back*. After only six weeks the play closed.

Several more plays that Massey directed or appeared in followed in quick succession. In February 1934, he and his wife returned to Broadway in the British play *The Shining Hour*. They had rehearsed the play in London before taking it, after a week's tryout in Toronto, directly to Broadway.

The play opened at Toronto's Royal Alexandra Theatre. Gladys Cooper and Raymond Massey, the stars, received rave reviews from the news media. But the critics were not too complimentary about the play. Despite the adverse comments it played to sold-out houses every night in Toronto.

It opened at the Booth Theatre in New York on February 14. The New York papers loved not only the actors but the play as well. It ran for five months before being transferred in its entirety to the St. James Theatre in London.

Alexander Korda, the only British movie producer of that era who turned out films to rival the best from Hollywood, saw Massey in the show. He went backstage and made him an immediate offer to appear in his next film, *The Scarlet Pimpernel*. Massey was cast as the evil Chauvelin.

The film was a huge success and made instant film stars out of Massey and Leslie Howard. The success led to another Korda film, the H.G. Wells story *The Shape Of Things To Come*. "It took us a whole year to make," Massey recalled later. "Korda spared no expense to make it perfect. I played two roles, John Cabal and his grandson Oswald, so was able to travel through the entire century over which the story moved."

The film was another triumph for Korda and Massey. It earned millions of pounds in England and many more millions of dollars in the United States, making it one of the most profitable films Korda ever produced and directed.

Two more plays took the Masseys to Broadway. Late in 1935 Adrienne starred in *Pride and Prejudice*. Raymond headlined in *Ethan Frome*, the play he always called "my favourite play of all."

Brooks Atkinson wrote in the *New York Times* these words about Massey's play: "When they hired Ruth Gordon, Pauline Lord and Raymond Massey for this play they nominated the trio to immortality."

Cary Grant, Raymond Massey, and Peter Lorre in *Arsenic & Old Lace*.

Between 1935 and 1958 Raymond Massey appeared with enormous success in twenty-two more plays. Included was *Abe Lincoln in Illinois*. In 1938 Raymond Massey returned to Broadway to appear in the play. "I had promised Bob Sherwood six years earlier that I would be there when he needed me," he said.

1938 was also the year he received a letter from his wife, Adrienne, that she felt they should go their own ways, they were so often apart. Three months later the divorce was finalized.

The play was a major accomplishment for Massey. Two years later, when the play was transferred to Hollywood, Robert Sherwood only agreed to sell the film rights if Raymond Massey was given the title role.

Later in his career, after he had portrayed Abraham Lincoln three times, he found this fact always headed the biographies sent out by studio press agents. "I'm sure I am the only actor ever typecast as a president," he said.

Others plays that brought him more applause included *Idiot's Delight*, *Candida*, *Doctor's Dilemma*, and *Pygmalion*.

In 1940, Raymond Massey was nominated for the highest honour given by Academy of Motion Picture Arts and Sciences, the Oscar, for his remarkable performance as Abraham Lincoln in the film version of *Abe Lincoln In Illinois*.

He lost the Oscar to Charlie Chaplin, who had made and starred in *The Great Dictator*, an appropriate film for that time, telling America the story of the villain of Germany, Adolph Hitler.

After the ceremony Charlie Chaplin walked over to Massey. "Mr. Massey," he said, "it is ridiculous for me to consider myself an actor with talents approaching yours." He smiled. "But I got the Oscar so I'm planning to keep it. You will get your own Oscar very soon, I'm certain."

Raymond Massey never did win an Oscar, but he collected numerous other awards and citations for his performances on stage in both London and New York and in films in London and Hollywood.

It was the play *Ethan Frome* that led the way to his illustrious film career on both sides of the Atlantic. Adrienne Allen's *Pride and Prejudice* was also the start of a memorable career for her on Broadway. But she was not a successful film actress, and this simple fact led to the breakup of their marriage.

In Hollywood Massey starred in *The Prisoner of Zenda* before returning home to team again with Alexander Korda and Flora Robson in *Fire Over England*. Both were box-office successes.

"It was at that time in my career I found I could no longer walk down the streets in California or England as I once used to," he said. "People stared at me and said loudly and rudely, 'That's Raymond Massey.' Younger people asked me for autographs. I liked that. But fame had destroyed the anonymity I once loved."

Two more films, *The Hurricane*, directed by John Ford, and *Under The Red Robe*, enhanced his popularity.

With his marriage over, Raymond Massey decided to make his permanent home in California. There he met Dorothy Ludington. They were married in 1939. The marriage lasted harmoniously until her death in 1982.

Among the films he made were *Arsenic And Old Lace*, *Desperate Journey*, *Hotel Berlin*, *49th Parallel*, *Dallas*, *Prince of Players*, and *East of Eden*. He remembered the last film vividly.

"James Dean would wander about the set in search of motivation to play the next scene," he said. "When he found that motivation he would blow a whistle he carried with him everywhere and director Elia Kazan and the rest of the cast were expected to be in their places by the time he reached the set. Kazan pacified us all by saying, 'Bear with me my friends, I'm getting pure gold out of this film.' Kazan's patience and intuition soothed us all and the resulting film was everything he said."

Raymond Massey returned home to Toronto on many occasions. "I was there when my brother Vincent was sworn in as Governor General of Canada," he said. "I reminded him of his comment many years earlier that predicted this lofty role would one day be his."

"Did I really say that," said Vincent. "I recall telling you that one day you would be one of the most accomplished actors on the face of the earth."

"If you said that, Vincent," said Massey, "thank you, but I don't recall that moment."

In 1961, Raymond Massey was lured from the big screen to the television studio to play the part of Dr. Gillespie in the TV series *Dr. Kildare*. "I took the role because I expected it would last no more than one season and leave me sufficient time to make more features," he said.

He was wrong. The series lasted six years. During that time he never found time to make even one movie.

Richard Chamberlain, who became a big star from *Dr. Kildare*, credits Raymond Massey with giving him the courage and knowledge to play the role. "I never knew when I met Raymond that he would become such a motivating force in my life," he said.

> I was only twenty-two when I was chosen to play in a teleplay, *Alfred Hitchcock Presents*. I don't know what I expected when I was told I would be working with Raymond Massey.
>
> Perhaps I expected to get eaten alive. Raymond had a reputation of not suffering fools lightly. I learned my lines to the letter and was ready when this big, hulking person with the rich, resonant, booming voice, walked on to the set.
>
> To my amazement we got on well. He brought my character alive. Two years later when I was trying out for the part of Dr. Kildare to his Dr. Gillespie, it was his approval of my acting that got me the role that made my life a continuing success.

In 1968, Massey made his final feature film, *Mackenna's Gold*. He was not the star. Gregory Peck, Omar Shariff, and Telly Savalas had the juicy roles. The film was not a box-office success, but Massey always prized the review he clipped from the *New York Times*. "All the big stars couldn't hold this film together," said the writer, "but had they chosen to enlarge the characters given to Raymond Massey and Lee J. Cobb they might have had a movie worth watching. These two showed why they are still among the elite of Hollywood's acting fraternity."

In 1972, he accepted a role in a film, *All My Darling Daughters*, made for television. Friends who knew he had been suffering dreadfully from arthritis, which had made getting around very difficult for him, were surprised when he agreed to appear.

"I just wanted to see if I still had what it takes," he said. "Now I know I haven't! My acting career is now at an end." He told a *Los Angeles Times* reporter that he estimated he had spent seven years of his life inside film studios. "That's enough for any man," he said.

In 1982, he welcomed CBC producer Harry Rasky into his Beverly Hills home. Rasky wanted to make a TV film, *Raymond Massey: Actor of the Century*, for Canadian audiences. "That's the least I can do for my beloved Canada," said Massey.

On July 30, 1983, before the tribute was ready for airing, he died, aged eighty-six, at his home after a six-week bout with pneumonia.

His final comment to Harry Rasky, during filming of the tribute that was aired on January 22, 1984, was this: "I must make it clear that I despise the unnecessary vulgarity and indecency in today's theatre. In my day we didn't need this to create a successful play or film. I believe the theatre and movies should be enchantment, make-believe and let's pretend. Today it is sex, obscenity and squalor. I am glad I will be leaving it all behind very soon."

Walter Pidgeon

"I would have liked to live forever. Life has been so good to me!" Actor Walter Pidgeon spoke these words on September 25, 1984, to his wife, the former Ruth Walker. "But," he added, "I'm afraid no one up there is listening."

They were the first words he had spoken at St. John's Hospital in Santa Monica, where had been rushed after suffering a series of strokes at his home in Bel Air, California. They were also his last words. One hour later he died, with, said his wife, "a wonderfully contented smile on his face."

"I too had a lifetime of joy," she said. "Although I'm alone I feel Walter is here and the memories will never go away."

Walter Pidgeon, born on September 23, 1898, at 23 Cedar Street in Saint John, New Brunswick, had every reason to be satisfied with his life, which had led him into his eighty-seventh year. He had succeeded beyond his wildest dreams in the motion picture industry, and not once in the fifty-nine years he had called California his home was any hint of scandal ever written or heard about him.

His co-star in eight successful films, Greer Garson, called him Hollywood's only real gentleman. "I never heard him raise his voice in anger," she said in 1980, "I never heard him say a bad word about anyone, nor did I hear anyone say a bad word about him. He was a gentleman and a gentle man."

Ninety years ago, in 1913, a trembling schoolboy celebrating his fifteenth birthday stood on the stage of the Imperial Theatre in Saint John, New Brunswick, to give his first public performance. But the young Walter Pidgeon was not there as an actor. He had been chosen to sing as a soloist in a musical concert presented by a number of local church choirs. Some stories have suggested he went on stage to substitute for his brother Charles, who had lost his voice with a bad cold. "Rubbish," said Pidgeon. "I was there because they invited me. Charles couldn't sing a note."

Walter Pidgeon, whose later well-documented singing accomplishments have often been eclipsed by his brilliant acting achievements, was a member of one of the church choirs showcased on stage. His outstanding voice earned him not one but two solos.

In 1983, relaxing on the lawn of the beautiful mansion that film success had enabled him to build at 230 Strada Corta Road, in exclusive Bel Air, California, he recalled his public debut seventy years earlier.

"My knees were shaking so much that I missed the piano introduction and the pianist had to repeat it before I was able to start singing," he said. "I was so scared I wasn't sure my voice would come out at all, but it must have been all right, I remember the applause to this day. It is probably my most wonderful memory of the city in which I was born. You forget all the boos and catcalls in your life but you never forget the applause."

In 1915, when he was seventeen, he enrolled at the University of New Brunswick in the provincial capital, Fredericton. "I didn't know what I wanted to be, if a pirate sailing the oceans doesn't count," he said. "But the next year, at eighteen, I left the university and joined the 65th Battery of the Canadian Field Artillery. I was full of adventure and ready to face the trenches in France, but fate intervened. In training I became trapped between two rolling gun carriages and spent the next sixteen months in a Toronto military hospital."

When the war ended, Pidgeon moved from Saint John to Boston with eighteen dollars in his pocket. "I had to take anything that was available, and found a job the day I arrived working five nights a week in the mail room of a well-known stockbroker," he recalled sixty years later.

He used most of the money he earned to pay for tuition at the Boston Conservatory of Music. "There was no thought of acting — unless you count the awkward movements I made on stage in the various musicals I did in the early twenties acting — but I did believe I was going to find fame as a singer."

Pidgeon married his first wife, Muriel, also hoping to find fame as a singer, while both were training at the conservatory. "It was tough at first, trying to keep both of us on one salary," he recalled. "But we survived because Muriel took an evening job as a salesgirl."

His acting can't have been so bad, because four years later, when he was twenty-three, he appeared in Canada again at both the Imperial Theatre in Saint John and the Grand Theatre in Moncton. This time he was singing a small but important role as a member of the Boston Light Opera Company.

The theatre critic for the *Moncton Times* singled him out, saying, "Mr. Pidgeon has a robust baritone voice that is enhanced by his masculine appearance and excellent stage presence. Mark my words, this young man will go far in the world of the theatre."

Pidgeon recalled in 1980, "The Moncton writer, who didn't get a byline, was the first critic who ever noticed me. I still have the clipping in my first scrapbook. You never want to lose moments in time like that."

Pidgeon had special memories of one singing role he won while he was still at the Boston Conservatory:

> I played the lead role of a Mountie in *Rose Marie,* and after a month on the road, during which time the producer often had me walk up and down the main street of each town in which we were playing, wearing my Royal Canadian Mounted Police uniform, I became so enthused with the red coat that I actually applied to join the force. When they saw the record of my military injuries they sent me a letter of regret. I have often wondered what my life might have been like had they accepted me.

Long before his own Hollywood fame, distinguished dancer Fred Astaire, a favourite, with his sister Adele, of stage audiences worldwide, spotted Pidgeon singing with an amateur company in Boston. He knew renowned singer and entertainer Elsie Janis was then in search of a new partner, and he suggested Pidgeon. She respected Astaire's evaluation and immediately travelled from New York to Boston to hear him. Walter Pidgeon was hired on the spot and joined the Elsie Janis show four days later.

"Miss Janis was a delight to work with," he said. "I learned from her more stagecraft than I had learned in the years before we met or have learned since. For more than two years I toured the United States and Canada with her. I still recall the glorious moment she told me we were going to Broadway."

Pidgeon's wife, Muriel, travelled with the company as understudy for Janis. "But just her luck," said Pidgeon. "Elsie Janis had a constitution like an elephant. She was never sick."

Walter Pidgeon relaxes while enjoying a few days off from
his MGM work at his Beverly Hills home.

At Home, the 1924 Janis revue that took Walter Pidgeon to London
and the Shaftesbury Theatre for ten months, brought him another
review that he never forgot. "I can find it if you'll bear with me," he said.

> It's in my first scrapbook, that's the battered one on the
> desk in the corner. This is what the *London Times* said
> about me. "It may be the Elsie Janis revue but the real
> star is Walter Pidgeon. His glorious voice, superb stage
> technique and ability to steal scenes from Miss Janis
> makes him the concert-master and puts her in the first
> row of violins." Elsie wasn't very happy with the review
> and cut my number of appearances down next night.

It wasn't exactly a financial bonanza playing second fiddle to Miss Janis. "I think I got about one hundred dollars when we were on Broadway in the revue *Puzzles of 1925*. Muriel got about twenty dollars. But that was a lot of money in those days," said Pidgeon. "We had been playing for about three weeks when one memorable night I received a standing ovation after a solo spot. Elsie was mad! Told me if that happened again I would be fired. It did, and I was! It was tough to accept but perhaps the best thing that had happened in my career so far. I was stuck as second fiddle to Elsie just as long as I stayed with her."

Most books about the history of Broadway list *Puzzles of 1925* as being Walter Pidgeon's New York debut. "That isn't correct. I had ventured from Boston to New York in 1923 and somehow managed to get an interview with the British actor E.E. Clive," he said. "He was producing *You Never Can Tell* on Broadway and despite my having a total lack of professional experience he gave me a small role. I still have a review of the play by a New York critic because the show was a huge success. This is what he said about me: 'Also in the cast is Mr. Walter Pidgeon.'"

Although movies were still silent in 1925, and Pidgeon at that time was considered to be a singer, not an actor, his good looks had attracted the attention of a number of movie moguls in Hollywood.

"Several talent scouts had come backstage to see me," he said, "and when Elsie Janis fired me, Muriel and I decided to use our savings and head by train to Hollywood to visit the different companies whose representatives had given me their calling cards." He continued:

> I remember leaving the New York rail terminal as clearly as though it was yesterday. As we waved goodbye to our friends my wife yelled out, "I should tell you all, I'm going to have a baby!" It was the first I'd heard of the news and I was quite stunned. I guess I worried all the way across the United States wondering whether I could succeed in motion pictures sufficiently to keep three people alive. By the time we reached Chicago we were so uncertain that we were ready to leave the train and return to New York where I knew stage work would be easy to get.

Once again fate intervened. The railroad company told the Pidgeons it was impossible to get their heavy trunks out of the sealed compartment destined for Los Angeles. "So on we went," he said, "both feeling very afraid of the future."

Tragedy struck his life on October 26, 1926, when Muriel died giving birth to their daughter. Hearing the terrible news, Pidgeon's mother, Hannah, got the first train from Saint John to Los Angeles to help look after the new arrival, whom Pidgeon's wife had named Edna weeks before the baby's arrival.

"There was no way in those days to know if the baby would be a boy or a girl," said Pidgeon, "but a fortune teller on the pier at Santa Monica told us that we could definitely expect a girl so we had the name Edna ready!"

That visit to California by Pidgeon's mother, when she was fifty-six, lasted thirty-eight years until she died peacefully in her sleep at his Bel Air home at the age of ninety-four. "Until she was eighty-five she went home to Saint John every year, spending a month there in the spring," he said. "She loved the old city especially in springtime."

When Edna Pidgeon was twenty she married John Aitkins, a man with no connection to the film industry, and she soon presented Walter Pidgeon with two granddaughters, Pat and Pam. "He was never happier than when he was with them," she said. "He became a kid again whenever he took them to Disneyland or the circus, and he was very generous to them, and all of us, before and after he died. Pat and Pam were ten before we told them their grandfather was a famous actor. Pat replied, 'I prefer him as a famous grandfather!'"

Pidgeon's first film, *Mannequin*, was, he said, "totally forgettable." He made several more "forgettable" films in the next three years before he called a halt and requested that he be given some sort of control over the films in which he was to perform. When none was forthcoming he returned to New York, where a lucrative starring stage role was waiting.

His return to Broadway in *No More Ladies* made him into a major idol of theatre-goers. "You can't believe the huge crowds that stood outside the stage door each night to applaud as I left the theatre," he said.

Producers were lining up at his door. "Literally," he recalled. "I remember answering the bell to my apartment door to find two of Broadway's most important producers standing there, arguing over who had the right to make me an offer first. It was so funny, I broke out laughing and they both marched away in disgust."

His two next plays, *The Night of January 16th* and *Something Gay*, the latter with Tallulah Bankhead, were major hits on Broadway.

"It was a bit like a see-saw," he laughed. "When I was in Hollywood, New York wanted me. When I returned to New York, Hollywood wanted me back. Since I had bought a small home for mother and Edna in Hollywood, I was more than happy to return to California."

Walter Pidgeon never became a difficult performer. "I didn't ever demand any control over the roles I was to play, as they do today," he said. "I asked nicely and discovered a secret that has stayed with me for my entire career, that a request spoken softly usually brings results and demands rarely do."

When sound arrived in Hollywood, the studios that previously saw him as a singer in silent movies suddenly now perceived him only as an actor. "I found myself cast in non-singing roles in musicals," he recalled. "But that is what is so lovable about the crazy Hollywood I have learned to call my home for so many years!"

In 1931, with the blessing of his daughter, Edna, he married Ruth Walker, a girl who had become his secretary. "I can truthfully say it was Edna who first suggested I marry Ruth. 'I'd like her as my mummy,'" she said. It was a marriage that lasted fifty-three happy years until his death.

In 1956 he returned to New York as a major Hollywood star, staying almost two years in the play *The Happiest Millionaire*. Before the play ended its Broadway run late in 1957, Pidgeon had received so many letters from all over the United States asking if the play would tour after its New York run ended that he decided to stay away from Hollywood for a while longer. In 1982 he recalled:

> I took a huge cut in salary and went on the road for fourteen delightful months. With my film fame and a wonderful play it was almost like being in heaven. Ruth came with me and we made the tour into a vacation

with pay. Every city we were in, Ruth and I went to see all the important places worth seeing. We were very contented tourists. I signed so many autographs during the run of the play that I doubt my signature could be worth more than ten cents today.

All my life in the film industry I have missed the applause when they liked you and boos when they didn't. If we could have made films before an audience, as they do in television today, I think my life would have been totally complete.

He was nominated twice for Academy Awards for *Mrs. Miniver* and *Madame Curie*. Twice the Oscar went to other actors. When James Cagney and Paul Lukas collected their statuettes, Walter Pidgeon was the first to congratulate them.

Pidgeon was on the board of directors of the Screen Actors Guild for thirty-three years, including five years as president. In 1974 the Guild, unhappy with the Academy's failure to give Pidgeon an Oscar, honoured him with their own highest award, "For outstanding achievement in fostering the finest ideals of the acting profession."

The framed award hung in a place of pride in his study. "It would have been nice," he said in 1983, "to have had an Oscar to put beside it. But it is too late now."

It was his proud boast that he had visited every one of the fifty American states. "Each year, between films, I marked one of the states on a small map I have on the wall of my den," he said. "Ruth, Edna and I chose the states in turn and we went by train, drove or flew to the ones we had chosen. Sometimes we were able to visit four or five a year."

In August 1977, Walter Pidgeon was rushed to St. John's Hospital in Santa Monica after a fall that had caused a blood clot to form on his brain.

When news leaked out on a television newscast that he was in a coma and unlikely to live for many hours, one Beverly Hills florist received nearly one hundred orders for floral tributes to be delivered to his home when the sad news was confirmed.

But this time "someone up there" did hear him, and by September 23, his birthday, he was ready to return home. As he left the hospital, sitting in a wheelchair, he joked with the group of photographers and newsmen who were waiting outside. He glanced up at the St. John's Hospital sign. "I started in S-a-i-n-t John, in Canada, and there was no way I was going to die in St. John's! That's in Newfoundland. If they had spelled it right I might have been more co-operative."

But it was to be a year before he was able to work again. "I'm unsteady on my feet," he said in the spring of 1978. "Can't do anything, can't even tend my geraniums, and you know how much I love to be surrounded by geraniums."

Regrets in life? "Only one, that because of a shortage of time I sometimes had to turn people away who asked for my autograph, I've felt pangs of regret for them all my life. I was so grateful to be asked." The *New York Times* reported that a tear ran down his face as he talked.

Walter Pidgeon was a hard worker all his life. In Saint John, as a child, he was the youngest paperboy in the city. "My paper route was cancelled when I accidentally threw a paper into the face of one of my customers who opened the door just as I launched the missile," he said. "But the other thirty customers on my route signed a petition requesting I be reinstated so I was. The paper had to send another boy, way off his regular route, to deliver the paper to the customer who no longer trusted my judgment or aim."

One of Pidgeon's grandfathers was a sea captain whose vessel carried products from Saint John to Boston and brought goods from there back to Canada. "He was a real old salt. With other boys around my own age, perhaps ten or eleven, we listened for hours to his stories about the great pirates like Captain Kidd," Pidgeon recalled. "Most of us were sure gramps really was a pirate too, masquerading as an honest sea captain. Of course we loved him for that and all of us wanted to spend our lives sailing the oceans in search of ships to rob and plunder."

At thirteen Pidgeon was employed-full time on weekends in his father's store, Caleb's Men's Wear, located at the corner of Main and Bridge Streets in an area he remembered as Indiantown. "My father sold just about everything a man needed in life, and a lot of things women needed too," he recalled. "It was more of a general merchandise store than just a men's wear store as the sign over the door suggested. I remember he caught me one day using a woman's corset as an imaginary accordion. There was no music, of course, but I was singing along to my make-believe instrument."

Pidgeon used every penny he earned to buy the fine quality clothing that became his trademark throughout his life. Did he buy them from his father? "Sadly, I must say no," he said. "I have to admit his clothing, though good value, wasn't the quality I wanted."

His wife recalled that often when he was expecting a newspaper writer to visit him at home he would peep out of an upstairs window to see who got out of the car. "If the reporter was scruffily dressed and his

Walter Pidgeon and Ilona Massey in *Holiday in Mexico*, 1946.

hair uncombed, Walter would tell me to say that he had been called away and the interview had to be cancelled," she said.

But there were two sides to that story, said Pidgeon. "If the reporter was neat and tidy I often invited him to stay for dinner, and on more than one occasion to stay overnight to finish the interview. Even lent him the spare set of pajamas we kept for unexpected guests and we always kept a few spare toothbrushes in the guest bathroom!"

In 1932, when a suit arrived back from a cleaner pressed so that two side-by-side creases could clearly be seen on the trousers, Pidgeon bought a professional pressing table, and from that day onwards no one ever pressed his trousers but his wife. "Our house staff would just stand by and watch," he laughed. "Think of the money we saved over fifty years," said Ruth.

Walter Pidgeon was always proud to display to visitors another item in his early scrapbook. It was the first letter he received from a fan after making his second film, *Old Loves And New*.

"Read it," he said. "It's a charming letter, thanking me for providing moments of satisfaction to the writer. It was dignified yet enthusiastic. I have re-read it many times for comfort in moments of uncertainty in my life."

Pidgeon answered the letter personally, as he did the majority of fan mail he received throughout his long career. In 1946, when he was making a personal appearance in Chicago, an elderly lady came up and introduced herself. "All she needed to say was, 'Perhaps you will remember a letter I sent you twenty years ago.' I knew who it was instantly, there seemed to be some sort of bond between us," he recalled. "We had supper together that evening, but I was saddened only three weeks later to hear from her grandson that she had died very suddenly."

Pidgeon recalled the early days of sound in Hollywood with pleasure:

> We worked then for the love of what we were doing.
> Everything was quite casual and relaxed. No one shouted
> or screamed as many directors and actors do today. We
> didn't have agents standing behind our chairs demanding

more pay or better conditions. I don't recall that I had an
agent in those wonderful days. It was a world that ended
when making huge sums of money became the only
thing in the minds of producers and actors too!

But there was more to him than just his acting. "Few people remember today that I, as a singer of popular ballads, made six records, the old 78s, back in 1930," he said in 1980. "They were all best-sellers, maybe sold fifty thousand copies or so, that was a best-seller then, but I doubt if anyone has one now, fifty years later. I wish I'd had the sense to keep a few. I'd like to hear now what I really sounded like all those years ago. I croak a little these days."

Walter Pidgeon made several early musicals like *The Bride Of The Regiment, Melody Of Love, Sweet Kitty Belairs, Viennese Nights,* and *Kiss Me Again,* but he believed his final transition to dramatic roles came in 1937 when he made *Saratoga* with Clark Gable and Jean Harlow.

"Jean Harlow was the big star of the film and when she died, tragically young, before the film was completed, Clark and I suddenly found ourselves being very critically judged on our acting abilities. I guess we passed the test because both our careers skyrocketed from then on," he said.

Clark Gable was one of the few actors in Hollywood that Pidgeon called a close friend. "We became very close when Harlow died, and I learned to respect his ethics. He never showed up late for any appointment, never took advantage of his position in Hollywood and, perhaps most important, was always considerate on the set of any film to every member of the crew," Pidgeon said. "Before a film was completed he knew the name of everyone on the set. When he died, the world lost a real man, and Hollywood wept."

He laughed as he recalled his first meeting with another important man from Saint John, New Brunswick, Louis B. Mayer, production head at the giant Metro-Goldwyn-Mayer studio.

I was called to his office to discuss a long-term contract
the studio wanted me to sign. He told me he had been
impressed by my work at other studios and that he felt
I would be an asset to MGM. He peered at me over his

glasses and suggested I tell him about myself. I started by saying I came from New Brunswick. "That's in Canada," I added.

"I know where New Brunswick is," said Mayer rather snippily. "Where in New Brunswick were you born?"

"Saint John."

Mayer jumped to his feet and thumped on his desk. "Young man," he shouted, "you can't influence me with lies like that. I'll fire the person who told you to say you came from Saint John."

Finally I quietened him down and convinced him I really was from Saint John. I had to tell him where half-a-dozen streets and buildings were that he remembered. But I left his office with a contract for much more money than I expected and we were friends until the day he died. On opening nights Louie, in his chauffeur-driven car, always picked Ruth and me up at our home to attend the performance.

When the Second World War was at its height, Louis B. Mayer offered Pidgeon to the Canadian government, with all expenses paid by Metro-Goldwyn-Mayer, as a morale-booster for the troops about to leave for Europe and the folks left behind at home in Canada. For more than a year he appeared at bond drives, troop shows, and concerts, and he often raised his voice in song to help raise money for the war effort. Apart from building morale, records show he raised more than $7 million in less than 12 months from the war bonds he personally sold.

When he arrived by train to start the bond drive in Saint John for the Third Victory Loan Campaign of 1942 he found hundreds of fans at the railroad station cheering and waving autograph books. "I stayed until I had signed every one," he recalled proudly.

It was at MGM that he made his most memorable films.

"They'll still call me Mr. Miniver on the day I die," he laughed. Had he still been able to laugh on September 26, 1984, he would have discovered his prediction had come true. The *Hollywood Citizen News* ran, as its front-page headline, "Mr. Miniver Dead At 87."

"I don't really mind the name," he said.

> It was a major turning point in my life. *Mrs. Miniver*, with Greer Garson as my co-star, made my life more secure that I had ever dared dream possible.
>
> It wasn't my first film with Greer, I'd made a very successful film, *Blossoms In The Dust*, with her in 1941. Later we made seven other films together, each a wonderful experience that I treasure. She was and always will be a real lady among the few in Hollywood. We never had a cross word between us.

Apart from Clark Gable and director William Wyler, few of Walter Pidgeon's real friends were important people in the film industry:

> I enjoy the company of the people who make the wheels turn, the sound men, electricians, the set builders, and one of my best friends was, until he died in 1973, a guard at the front gates of MGM. I won't name him because in the silent days he had probably been a much more renowned actor than I'll ever be. But he didn't have the voice for sound movies. He was happy as a gateman at MGM, Louis Mayer saw to that, and I was happy to have him in my home. He often regaled the other guests with hilarious stories from the early days of the silent era and my friends who met him often invited him to their homes too as a welcome guest. If we made the last years of his life more cheerful we were all very content.

Since both Walter Pidgeon and the MGM gateman have left this earth, neither would be annoyed that the gateman's identity be now revealed as the former major star of silent movies, King Baggott.

Pidgeon aged gracefully through the years, and there was no gap between his days as a romantic leading man and his move into character roles.

"Somehow I just muddled through," he said. "I don't know quite when I started to get old, but I recall very clearly, when I played opposite Elizabeth Taylor in 1954 in *The Last Time I Saw Paris*, thinking how young and beautiful she was and how old I had suddenly become."

Walter Pidgeon returned to Saint John without any ballyhoo many times to see members of his family and old friends. "I always had someone drive me to Cedar Street to see the house in which I was born," he said. "It changed its face over the years but I always thought of it very lovingly."

Among the friends Walter Pidgeon never forgot was Helen Russell (then Helen Campbell); he always visited her Rothesay home on his Saint John visits. "We had been friends since we first met in Grade 7 at Alexandra School," said Pidgeon.

Walter Pidgeon in *The Neptune Factor*.

In 1959 he returned to New York once more, this time to play in the highly successful Broadway musical *Take Me Along*, co-starring Jackie Gleason.

"Gleason is a master at everything he does. Ad-libbing with him was a special delight that we carried out every night after the final curtain," Pidgeon recalled. "Sometimes for as long as ten or fifteen minutes, and the audience loved it. I have wonderful memories of a great man and brilliant performer. I must credit Elsie Janis for giving me the ability to hold my own with Jackie Gleason. She and Jackie would have made an incredible vaudeville team."

Many films made by Pidgeon are still seen on late-night television and are available on videocassette. They include the unforgettable *Mrs. Miniver, How Green Was My Valley, The Girl Of The Golden West, Madame Curie, Mrs. Parkington,* and *Funny Girl* in 1968, in which he played Florenz Ziegfeld.

An avid reader of everything from history books to the classics by way of Erle Stanley Gardner mysteries, he could talk knowledgeably about any subject that was raised in his hearing.

"I am proud to say that I never once corrected anyone, or embarrassed them, if they tried to be clever by making a statement in my home that I knew was not true," he said. "But I made sure he, or she, never got another invitation. There are a lot of stars who think they know everything. They have no place in my life. None of us know everything."

When television grew in popularity he declined many times the roles offered him, as did the majority of the stars of Hollywood's golden years, but eventually he agreed to help out a friend in need.

"In 1963 when Raymond Burr, playing Perry Mason, was taken ill and four substitute 'lawyers' had to be hired to keep the show running for a month, Erle Stanley Gardner himself, who I had met many times, called and asked me to be one of guest hosts, and I agreed."

There was an amusing sequel on a very unhappy day for Pidgeon. "I attended Gardner's funeral in 1970 and saw a man point me out. Then I heard him telling his wife, 'I don't know his name, but that's the man who played the replacement lawyer when Raymond Burr was ill.' Such is fame!"

Having enjoyed his one week on a television set he started to appear regularly on many TV shows. "Perhaps fifty or sixty all told," he said. But his total of more than a hundred feature films was never in danger of being beaten.

In 1941 he told Sidney Skolsky, the Hollywood columnist, that he would work just ten more years before buying a boat so that he and Ruth, Edna, and perhaps a couple of close friends "could sail away into the sunset." He actually planned a world ocean voyage that would have taken at least three years to complete. But Hollywood, and Broadway, always refused to let him retire.

A grand piano that Pidgeon claimed he personally polished every week stood majestically in the corner of his spacious living room. But few ever heard anyone play it.

The great concert pianist Jose Iturbi, visiting the Pidgeons, asked who played the instrument. Iturbi recalled:

> Edna told me her father was a very good pianist but would never play in public. Somehow I convinced him to join me at the keyboard in a duet and I was amazed how good he was. Obviously the piano was tuned regularly, and perhaps Walter played when there was nobody around. I offered him the opportunity to play a duet on two pianos with me in a film I was making for MGM, but after thinking it over he declined. Walter Pidgeon had more talents than any other man I knew.

In 1982 Walter Pidgeon shed a tear when asked if he ever planned another visit to his hometown, Saint John. He dropped his head for a moment, wiped away the tear, and paused before answering. "I have nobody there now, nothing to come back for. The city is not what it was when I lived there," he said. "New Brunswick is one of the most beautiful places in the world, but Saint John is damp and cold and my rheumatics don't like that. I can still hear those fog horns croaking on Partridge Island. But I'll think about it and let you know before I make another trip."

Sadly, he never did return, and fifteen months later he died at the age of eighty-seven. Among the floral tributes at his funeral were dozens of bouquets of his favourite geraniums.

His wife, Ruth, told this delightful story:

> Our garden was in full bloom when Walter died. I remember answering the doorbell the next morning to find a young girl, perhaps fourteen or fifteen standing there. "I know Mr. Pidgeon loves geraniums," she said, "but I can't afford any. Could I pick a few of yours to send with a little note saying 'I love you?'" I helped her pick about two dozen of the best flowers and we packed them carefully in a bouquet. I was thrilled to see them prominently displayed in the chapel before the service. Many times I have wondered what became of the young girl and regretted that I never asked for her name or address. If I could have located her, I know Walter would have wanted me to help guide her through the life that lay ahead of her.

It was said in Hollywood that you were really accepted as his friend when he told you to call him "Pidge." Not too many people earned that right, and if a guest, not a special friend, copied the nickname after hearing it, Pidgeon would quietly ask that he be called Walter.

The city of Saint John, New Brunswick, has boasted on many occasions that Walter Pidgeon was born there, but at the time of writing nobody in authority had chosen to name a street or perhaps a square or park after this gracious star, who brought nothing but credit to the city in which he started life. If anyone out there is listening, perhaps it is still not too late to make amends.

John Qualen

Although Vancouver-born John Qualen appeared in more than one hundred films and on television in at least one thousand dramas and comedies, few people today can put a name to his very familiar face.

Remember the neurotic elevator operator on the Danny Thomas television series *Make Room For Daddy*, which ran for seven years? That was John Qualen.

Did you hate Muley in *The Grapes of Wrath*, which starred Henry Fonda? That was John Qualen.

Do you remember the only occasion on TV when Mr. Ed, the talking horse, spoke to someone other than series star Alan Young? That someone was John Qualen.

Only once during the forty-six years John Qualen worked in Hollywood did his name appear above the title of the movie. When the Canadian Dionne quintuplets were front-page news in 1935 and Hollywood decided to make a film, *The Country Doctor*, about the "miracle births," John Qualen was given the lead role as Papa Dionne, the girls' father.

The casting caused a furor in Canada. Questions were asked in the House of Commons why a Canadian could not have been given such an important role in Canada's history. Newspapers published editorials denouncing the choice of John Qualen.

Then John Qualen spoke up, and surprised even the film company. "But I am Canadian," he said, "from Vancouver." He produced a birth certificate for reporters hastily called to a press conference by the now gleeful film company, which was about to get front-page stories around North America.

The company sent Qualen on a three-month trip, all expenses paid, travelling from Vancouver to Halifax by train, stopping in every city where the film had been or was to be shown. Papers made his visit into headlines, and the film became one of the biggest box-office hits of the year.

He stopped off the train in Callender, Ontario, so he could greet the quintuplets again. There he received the shock of his life. The real Papa Dionne greeted him with yells and screams. He had to be forcibly restrained from hitting Qualen by the film company representative travelling with him.

"What have I done to upset you?" said Qualen.

"You've destroyed my life," said Dionne. "Until that damned film came out I was signing and selling about five hundred autographed photographs every day. Now the visitors to see the girls just ignore me. I sit in my little store with a pile of photographs and few people come in to buy a picture," he complained. "They tell me I'm not the real Papa Dionne. They tell me I'm a phoney. Everyone believes the man they saw in the film is the real Papa Dionne. Look there are no buyers for my signed pictures."

"I looked," said Qualen, "and he was right." He continued:

> When the real Papa Dionne sat behind the table he signed no more than twenty photographs an hour. I thought maybe I could help a little. I told him to go in the main house and I sat behind the table in the store. In minutes there was a line one hundred yards long. So I signed Papa Dionne on all the pictures and sold about three hundred in record time. I only closed Papa Dionne's little store when the quintuplets' visiting hours were over for the day. I'd been there three hours signing autographs as someone other than myself and the autograph buyers loved it!

John Qualen handed the money he had made over to Papa Dionne and headed back to the railroad station.

That should have been the end of the story, but it wasn't. Two days later, in Toronto, John Qualen was served with a writ from the real Papa Dionne claiming damages for loss of income due to Qualen's total acceptance as Papa Dionne.

"I handed the writ over to a lawyer and heard no more until I had been back in Hollywood for several weeks. The Toronto lawyer told me that the Canadian courts had dismissed the action as being frivolous, without merit, and time-wasting," Qualen recalled.

With the immense popularity of *The Country Doctor*, everyone forecast stardom for this highly competent actor who had attracted the attention of millions of moviegoers. But it wasn't to be. He found he was typecast, and when two sequels to the original film were made, the situation got worse. Although he was given excellent roles in other films, audiences still thought of him as the nervous and insecure Papa Dionne.

So stardom still eluded Qualen. He made films with stars like Janet Gaynor, Carole Lombard, and Irene Dunne. They all praised his acting talents and all, like Henry Fonda, loved Qualen's charm and became his friends for life.

His modest home in Hollywood was a quiet place away from the studio for many of the film industry's top stars, including Sylvia Sidney, Thelma Todd, Ida Lupino, Franchot Tone, Carole Lombard, and Greer Garson. When fans discovered this was where the stars went for a quiet evening, they hung around his home waiting to collect autographs of his visitors.

"But I don't ever remember any one of them asking for my autograph," said Qualen with a wry smile. "I was just the guy who knew the famous people."

John Qualen was born in Vancouver, British Columbia, on December 8, 1899. His father, who had emigrated from Norway to Canada several years before John arrived in the family, was minister of a well-attended Norwegian church in the city.

After graduating from high school in Vancouver, Qualen attended the University of Toronto for four years before deciding the university drama group was much more fun than studying, so when offered a professional job he joined a travelling company based in Toronto.

When the company reached Vancouver, Qualen looked up an old girlfriend from his high school years. Two weeks later he and Pearle Larson were married. Pearle joined the company as costume mistress.

When the company returned to Toronto, Pearle and John decided to create their own touring group, The Qualen Concert Company.

> I had written a comedy play so we decided it was time to try it out on the public. I played all the male roles, a little like Neil Simon's *Plaza Suite*. I had four ladies in

the company and they played in individual scenes. We didn't make much money but we were never broke. Pearle went around all the newspapers with photographs and stories and we got a lot of free publicity. After two years on the road in theatres from Chicago to New Orleans and over to Boston, we thought it was time to head to New York to see what the theatre market was like down there.

From the applause I had received every night and the wonderful comments from people waiting around the stage door after the show, I felt sure I had what it took to play on Broadway.

I must admit that between plays I sold aluminum cookware in the suburbs of New York. We had no car so I had to pull a small handcart containing the pots and pans. I can't have been too bad as a salesman, I made more money from the cookware than I did as an actor.

(Left to right) Henry Fonda, John Carradine, and John Qualen in Darryl F. Zanuck's production of *The Grapes of Wrath*.

For three years he played small roles in the New York theatre until, in 1929, an accidental meeting with Elmer Rice gave him the chance to play the Swedish janitor in his play *Street Scene*.

"It was the opportunity of a lifetime. Nobody knew the difference between a Norwegian and a Swedish accent. I was perfect for the Swedish janitor in *Street Scene*," he recalled. "It was the easiest role I ever had."

And probably the most successful — the play ran three years and won the Pulitzer Prize, earning John Qualen a trip to Hollywood to repeat the same role in the film version of *Street Scene* for Samuel Goldwyn.

Elmer Rice called him back to New York in 1930 to star on Broadway with Paul Muni in *Counsellor-at-Law*. It was another huge success, and once again Hollywood called him to repeat his New York role in the film version.

"Pearle and I didn't hesitate," he said. "We had enjoyed our first stay in the California sunshine and adored the homes with lawns and flower gardens like we had in Vancouver. It was an easy decision." This time the Qualens stayed in California.

Other important films he appeared in include *All That Money Can Buy* with Walter Huston, *Casablanca* with Humphrey Bogart, *Captain Kidd* with Charles Laughton, and *Tortilla Flat* with Spencer Tracy.

In 1934 John Qualen appeared in ten feature films. "I could have had ten more," he said, "but there just wasn't enough time. My agent, who had been quite unimportant before I arrived in his office, told me actors were now clamouring for him to represent them, and studios were suddenly calling all hours of night and day for me, at first, then all the other young people he took on as his clients. I had created quite a stir, and although my agent got me good money for every film, stardom never happened."

In 1936 John Qualen had a small role in *The Farmer Takes A Wife*, a year before *The Country Doctor* was released. It was the film that made Henry Fonda an important star. Fonda was so incensed that Hollywood was ignoring Qualen's superb acting talents that he insisted on a clause in his contracts that John Qualen must be given a role in every film he made.

Henry Fonda had this to say about Qualen in an interview with the *Hollywood Reporter*: "He never muffed a line, knew his dialogue after one reading, and taught me a great deal about film acting when I made my film debut."

In 1940 Fonda got Qualen the memorable role of Muley in the *Grapes of Wrath*. That same year he met John Wayne when he was cast in *The Long Voyage Home*. Wayne had been alerted by Henry Fonda to Qualen's scene-stealing abilities, and to the news reporters attending the film premiere, Wayne said, "I'll take a bet that people will come out of the theatres talking about John Qualen first and John Wayne second."

He was right. Qualen stole many scenes, but Wayne loved it. Like Fonda, he put a clause in all his contracts demanding that John Qualen appear in each of his films.

Director Tay Garnett, who asked for Qualen to be in the cast of *Joy of Living* in 1938, said this of Qualen in 1965: "How wonderful it would be if every actor in Hollywood was as dedicated as John Qualen. He is faultless with his lines. Seems to know exactly what I am looking for in his role. If I was asked, back in the early forties who I considered the best actor in Hollywood I would have said emphatically, John Qualen."

Qualen's love of animals led to a lifelong friendship with many stars, including Lucille Ball, Barbara Stanwyck, and Penny Singleton. With the support of many other actors and directors, they were the quartet who formed the Motion Picture League of Animals.

"It was designed to stop abuse of animals in the movies," said Lucille Ball in 1980.

> Until we started the group, producers, directors and actors could get away with anything. Hundreds of animals were hurt or even killed in the stunts they were expected to do. Horses in particular, in the big war pictures, had to be shot after they broke their legs when actors pulled on a wire and made the horse trip. It was utter cruelty. If John, Barbara, Penny and I did nothing else in Hollywood other than creating this protection for animals, which later became the law, I believe we spent our lives on earth doing something worthwhile.

John Qualen made friends for life with many of the stars with whom he worked. A reporter from *Film Weekly*, interviewing John Qualen, had found it impossible to get an audience with John Wayne, who had demanded Qualen in all his films. "I wanted to get quotes from the stars with whom he worked," said Brent Carter. "But many like John Wayne had retreated into the privacy of their homes and wouldn't talk to anyone. I mentioned this to John Qualen. He picked up the phone and was immediately talking to John Wayne. He spoke briefly to Wayne, explaining my problem, and hung up the phone"

"If you can be at his house at three this afternoon," said Qualen, "he'll be happy to talk to you, not about himself, but me."

Brent Carter said in his story he expected to get a ten-minute interview with the reclusive John Wayne, but he spent more than two hours with him. During that time Wayne called four other stars Carter had wanted to talk to about Qualen, but with whom he couldn't get appointments. Said Carter, "He set up appointments for me with Myrna Loy, Janet Gaynor and Barbara Stanwyck. In addition he gave me his own unlisted telephone number and told me to be sure to let him know if there was anyone else I wanted to interview. He added: 'But to talk about John Qualen, not the stars you are going to see.'"

John Qualen tried to enlist in the U.S. Army, the U.S. Navy, and the U.S. Army Air Corps during the Second World War. "They all turned me down," he said. "I'd had rheumatic fever when I was about ten and it had left me with a heart murmur that one army medical officer warned me might make me die at any moment. He advised me to work only short periods every day and suggested I limit my work to non-stressful things."

But Qualen didn't slow down at all. In 1943, 1944, and 1945, he appeared in good supporting roles in more than twenty major films.

When the Hollywood Canteen, the place for servicemen and women to go to meet the stars and hear the big bands like Harry James and Benny Goodman, opened its doors, Qualen was inside ready to serve food to the visitors.

"Very few knew me," he said. "Some would say they recalled seeing me in this or that movie, but they went away to join the line-ups to get autographs of the big stars like Bing Crosby, Ingrid Bergman, Merle Oberon, Humphrey Bogart, and Ida Lupino, who were there night after night."

It was his proud boast that from the opening day of the Hollywood Canteen to the day it closed its doors when the war ended he had only missed working there as a volunteer for six nights. "My film schedules kept me working until midnight or I would have been there those days too," he said.

John Qualen brought his parents, Olaus and Anne, down to Hollywood during the war years:

> They were both getting old and Pearle and I wanted to have them around. Although dad was nearly seventy-five he didn't sit around and do nothing. He heard that a local church, close to where we lived in Westwood, was having to close its doors because the congregation couldn't afford to pay their preacher. For three years he kept that church going, never taking a cent for his work in the church and in the community. Mother formed a ladies committee and I couldn't begin to tell you all the good things they did.

When the Second World War ended John Qualen found himself in demand to the newest entertainment medium, television. When TV first began, most shows were aired live. John Qualen became the actor every producer wanted. "His ability to memorize lines at sight and pick up lines dropped by other lesser talents should have made him a star, but for some reason it didn't," said Danny Thomas. "But often he got a higher salary than some of the stars because he was so valuable."

When Mr. Ed, the talking horse, spoke to him on TV the story was sent around the world on the news wires. "That one small part brought me more fan mail than many of the better and bigger parts I played," he said. "Until that week Mr. Ed could never be heard talking to anyone other than Alan Young."

John Qualen holds a record in Hollywood that will likely never be beaten. In one week he played different roles in twelve different comedy and drama series on television:

I remember one day I was asked to play three different parts. CBS provided me with a car and driver to take me to the different studios. We had worked out an intricate system of timing that allowed me to hop from one rehearsal to another and back again for final tapings. In the car I read my script for the next show and by I reached the studio I was word perfect. I can honestly say that they never needed to make a second shot of any of my different scenes. The makeup people had the toughest job. They had to change me from one character to another, often in as little as fifteen minutes. So much for my supposed troublesome heart. It never missed a single beat, but I did sleep well every night that week.

On Friday of this exhausting week he arrived home at seven o'clock. "I was ready for supper and an early night, perhaps a whole weekend in bed," he said. "Pearle met me at the door. In her hand was a message she had taken down from a caller. The series *Ironside* with Raymond Burr was scheduled to work on Saturday and Sunday due to the illness of one

John Qualen and John Wayne in *The Searchers*.

of the cast. I spent the next two days on the *Ironside* set before falling asleep at home before supper."

John Qualen kept in his home a diary showing that he had, between 1950 and 1978, appeared in more than one thousand different segments of television shows. Add to that appearances in more than one hundred films, and there is little chance his amazing record will ever be eclipsed.

For seven years he appeared weekly with Danny Thomas in *Make Room For Daddy*. "They may not remember John Qualen's name," said Thomas in 1964, when the show was taken off the air, "but they'll never forget the Swedish janitor in the series. That was John Qualen." He continued:

> He got a huge fan mail each week and we gave him two hundred dollars a week extra so he could hire a secretary and pay for all the photographs he had to send out. I used to get letters to me asking if I would give the enclosed letter to the Swedish janitor whose name they didn't know. As a result of these letters we started giving John's name more prominence on the show credits. He was a major part of the show's success. I never saw *Street Scene* in which he created the Swedish janitor both in New York and here in Hollywood on film, but he told me he simply relived *Street Scene* to create the character in my show.

But John Qualen had one more talent that few, apart from his family, ever knew about. "From a youngster of eight in Vancouver I learned to play the flute," he said. "When I was in Toronto, at the university, I continued my training and on several occasions played in professional orchestras there for the fun of it."

Pearle Qualen added the following: "He has never boasted about it, but I must tell you that on at least six occasions he played the flute in the Hollywood Bowl Orchestra. Once he was chosen to play a solo, and I think that this was the greatest highlight of his entire career. He could have earned a good living as a musician if films and television hadn't got in the way."

Over the years the Qualens added three daughters, Betty, Meredith, and Kathleen, to their family home. All married well: Betty became Mrs. Erle Bacon, Meredith married David Kilpatrick, and Kathleen found a good husband in Tom Roberts. None were involved in show business, and the fifteen grandchildren they gave John and Pearle Qualen in turn gave them six great-grandchildren, none of whom went into the world of entertainment.

"He was a great actor but a much greater father," said Meredith. "No one could ever have asked for better parents," said Betty. "My autograph book is full of all the stars who came to our home," said Kathleen. "Because he knew Mary Pickford all of us and our friends were able to swim in her pool whenever we wanted. If we called she sent her car for us. All we had to do was call Mary on the phone and she immediately told us to bring over any of our friends we wished."

John Qualen in 1970 remembered the friendship of Mary Pickford. "She was the first lady of Hollywood. I made sure my daughters didn't overdo her generosity, but that would have been difficult, Mary's generosity was boundless," he said. "When it became time for my oldest daughter to go to college, I recall her dropping by the house just to ask if we had enough money for university costs. Happily, Pearle had handled our money wisely and we had ample for all our needs and some left over for ultimate retirement."

For several years before he retired, John Qualen was the official, unpaid historian for the famed Hollywood Masquers Club. He spent countless hours compiling biographical material about former members of the Masquers who were no longer alive.

"I enjoyed the research," said Qualen in 1978. "Perhaps in another life I will come back as a writer. If I helped keep history alive it was more than worthwhile."

In 1978 John Qualen finally retired. His eyesight was beginning to fail. Without realizing it, he had suffered from diabetes for many years.

In 1983 John and Pearle Qualen moved from the small home they had occupied for fifty happy years in Westwood Village to a beautiful retirement complex in the San Fernando Valley.

John Qualen, 1967.

His proudest possession was the medal presented to him by King Haakon of Norway. The citation that accompanied the gold medal praised him for his many portrayals of Norwegian men in the movies and on television, "without once allowing his characters to riducule the land of his father's birth."

On September 12, 1987, John Qualen, aged eighty-eight, suffered a stroke from which he never recovered. Pearle and his three daughters were at his bedside when he died the same day in Torrance Memorial Hospital.

A lot of the stars who had been his friends had gone before him, but at the service in a Torrance Church many of the biggest names in Hollywood were present. The church was packed. Among the mourners were Anthony Quinn, Frank Sinatra, Barbara Stanwyck, Greer Garson,

Eddie Albert, Buddy Ebsen, Ann Sothern, Roy Rogers, Dale Evans, Gene Autry, Dorothy Lamour, Red Skelton, Danny Thomas, Milton Berle, and Charles "Buddy" Rogers, representing Mary Pickford, who had died six years earlier.

Gene Autry spoke the eulogy: "He may never have been a star in the movies but he was a star in his personal life and the type of person everyone hopes to have, as I had, as a lifelong friend."

Ned Sparks

Although Ned Sparks had one of the most recognizable faces in Hollywood, with a gruff and gravelly voice that matched his deadpan face to perfection, little has been written about him throughout his successful career in New York on the Broadway stage or later in Hollywood in both silent and sound films.

Perhaps he was overlooked because he refused on many occasions to sign long-term contracts with the major studios in Hollywood, and their publicity departments were apparently interested only in those actors who were going to be around for a long period of time.

Buster Keaton, the most celebrated deadpan face in the history of movies, said, in 1965, when he was struggling to get even small roles in the sound era, that had he been blessed with Sparks's raspy voice he might still be a major star.

Ned Sparks left the film capital in 1948 and never returned, even though producers were still bombarding his agent with offers of work five years later.

His only explanation was that everyone should retire at sixty-five. "That's precisely what I am doing," he said.

Ned Sparks was born Edward Sparkman on November 19, 1883, in Guelph, a small town in Ontario, Canada. Some biographies, including excellent books like *Close Ups From The Golden Age of the Silent Cinema*, give his birthplace as St. Thomas, Ontario, and the date as June 17, 1884. In 1960, his daughter, Laura, still living on the ranch that Ned Sparks had called his home for many years before his death, produced a birth certificate that confirmed Guelph and 1883 as the correct place and date.

"My father was a Canadian until the day he died," she said.

> He would, at any time in his successful career, willingly have returned to his homeland had there been a film industry up there in which he could work. He told me his parents moved from Guelph to St. Thomas, in Ontario, only a few miles away from his birthplace, when he was only five years old.

But he always thought of St. Thomas as home, and every year he went back to relive the memories that were so important to him. His sister Gladys and brother Reuben both still live in St. Thomas.

Newspaper clippings in the Lincoln Center library in New York City quote him as saying he took part in the Klondyke Gold Rush when he was only sixteen in 1898.

He told an unnamed writer in the *New York Post* that he had his parents' blessing when he got a job selling candy, fruit, and cookies to passengers on the Trans-Canada Railroad from Toronto to Western Canada.

"They thought I was coming right back to Toronto when the train returned," he said. He went on:

> I didn't say anything about the gold fields but I deserted the train in Alberta and worked my way to Dawson Creek in the Yukon by hauling a food sled belonging to other prospectors.
>
> I tried prospecting for gold near Dawson City but had no luck. When I ran out of money and hadn't eaten for several days I decided gold panning was not for me. I'd always had a good tenor voice, much richer and rounder than the average youngster at sixteen, so I approached the manager of a barnstorming musical company that moved from tavern to tavern in horse-drawn trucks. I sang him one song and he hired me on the spot. They gave me a place to sleep, my food, and five dollars a week. This was much better than no place to sleep, no food, and no dollars a week so I accepted.

The company travelled around the gold fields area from Dawson Creek to Skagway, Juneau, and Ketchican. "Often we left hurriedly overnight when unhappy audiences threatened to tar and feather the lot of us if we were there next morning."

For two years he travelled with the show. He recalled:

Our leading lady had five gold teeth each of which was studded with a diamond. But she did know how to belt out a song and entertainment in the gold field area was very much in short supply. Every night after the show she offered herself to the best bidder in the audience who could prove he had a warm and comfortable room in which they could sleep and do other things her offer implied. I recall one night she got a hundred dollar offer from a miner who had struck it rich. She used to keep all her ill-gotten money in a sack on which her very fierce dog slept.

One morning she didn't return from an overnight stay and nobody ever heard from her again. I noticed her sack of money and her dog had gone too. One of the company's four dancers, I remember only as Millie, said she could sing as well as dance and without the benefit of gold teeth and diamonds, she took over the former singer's act, including auctioning herself off every night to the highest bidder.

Ned Sparks was always seen with a cigar in his mouth, but a secret about that was revealed by Bing Crosby thirteen years after Sparks's death.

At the end of his two years with what he described as "surely the worst show any company ever staged anywhere," he returned to his parents' home in St. Thomas, Ontario, with more than five hundred dollars in cash that he had managed to save.

His daughter, Laura, believed his gold rush stories were genuine. In 1959, two years after Ned Sparks died, she said to *Hollywood Citizen News* writer Sidney Skolsky, who had tracked her down to her ranch in Victorville, "He talked about those days in the Yukon many times, reliving many moments of humour and fear. The stories were all genuine, nobody could have described the conditions up there who had never seen them first hand."

Her home was close to the ranch owned by Roy Rogers and Dale Evans. Laura said, "Although my Dad left me plenty of money on which to live for the rest of my life, every day I earn a little more by exercising Roy Rogers' horse Trigger in the fields around their ranch."

To please his family, Ned Sparks entered a theological college in Toronto when he was nineteen, but quit after two years of study. "I decided I wasn't cut out to be a minister," he said. "My gruff speaking voice, which contrasted rather frighteningly to my rich tenor singing voice, was not looked on favourably by those in charge of the college so there were no tears shed when I left. They had even tried putting butter in my mouth to take away the raspy sound of my voice before I read my daily passage from the Bible, but it didn't work at all. In fact it was quite scary, I looked like I was foaming at the mouth."

For the next three years he worked for the railroad in Toronto. "I did odd jobs, helped keep the passenger ledgers up to date and sold tickets. But more satisfying was the job I got playing a non-speaking part in an important play in Toronto," he recalled. "You'll never believe that I smiled in those days. The deadpan look didn't arrive until six years after I reached Broadway. I got several speaking parts in plays and soon was able to quit the railroad."

At twenty-four, in 1907, he decided to try his luck in New York City. "I'd heard from some of the better actors who were in touring plays in which local people, like me, were called on to augment the company in

Toronto, that the theatre on Broadway was growing in strength so I headed down there, again with the blessing of my parents."

In New York the work didn't arrive as easily as he had been led to believe. "I got a few small parts but was working behind the bar in a seedy tavern when a theatre booking agent heard me talking and offered me a small part in a play just about to open. 'The audience will love that voice,' said Herbert Wallace."

Considering it was his first sizeable acting role, Ned Sparks took a chance and changed the role he was given and created a unique character that remained with him throughout his career:

> I'd been in New York six years and the smiling-faced insipid characters they called on me to play were exactly what I had been offered in *Little Miss Brown* which starred Madge Kennedy. It was Madge who suggested that I might enhance my small role if I created my own character. So I rehearsed the play exactly the way the director wanted it to be done, but on opening night the meek, smiling, hotel desk clerk, that my character was supposed to be, turned into a gruff, deadpan man with only one desire in life, to annoy the customers. On opening night Madge Kennedy actually burst out laughing on stage at my new character and for a few minutes couldn't continue. The audience loved it. Only the director was mad.
>
> "You are fired," he said.
>
> "No he isn't," said Madge Kennedy to the director. "That gruff quality is exactly what this play needs. Either you accept the character or I'll have you fired."

Newspaper critics who attended the opening night picked out Ned Sparks's desk clerk spot as one of the show's highlights. The producer called him to the front office, shook his hand, and doubled his salary.

"I was so ingrained with my new non-smiling creation that I didn't even smile when he offered not only to double my salary but to put my name under that of Madge on the posters," he recalled.

From that day on Ned Sparks is said to have never smiled again. He went from success to success, quickly becoming one of the best-known comedy actors on Broadway.

In shows like *The Show Shop, The Younger Son, Nothing But The Truth,* and Victor Herbert's major hit *The Golden Girl,* he received excellent reviews, often eclipsing those of the stars. He appeared with Alice Brady, Rose Stahl, Effie Shannon, George Nash, and William Collier, who later played a major role in establishing the Ned Sparks deadpan face in Hollywood.

One of the few established film actresses to remain in the New York area when most of the movie companies moved out west to sunny California, Constance Talmadge saw Ned Sparks in *Nothing But The Truth.*

"I was so enchanted by his funny portrayal of a kind-hearted man who tries to be gruff and tough that I went backstage immediately after the show and invited him to visit our Vitagraph film studio. I told him what street car to get to our front door," she said in her biography.

Ned Sparks described his first day at the studio in a story printed in the *New York Herald Tribune.* "I walked in, spoke briefly with a man I later discovered was the director, waved across at Miss Talmadge, and was told to sit down in the chair beside her. She looked beautiful wearing what looked like an abbreviated toga so I didn't argue," he recalled. "That was how I made my first silent film, deadpan, of course. To this day I have no idea what the film was about but Miss Talmadge told me it was called *Sawdust and Salome.* I have to think that she was Salome and I was merely the Sawdust!"

Ned Sparks's film debut was apparently satisfactory to the company. "In the next two months I played in four more films with Talmadge and began to enjoy the relaxation of filmmaking. I worked in the studio in the day, then travelled by street car to the theatre and appeared there at night. It was the first time in my life I had money to spare."

Although there was plenty of work being offered to him in the New York theatres, Ned Sparks couldn't stop thinking of the fun he had making movies.

"When a letter arrived for me from William Collier, who I had worked with on Broadway, but who was now an established film director in Hollywood, I decided in 1920 to head out west."

Ned Sparks never talked about his work alongside two other Canadians, Berton Churchill and Marie Dressler, on behalf of the underpaid dancers and chorus singers on the New York stage.

But Marie Dressler, in her autobiography, said:

> It was as though Canadians were organizing the revolt. American actors had not bothered to stand up for the poorly paid small part performers, and we three were in the forefront of the fight to establish Actors Equity.
>
> When the 1918 theatre strike began, closing every theatre in the United States, theatre managements were forced to accept a minimum wage, the managements didn't give us and the Americans who had dared to defy the big bosses any work. I was blacklisted for several years. Berton Churchill and Ned Sparks got out quickly. They headed for Hollywood where talent, not political and union leanings, was important. Berton got work immediately, Ned, with a few dollars in his pocket, waited for them to call him. Bill Collier, then a director in California, made the first overture and Ned never looked back.

Ned Sparks checked into the Hollywood Hotel on Hollywood Boulevard and waited for someone to contact him. He later recalled:

> I was there several months before Bill Collier called and asked why I hadn't been to see him. I told him I had plenty of money and enjoyed sitting around in the sunshine but would be happy to work if he had some to offer.
>
> You must remember that this was 1921 and sound wasn't yet around. I'd discovered that my deadpan features photographed well in the Talmadge films, but I worried a little that no one would be able to hear my

voice which had become an essential part of my life in the New York live theatre.

Most film listings for Ned Sparks suggest he started his movie career in 1925 in the MGM silent picture *Bright Lights*, but after his death his daughter, Laura, produced a handwritten ledger that she said had been kept by her father since the day of his arrival in Hollywood. "He was most meticulous about paying his income taxes and had these records to prove he never failed to return any money he received."

The ledger showed that his first film was in 1923, called *Quickly Please*, followed by more than a dozen rather forgettable films before his first MGM movie, *Bright Lights*, in which he was given billing equal to the star, Pauline Starke.

For *Quickly Please,* directed by William Collier, he reported receiving $15. By the time MGM gave him his first opportunity at a big studio, he was earning $70 per film. It was at MGM he signed his only short-term contract in Hollywood.

When he was sixty-five, Ned Sparks, at the height of his successful career, shook hands with all of his friends in Hollywood and retired to a ranch in Victorville, miles away from the movie studios.

"Louis B. Mayer convinced me that his studio was going to be the biggest studio in Hollywood and signing with him would be an intelligent move on my part. I signed to make six pictures over the next twelve months. The contract offered me $100 a week for fifty-two weeks," he said to the *Los Angeles Times* in 1947. "That was a lot of money in those days. I rented an apartment and paid five dollars a week for one bedroom, a sitting room and a kitchen."

By 1929 he had made thirty-seven films. "I decided I wouldn't sign with any studio for more than one film," he recalled in 1943. "My minimum salary, per picture, had gone up to three hundred dollars so you can see why I would not sign to anything longer than a one-picture deal. The year I spent at MGM I found my contract said they could use me in crowd scenes or small unbilled roles as often as they liked. I lived at the studio each day that year for eight or nine hours."

Did he ever smile in the small roles he was called on to play at MGM? "I'll never tell," he said without a glimmer of a smile. "My image would be destroyed."

In 1928 he made his sound debut in *The Big Noise*. It is listed in film records at the Academy of Motion Picture Arts and Sciences in Hollywood as the second sound film ever made.

His gravelly voice, added to his deadpan face, made Ned Sparks an actor audiences looked forward to seeing on their screens.

Still living in the same five-dollar-a-week apartment in 1929, he had become friendly with a young lady, Mercedes Wilson, living down the corridor from his apartment. "She used to call me into her apartment to share the wonderful meals she made," he recalled.

In time for a Christmas celebration together, he rented a much larger apartment and married Mercedes in a quiet civil ceremony in Hollywood. If any paper recorded the event it is long lost in the mists of time. But in 1934, when Mercedes sued for divorce, saying her husband had slapped her, he was sufficiently well-known to interest national and international newspapers.

"It was a grave mistake that we ever got married," said Sparks to the judge. "I deny completely the allegations that I ever struck her. It is not my habit to strike women. In fact, apart from in one film where the script called for me to do just that, I have never in my life struck any man, woman or animal."

He added, "Mercedes and I had agreed on a Mexican divorce and went through with it." He produced papers to prove that this court case was merely an attempt by his wife to get more money than they had already agreed to in Mexico.

The judge examined the Mexican divorce papers and agreed with Ned Sparks that there was no basis for this new application for divorce.

"This is a remarkable agreement," said the judge, "I see you, Mercedes Sparks, have agreed that your former husband will get custody of your daughter, Laura. Am I correct?"

When Mercedes confirmed this decision, the judge ruled quickly. "I can't accept the plaintiff's application for divorce when she and Mr. Sparks are obviously no longer married."

As she left the court, Mercedes Wilson told the newspaper reporters, "I was wrong to say Ned struck me. He is a kind and gentle man. I tried to be clever and it is obvious that the court didn't believe me."

In 1957, after Sparks died, Laura said her mother had died only two years after the divorce. "Dad and I attended the service," she said. "We were the only people there. I cried a little."

Sparks never allowed photographers to take pictures of him with his daughter. He hired a full-time caregiver to look after her every want, and this lady, after Sparks's death, said, "He was completely devoted to the child and spent every spare moment he had with her. He actually taught her to read and write before she was four years old."

With his career now enhanced by sound, he hired his own publicity man to make sure his pictures and stories were planted in newspapers around the world. The publicist can't have done too much to earn his money, because clippings are almost non-existent in both the Lincoln Center and Academy libraries.

In 1934 he was hired by Cosmopolitan Films, the company owned by newspaper magnate William Randolph Hearst, to play a good part in *Going Hollywood*. The movie was to be shot in the MGM Studio, where Louis B. Mayer permitted films starring Marion Davies, who was Hearst's mistress, to be made. In return Hearst promised his columnists would never write any bad stories about MGM and its huge stable of stars.

This was to be her last film at MGM, although Davies, Hearst, and Mayer didn't know that when shooting began.

Bing Crosby told this story at a party in Hollywood in 1960. Ned Sparks, who had been waiting for more than two hours for Marion Davies to complete a scene to the satisfaction of director Raoul Walsh, was asked by a stranger on the set what he thought about Marion Davies' talents as an actress. Obviously frustrated at waiting for his own scene, he said, "I have more talent in my big toe than she has in her whole body." The stranger turned on his heels and walked off the set.

Crosby, who was also waiting for Davies to satisfy Walsh, heard the remark and walked over to Sparks. Crosby asked if he knew who he had been talking to.

"No," said Sparks. "Why do you ask?"

"That was William Randolph Hearst," Crosby told him.

From that day onwards Ned Sparks's name was never mentioned in any of Hearst's newspapers. Hearst issued a statement to every one of his many editors saying that to mention Ned Sparks would be to ask for instant dismissal.

This may be the reason why brilliant performances by Sparks never received the credit they deserved in major newspaper columns.

Hearst was so incensed that Sparks had been permitted to make this comment about his mistress that he went to Louis B. Mayer, repeated the conversation, and urged that Sparks be banned from MGM from that day on.

Mayer, perhaps fed up with Hearst's dictatorial ways, had the courage to tell the newspaper magnate that what Sparks had said was probably the truth.

Hearst blew up and threatened to take his Cosmopolitan Film Company to another studio, adding, "And I'll have Marion's seventeen-room cottage I built at MGM dismantled and moved to wherever we decide her next film will be made."

Mayer, who had been unhappy with Hearst and Davies for some time, told him to move away from MGM as fast as he liked. He turned on his heel and walked back to his office. Hearst kept his threat, and

MGM actors had to watch their activities from that day on. Hearst told his editors to dig up any dirt they could on MGM and its stars.

In 1936 a major story was printed in the *New York Times* that Ned Sparks had insured his deadpan face for $100,000. Lloyds of London said that they had agreed to pay that sum to Sparks if a photographer ever caught him smiling.

"The newspaper cameramen get around everywhere these days," said Sparks. "I actually have to lock my doors at night and sleep with my windows covered by blinds. I'm not sure the policy is worth all that trouble."

Some years later he told the *Hollywood Citizen-News* that the whole thing was a publicity stunt. "Lloyds did insure me, not for $100,000 but for $10,000. They agreed I could use the inflated figure because it was good publicity for Lloyds. But they didn't stand to lose even a cent. The $10,000 policy cost me $10,000 in premiums!"

In 1936 it turned out that the teeth he never showed were not really his own. The *Los Angeles Examiner* reported that Sparks was present in the United States Circuit Court of Appeals, which was hearing his request to deduct from his taxes the three-thousand-dollar set of false teeth he had to buy.

"I earned $137,380 in 1935," he said. "Like a good taxpayer I paid all the taxes I owed on that amount, but I didn't like the tax assessor's refusal to permit me to deduct the cost of my false teeth."

He contended that the teeth were a business investment, necessary to keep him from hissing his lines into the primitive microphones of that era.

The appeal judges ruled against him. "Mr. Sparks," said the panel of three judges, "we have watched your performance in this court, and all of us have seen and enjoyed your films, but we can not collectively recall ever seeing your teeth. If you smiled occasionally, our decision might have been different."

Ned Sparks is said to have left the court without a smile on his face.

A *Los Angeles Examiner* reporter said he refused to confirm that in his work with young people in need of guidance, which he did two or three nights every week, he actually smiled at the children.

"You cannot know whether that is a fact or not," he said. "No cameras are allowed into the sessions so you will never know."

For a while cameramen hung around the guidance centre where he volunteered, but they never caught him smiling.

In 1938 he found a new career. CBS radio hired him to be a miserable grouch on their Texaco Star Theatre. Whenever the rest of the cast got too happy the writers added a few lines from Ned Sparks to stop the fun.

"I squelched more good ideas than you can count," he said.

> But what surprised me was the fact the radio audiences decided to love me. I got more fan mail than other stars like Una Merkel, Charlie Ruggles and Jimmy Wallington got for their appearances. Would you believe I got more than fifty proposals from women who sent their photos so I could see what I might be getting. I answered each one with a polite "no." One marriage in a lifetime is enough for any man especially if it was like mine, a failure.

In 1943, with his film earnings invested wisely, he bought a seventy-acre ranch at Victorville in Apple Valley, fifty miles away from Hollywood. He built a seven-room house on the property, had the grounds landscaped, and every weekend went out there with his daughter, then eleven, to ride the horses he had bought. Laura recalled, after his death, that only one of his Hollywood friends was ever invited to visit them on the ranch. "Bing Crosby was here many times, but none of the others," she said.

Ned Sparks's fame grew with every film he made. In 1933, in *42nd Street*, the stars were Ruby Keeler, Warner Baxter, Bebe Daniels, and Dick Powell, but the most favourable reviews for what is still today a well-watched film on videocassette went to Ned Sparks.

The same happened when *Gold Diggers Of 1933* was released. He again stole the film from Joan Blondell, Ruby Keeler, and Dick Powell.

In 1970, Bing Crosby, reminiscing about the "good old days in Hollywood" told this story about Ned Sparks:

The film *Gold Diggers* was spectacular. In one scene
they put thirty-six grand pianos side by side and playing, or supposed to be playing, were thirty-six beautiful
girls. It was a great scene, but if you look carefully at the
very end of the line of pianos you will see Ned Sparks.
He was in the studio but not working that day, so he
gave one of the girls fifty dollars to lend him her wig
and dress so he could sit at the piano furthest from the
camera. But he did it in style. He never took the cigar
out of his mouth and you can see it quite clearly if you
look closely at the scene.

Crosby, famed for smoking a pipe, told a *Los Angeles Examiner*
reporter that although Ned Sparks was never seen without a cigar in his
mouth, he never smoked them. "In the early 1930s he was important
enough to convince the producers to put a clause in his contract that
they would supply an actor to light and get the cigars smoking before
every scene," he said. "When they were ready to shoot he took the cigar
from the other actor and put it in his mouth. All he did was chew on the
cigars, never inhaled the smoke, puffing occasionally to show the cigar
was actually lit."

The Ritz Brothers, Al, Jimmy and Harry, told the *Hollywood
Reporter* that when they had appeared in *One In A Million* with Sonja
Henie and Adolphe Menjou, they tried every trick in the book to make
Ned Sparks laugh. "We never did it," said Harry. "I think he had his lips
sealed. He was the best deadpan we ever worked with. A great guy who
never smiled at anything. Certainly not when anyone was looking."

Ned Sparks saved and invested his money well. In 1937 and 1938 he
earned more than two million dollars. "My one extravagance was to buy
a Lincoln car and hire a chauffeur to drive me everywhere I wanted to
go. I never did learn to drive and was tired of street cars. I looked a little silly sitting on a street car when I was earning so much money."

The car and chauffeur came in handy in early 1940. Canada had
entered the Second World War, and Sparks didn't hesitate when he

received a call from a man he had known since his school days, by then Ontario's elected premier. Mitchell Hepburn asked if Sparks would travel to Toronto to take part in a new weekly radio series that would help to sell Victory Bonds to aid the war effort.

Ned Sparks put his career on hold for almost two years. He had his chauffeur drive his car to Toronto while he headed north by train.

Toronto newspapers all used photographs of Sparks, with a cigar in his mouth, leaning out of the Lincoln driven by his uniformed chauffeur. Mitchell Hepburn recalled after the war that Sparks went everywhere in the luxury car. "The car drew attention to our radio show and helped make it a major success. We put him into a suite of rooms at the Park Plaza Hotel and because he wanted his chauffeur to be near at hand, he convinced the hotel management to knock a hole in the wall of one of the suite rooms so it led directly into the chauffeur's bedroom."

When Ned Sparks left Toronto to return to Hollywood he sent his chauffeur back by train and had the huge car, which had cost him $16,000, a large amount to pay for a car in the 1940s, put in a Toronto garage. "I'll be back for it," he said.

But he never did return to Toronto, and for fifteen years he sent along an annual cheque to pay the car storage charges.

"When Dad died in 1957 I suggested the car should be sold and the money given to charity," said Laura. The aging car was sold to a Toronto used-car dealer, Craig Patton, for nine hundred and fifty-five dollars. Patton tried for several years to find a buyer for the car, which he said only got about ten miles to the gallon, but nobody wanted it. It ended its days in a Toronto scrapyard.

Hollywood welcomed Ned Sparks back home. But he only made two more films. One, *Stage Door Canteen*, he often said was merely to show respect for the thousands of New York stars who gave of their time to volunteer their services to the glamorous canteen that welcomed servicemen and women for an hour or two of relaxation in Times Square, New York. "It was as a tribute to my many friends in New York who made the Stage Door Canteen a place in which many service men and women made memories that will last all their lives that I agreed to appear in a film about a place I was never able to visit," he later said.

For his final film, *Magic Town*, in 1947, he was lured back from his ranch in Victorville by a friend he had known for many years, James Stewart.

His daughter recalled that Jimmy Stewart arrived at their door one day to thank her father for letters he had sent Stewart while he was serving in the United States Air Force in Europe. She said:

> Stewart told Dad that his letters were cheerful at times when he most needed to be cheered up. He asked Dad if he would go back to Hollywood for just one final film, *Magic Town*, in which he was to star. Dad thought about it and told Jimmy Stewart that because of their long friendship he would agree. "But no publicity at all," he said. Jimmy agreed and a week later I drove Dad into town. We stayed a week until his part was completed, then Jimmy surprised us both. He had a huge cake brought on the set. The words on the icing read, "To honour a great actor and a fine man, Ned Sparks." It is the only time I ever saw Dad cry.

Ned Sparks died early in the morning on April 3, 1957, at the St. Mary's Desert Valley Hospital in Apple Valley, near the home he and his daughter had shared for nine years after his retirement from the film industry. Doctors said an intestinal blockage that could not be cleared was the cause of death of the seventy-three-year-old actor who had never before suffered anything more serious than a bad cold, and who had never once missed a day's work in the New York theatre or the Hollywood studios.

He was buried in the Victor Valley Memorial Park in Victorville, San Bernardino, California. There is no headstone at his grave, just a simple ground marker three feet wide by one foot in depth. It reads simply, "Ned Sparks — 1883 to 1957."

There were only seven people at his funeral: his daughter, Laura, the two hired hands on the ranch, Roy Rogers and Dale Evans, who were his closest neighbours on the next ranch, and Bing Crosby.

After Ned Sparks died, Bing Crosby issued this statement about his good friend Ned Sparks. "He was the most honest man I ever met," said Crosby. "I would like to share with you this saying, which Ned repeated over the years to his closest friends. 'If you go through life treating everyone a little better than they treat you, your life will not have been in vain.' Ned Sparks life was not in vain. He was loved by more people than he ever realized."

In 2003, fans are still enjoying the deadpan activities of Ned Sparks. Twelve of the films he made, including *42nd Street*, *Gold Diggers of 1933*, *One In A Million*, and the final Marion Davies MGM picture, *Going Hollywood*, are still available on the internet.

Hopefully, after this story is printed, those owning the *Gold Diggers of 1933* will look a little closer at the beautiful blonde piano players to see Ned Sparks in an unscripted, unpaid, and unusual role.

Asked by Sidney Skolsky in 1959 if her father ever smiled at her, Laura just smiled at him and said, "What do you think Mr. Skolsky?"

"Now I'll never know," wrote Skolsky.

Jack Warner

Jack L. Warner was sixty-six before he became president of Warner Brothers. For forty-one years he had been in charge of all production at the studio, but until his brother Harry died in 1958, the top job was denied him.

His older brother Harry Warner, president of the company, was the moneyman of the organization. Working out of a New York office with another brother, Albert Warner, he was the genius who found whatever cash young Jack needed to fulfill his dreams.

Sam Warner, the fourth Warner brother, stayed with Jack in Hollywood. His chief job was to oversee all technical aspects of filmmaking. He is enshrined in Hollywood's record books for the only film he directed. It was the first talking picture, *The Jazz Singer*, starring Al Jolson.

The New York Warners approved just about everything Jack proposed. In his long career in Hollywood, Jack Warner produced or supervised the making of more than five thousand films. Three thousand of these were full-length features, two thousand more were the short films, comedies, travel films, educational films, or cartoons, including the immortal Bugs Bunny, that made Warners stand out from the crowd with its originality.

Jack L. Warner, the eighth of twelve children in the Warner household, was born in London, Ontario, on August 2, 1892. The August 2 date is approximate since nobody in the family was ever able to produce a birth certificate. Warner himself chose August 2 because it was the birthday of his mother, whom he revered.

Although he had no second given name, Warner added the L to make his name Jack L. Warner. He officially made his L into Leonard because, when he was only thirteen, he adopted the name Leon Zuardo when he was a singer at weddings and funerals. "Italian singers were very popular at that time," he said in 1943. "Fortunately nobody ever asked me to speak Italian. All I ever knew was how to say thanks when people gave me money."

Today most people remember Jack L. Warner alone of the four brothers, because it was his creative mind that first saw the possibilities of making films into works of art, not just strings of scenes put together for no apparent reason.

Jack Warner chose every script, had final approval in casting, and could hire and fire anyone he wished.

Harry Warner, the oldest of the Warner Brothers, was the salesman who convinced bankers to provide them with the money they needed to experiment with movies in the silent era, experiments that led to the making of *The Jazz Singer*, the first real talking picture, in 1926.

Sam Warner was a mechanical expert who contributed greatly to the modernization of equipment and the improvement of cameras used in both silent and sound filming.

Albert Warner kept the company's books accurate to the last penny. Jack Warner once said of Albert, "He is the most honest man on the face of this earth."

Jack Warner never forgot his brothers' importance to the founding and growth of the giant Warner studio in Burbank, and whenever he was asked to speak at industry functions, he always stressed that Warner Brothers' success was not due to just Jack L. Warner but to the combined talents of himself and his older brothers, Harry, Sam, and Albert.

The Warner family had been in Canada for two years when Jack Warner (christened Jacob) was born. His father, Benjamin, and his mother, Pearl, had been struggling to make a living in the United States but had moved to Canada because they were told foreigners, especially Jews, were receiving a warmer welcome north of the border in Ontario.

Ben tried trading metal pots and pans to the trappers in Canada's north for furs. The idea was good until a partner ran away with all the furs and money, leaving Ben with only his horse and cart and a pile of unsold metal products. He lost enthusiasm for fur trading and concentrated on selling his goods to the people of London, Ontario.

Before Jack arrived, seven young Warners, Cecilia, Anna, Henry (later known as Harry), Samuel, Albert, Rose, and Fannie, had already been born when the family lived in South Baltimore, Maryland. Cecilia died from pneumonia when she was only three and Fannie died in the bitterly cold winter of 1896 and is buried in a cemetery in London.

One more Warner arrived in Canada, two years after Jack. David Warner listed his birthplace as Hamilton, Ontario. David went to university and might have joined his brothers in the film industry, but he died unexpectedly in 1918 when he was only twenty-eight.

Jack Warner told a very special story about his parents' stay in Canada to everyone who would listen:

> They were probably the only Polish Jews in London at that time. They had never felt more isolated than when Fannie died. Then a miracle happened, neighbours arrived at the house bringing pies, hot food on plates and soup in bowls. It was the first time in their lives they had ever felt wanted. The neighbours arranged and paid for Fannie's funeral and took the other children, including me, into their homes to help us through this time of sadness. My father and mother told me never to forget what the people of Canada did for them at that important time in their lives.

Four decades later Jack Warner remembered that kindness when Canadian Prime Minister Mackenzie King turned to him for help.

Altogether Pearl and Benjamin Warner produced twelve children, the last three born after the family returned to the United States in 1898.

This time the Warner family settled in Youngstown, Ohio. They had travelled from Canada in a small truck resembling a covered wagon over roads that at times were almost non-existent. In Youngstown they found a house to rent, and Ben Warner started a small grocery store in the basement.

Many years later Jack Warner said, "To provide us all with food, clothing and a place to live meant everyone of us had to find some way to bring money into the house even when we were very young."

Warner had little schooling after the age of thirteen. "I just wasn't able to concentrate on learning things, especially the Hebrew which my mother and father had made compulsory in the family," he said in 1943.

Every member of the family had to contribute to the family income. Jack was selected to drive the family's small wagon and horse around the neighbourhood, starting at six every morning, making home deliveries of groceries ordered from the store the previous day.

Many years later he remembered the early-morning work:

> I learned that my father chose me to make the deliver-
> ies because I groomed Bob, our horse, every night and
> really loved the animal. Father knew I would never ill
> treat Bob by making it race through the cobbled streets
> to get home in time for breakfast. I was devoted to Bob
> and often missed breakfast because the roads were slip-
> pery and I didn't want to risk putting him in danger. I
> was only eleven and had to make all the deliveries
> before I arrived at school at nine each morning. It was
> not easy work, especially in winter, but I was bringing a
> few dollars into the family each week. If I got a tip of
> more than a dime at the homes to which I delivered
> groceries I was rich and the family coffers grew.

Harry showed signs of the inventiveness that later built Warner
Brothers when he opened a small shoe repair store in the front room of
the house next door to the one in which the family lived. Knowing that
few people owned more than one or two pairs of shoes in that era, he put
a crudely scribbled sign in the window: "Shoes Repaired While You Wait."

The sign brought a lot of customers to Harry's speedy repair shop,
and he became so busy that he trained Jack as his assistant to help when
he was getting behind with his work. One of the first "while you wait"
customers questioned his window sign. "Does that sign really mean
what it says?" Harry nodded his head and directed him to the old but
clean and comfortable chair in which customers were asked to rest while
he worked on their shoes. In front of the chair was a thick cushion on
which they could rest their shoeless feet.

Henry Garlick, the customer, recalled the incident years later when he
became an important financial partner with the Warner brothers on many
projects. "I had hardly read two pages of my morning paper when Harry
brought over the repaired and resoled shoes. I was so impressed, I gave him
my business card and said if ever I could be of help to contact me."

Harry tucked the card away safely. It told him Henry Garlick was
president of the First National Bank of Youngstown, Ohio. That card

proved to be the turning point in the existence of Warner Brothers Studio, when they badly needed millions of dollars to finance their ambitious plans.

Henry Garlick never forgot the first impression he had of Harry Warner, and he convinced his bank to give Warner Brothers money when nobody else considered them to be a good risk.

Jack, Harry, Sam, and Albert Warner first became interested in the world of entertainment when they joined a musical theatre group that met every week in the basement of a downtown store.

Harry, Sam, and Albert played small roles on stage but big roles off-stage. They were the trio chosen to raise money for scenery and to convince audiences to come and see their shows.

Jack Warner soon realized he had an outstanding soprano voice. At twelve he was playing lead roles in the group's productions of Gilbert and Sullivan operettas like *The Mikado*.

His singing brought him to the attention of wedding and funeral planners. Soon he had a flourishing business going that saw him singing happy songs at engagements, weddings, and other festive times, and sad songs, which the Youngstown paper described as "soulful enough to make even the hardened ministers cry," at funerals and other solemn occasions.

When there was no pianist to play for him, his sister Rose, an accomplished musician, played his accompaniment. "The fee was fifty percent more for the two of us," he said, "and we called her Rosa for the Italian evenings."

It was then that he became known, for a while, as Leon Zuardo. "The Italian families weren't too keen to hire a Jewish singer for their functions so I hired myself out as Leon Zuardo to Italian functions and Jack Warner to all the others," he recalled. "Fortunately for me the two groups rarely met at social or family events so I got away with it for a few years until my voice changed."

Asked which group was the most generous with the tips left in the hat on the stage beside the piano, Jack Warner laughed. "The Italians, of course," he said. "That's why the Jews had enough money left to

develop the studios in Hollywood. You don't see too many Italians running film studios."

Harry was the mover and shaker of the Warner family. A persuasive
salesman, he helped convince Harry Garlick to invest in many Warner
Brothers projects.

Jack Warner's education finished when was only thirteen. The rabbi
who taught him arrived at the Warner house one afternoon after school
with Jack in tow, hauled along by his ear. Ben and Pearl learned that Jack
had refused to learn Hebrew and had pulled the rabbi's beard violently
in protest at getting jabbed with a long pin when he couldn't learn to
spell. "He is expelled from the school as from now," said the rabbi.

Jack recalled that he was surprised that his parents showed little
concern that his education had come to an abrupt stop. "The grocery
store was flourishing," he said, "and they needed someone to work in the
storeroom and deliver groceries. So I was back to delivering with Bob
and the wagon but now I didn't have to get up so early."

His debut in the world of silent films had started when he was only
eleven. Two of his parents' friends hired him to sing along with the slides
showing lyrics of popular songs that were shown on the screen with a
simple projector. This method was used to keep the customers happy
while the first film of the evening was being rewound in preparation for
showing of the second film. He soon became a popular nightly star at
this downtown Youngstown nickelodeon. The theatre owners allowed
him to put a hat near the exit door with a handwritten sign that read,
"Help with the education of our wonderful boy singer."

These primitive movie houses drew all kinds of people. The one
Jack Warner remembered most was the sedate manager of the dignified live theatre, the Youngstown Opera House. Someone had passed
on the word that a young man with a beautiful voice was appearing at
the nickelodeon. "He deserves a better place to exhibit his talents," said
the informant.

So Jack Warner became a Sunday night fixture at the Opera House.
"I got ten dollars for each performance, and I still was able to continue
earning another eight dollars a week at the nickelodeon. Sometimes the

hat at the door brought be in another three dollars a week," he said. "I'd never seen that sort of money before."

From the Youngstown Opera House Jack Warner, at age sixteen, went into vaudeville. The proprietor of a small chain of vaudeville houses heard him at a Sunday show and offered him the opportunity to team up with another Youngstown entertainer, Pete Richard.

"We went out as a song and dance duo," said Warner. "We weren't very good, and the theatres we played were small and dirty. The rooms in which we stayed were disgraceful after the spotlessly clean home I had always been used to."

After one tour of fourteen theatres he returned home and told his sad story to his brother Sam. Sam warned Jack that his soprano voice would soon be changing and urged him to forget being a performer. "You'll never make any money on stage," he said. "It's the theatre managers who are making the profits. You should think about getting into theatre management."

It was also Sam who pushed the Warner brothers into the film industry. At the Ohio State Fair he saw Thomas Edison's first film projector, the kinetoscope, on display. It provided a primitive show with films no more than two or three minutes in length projected on to a screen, usually a white sheet tied at the corners to a wooden frame.

Sam became so enthusiastic about the flickering movies that he found a job as a projectionist at a nickelodeon in Youngstown. Not content with just projecting the images, he stayed late after the nightly shows pulling the kinetoscope apart, learning what each wheel and cog did in the projection process as he reassembled the machine.

Jack became as enthusiastic as Sam about this new form of show business. He learned that a man living nearby whose nickelodeon had closed had a kinetoscope that he wanted to sell. But the asking price of one thousand dollars for the equipment, including one film, *The Great Train Robbery*, was more than Sam and Jack could raise.

Harry called a family conference and convinced everyone that the purchase would make many thousands of dollars, but even when all the family cash was pooled they were still short of the thousand dollars.

Ben Warner agreed to pawn his gold watch. The family got a loan on old Bob, their horse, and finally reached the thousand-dollar mark.

Jack Warner with actress Rossana Podesta from Italy. She was one of the many starlets he was seen with at every public function in Hollywood.

Once they had the projector home, they discovered the reason it was for sale. It needed a lot of repairs. Fortunately Sam's training at the nickelodeon had given him the knowledge required to get the machine ready for its debut.

In a vacant store in downtown Youngstown they put up signs saying the greatest film ever made, *The Great Train Robbery*, would open in seven days' time. They reduced the number daily on the poster, to six, five, four, three, two, until finally it read "Tonight." It was the Warner brothers' first successful teaser promotion, and half an hour before the show was due to start there was a lineup of customers waiting to enter the theatre.

All four brothers worked at converting the old, abandoned store into a makeshift theatre. There was only one problem: they had no chairs and no money to buy them. Harry and Jack convinced the proprietor of a funeral home two doors down the road to rent them ninety-nine chairs every night if they guaranteed that the chairs would be back in the funeral home before nine the next morning. "I think we paid two dollars a night rental," said Jack Warner in 1943. "When the last customer had left all four of us carried the chairs back to the funeral parlour and set them up in lines ready for the next day's burial service."

Why ninety-nine? "Ninety-nine chairs was the limit," said Jack to the *Los Angeles Times*. "One more seat and the store would have been subject to fire inspections and safety regulations that we doubted we could pass."

Rose sold tickets at the door. When all the seats were full she ran down the aisle to the old piano they had purchased for ten dollars. She played while Jack sang the popular songs of the day to the projected slides showing the lyrics on the screen.

At the end of the first week they had made almost three hundred dollars profit. Flushed with success they moved to other Ohio towns, renting stores or empty vaudeville theatres. They went further into Pennsylvania, playing the smaller towns that had not yet seen a kinetoscope.

The tour ended when the patched-up film of *The Great Train Robbery* fell to pieces. The sprockets on the film were so worn that even by turning the projector handle as fast as they could the film refused to move.

Dave Robbins, who had married Warner daughter Anna, joined with them in creating a real theatre in New Castle, Ohio. The comfortable chairs and the presentation of new films the Warner brothers had managed to rent made the theatre so popular that they changed the one-show-a-night policy of most theatres to two shows a night.

Their biggest difficulty was getting the audience out of the theatre in time to seat the second set of house patrons. By this time Jack Warner's voice had started to change. His high soprano at times suddenly became a rusty tenor, so Rose had a brilliant idea. "After the first show," she said, "I'll play piano and Jack will sing."

"I was embarrassed and uncomfortable," he said years later. "When they heard how badly I sang they left their seats as fast as they could, just as Rose had hoped."

Soon the Warners had two theatres but found a great shortage of films good enough to attract customers. Sam went to New York and bought several trunks full of film that he shipped back to Pittsburgh, where the Warners had started their own film exchange, the Duquesne Amusement Supply Company. They quickly signed up more than a dozen theatres to receive their product exclusively.

"No respectable shipping company would have transported that highly inflammable film today, but somehow the trunks reached us in good condition and we didn't burn any wagons down," recalled Jack.

Harry, Jack, Sam, and Albert were working together as a business team for the first time. It was the first step toward the creation in Los Angeles of a Warner Brothers Studio many years later.

It quickly became apparent to the Warner brothers that the only way to get enough good films to satisfy their growing number of customers was to make the films themselves. They bought an old barn in St. Louis and made two or three one- and two-reel films before realizing that to make a film of any quality they needed a real studio.

It was at this stage of the growing film industry that Thomas Edison came to the conclusion that too many people were getting rich on the benefits of the cameras and projectors he had invented. Edison got together with most of the major filmmakers, including Biograph, Vitagraph, Kalem, Essanay, and Pathe, and they formed the Patents Company. The company decreed that no film could be made or shown in the United States unless the company licensed the cameras and projectors. These licenses were granted only to Patent Company members at fees that made Edison a wealthy man but kept most new young filmmakers out of the industry.

Realizing they were beaten, Jack, Harry, Sam, and Albert returned to their parents' Youngstown home with a lot of money in their pockets, but seemingly little future in the film industry.

But for the enterprising Warner brothers it was only a temporary setback. They heard that a film made in Italy, *Dante's Inferno*, was coming to the United States. Rights to show it in three eastern United States were being offered at a reasonable price. It was the first five-reel film they had ever seen.

Because the film was made outside the United States, the Patents Company had no jurisdiction over it. The Warners gloated a little at their unexpected good fortune.

Their actions when the film opened in Hartford, Connecticut, were perhaps an omen of the sound films they were later to create in Hollywood. The film was described on posters as "the experience of a lifetime." Jack stood out of sight behind the screen, using a thin sheet of metal to create thunder, a wind machine to give the effect of a tornado, and a red lantern, which he could turn on and off with a touch of his foot — *Dante's Inferno* really was "the experience of a lifetime."

As a bonus they hired actor Jonathan Willcock to recite the Dante poem from the wings. If his voice was somewhat muffled by the thunderclaps it was perhaps just as well, as Jack revealed many years later that the actor swigged substantially from a bottle between verses of the poem and by the end of the show was often muttering words that had no relation to the author's poem.

In 1912, with substantial profits from their venture as distributors and showmen, Harry decided on the move that was to enshrine their names in the motion picture industry for all time.

He sent Sam to Los Angeles and Jack to San Francisco to open film distribution houses there. By that time, Carl Laemmle, an immigrant from Germany, had battled the Patents Company head on. He had formed the Independent Motion Picture company (IMP) and soon convinced the federal government that they should move to end the Patents Company's unhealthy monopoly, which was stifling the progress of the industry. Other independent producers joined him. Harry Warner was one of the first to offer his support.

Jack Warner loved San Francisco. "They were still rebuilding after the earthquake and the city was wide open for anyone with original ideas," he said in a *San Francisco Chronicle* article in 1963.

Among the many people with whom he cemented lifelong friendships was Sid Grauman, who later became the builder of Grauman's Chinese Theatre on Hollywood Boulevard, still the home of handprints and footprints of many of Hollywood's greatest film personalities. "We made sure all our stars were there," said Jack Warner.

It was in San Francisco that Jack Warner met the girl who was to become his first wife. Irma Rogell and Jack Warner were married on October 10, 1914. Two years later she bore Warner a son, appropriately named Jack M. Warner.

The first film the Warner brothers made nearly ended in disaster. Harry had purchased the film rights of Ella Wheeler Wilcox's poem, *Passions Inherited*. Then he made a big mistake. Instead of moving immediately to California and using local people, he hired a British director, Gilbert Hamilton, supposedly with a track record of moviemaking in England. Harry gave him the money to hire a crew and cast and sent him to Santa Barbara, where he had been told the scenery was magnificent for filming purposes.

The $15,000 he gave Hamilton to make the movie vanished quickly, and after two more payments of $5,000 were requested by Hamilton, he told Jack to drive down to see what was happening. Why Sam, already in Los Angeles, was not selected to check out the movie has never been explained.

Jack drove his old car down to Santa Barbara and discovered Hamilton had spent a great deal of the Warners' money buying expensive clothes, cars, and gifts for the film's leading lady, whom he had successfully lured into his bed. Jack drove to Hollywood to the laboratory that had processed all the film already taken. He spent three days editing the film and decided there was enough footage to call a halt to any further shooting.

"I pulled the plug on Gilbert Hamilton," he said. "I repossessed the two cars he had bought and sent two tough friends to visit the hotel where he and his girlfriend were staying. They literally stole the clothes off their backs and left them as penniless as they were when the shooting began. The whole package cost me less than a thousand dollars and I had two cars to sell!"

Harry had now arrived in California with Albert to oversee what he hoped would be a successful conclusion to the family's first real movie. He convinced Jack to move his family to Los Angeles, where Sam was already established, and once more the four brothers were united.

Passions Inherited was a failure. With the First World War raging in Europe, moviegoers had no patience with the morality poem that depressed rather than entertained them.

Harry, getting close to forty, was too old for military service. Jack and Sam both tried to enlist. Sam was turned down on medical grounds. But the army thought Jack would be more valuable as a film-maker because they urgently needed informational films for the men and women in uniform.

Warner Brothers' first really successful production, *Open Your Eyes*, depicted something never before seen on America screens. Its topic was venereal disease. The Warner brothers paid all the costs of producing the film after getting a guarantee from the army that after the war they could show it to the general public in theatres across the country.

For some remarkable reason they chose Gilbert Hamilton, director of their first film fiasco in Santa Barbara, to handle the production. They decided to shoot in the Biograph Studio in New York, and Jack was sent east along with the director to ensure there was no hanky-panky on the new production.

It was in *Open Your Eyes* that Jack Warner made his one and only appearance as an actor. He appeared as a young soldier affected with venereal disease buying a bottle of fraudulent medicine from a phoney doctor. Many years later when asked why he decided to become an actor, he replied, "Simple, it saved us paying five dollars for a real actor."

The film was a huge success. It scared the heck out of a lot of soldiers by graphically showing the dangers of the diseases that came from having too good a time in their off-camp hours. In 1918, after the war, the film made a lot more money playing at hundreds of theatres nationwide.

Despite this success, the Warner Brothers were still not ready to plunge wholeheartedly into production. Their film exchanges were making money hand over fist, and other major filmmakers were offering their films first to the Warner exchanges because they had sole booking rights for hundreds of the best theatres in the country.

But they did not ignore the fact that their friends Adolph Zukor, Carl Laemmle, Jesse Lasky, and William Fox were establishing themselves in new studios they had built in or near Hollywood.

In 1917, only three years after his marriage, Jack Warner began to realize that having a wife and son to be looked after was not what his ambition had led him to visualize. The couple separated, with Irma moving back to San Francisco, but it was not until 1925 that the marriage ended in divorce.

It is interesting to note that in Jack Warner's autobiography, *My First Hundred Years In Hollywood*, published in 1964, he never mentions his first wife or the existence of a Jack Warner Junior.

Harry and Albert were back in New York looking after distribution there. Sam remained in Los Angeles with Jack. An avid reader, Sam found a book called *My Four Years In Germany*, written by James Gerard, a former American ambassador to Germany. He told Jack the book had all the ingredients of a blockbuster movie. Harry agreed and approached Gerard to see if he would sell the film rights to the Warner brothers.

It was Harry's salesmanship that won the day. Gerard was guaranteed $50,000 for the film rights plus twenty percent of profits from the film's distribution. Gerard said later the $50,000 Harry offered was less than half what other producers had suggested. "But Harry Warner convinced me that his company would give the film the treatment the book deserved," he said. "He was a persuasive man and I never regretted my decision."

To raise the money needed to make the film and pay the author, Harry Warner called in a marker from many years earlier. He went to visit Henry Garlick, still president of Youngstown's First National Bank. Garlick came though. "I never go back on my word," he said. "I had told Harry to contact me if he had an idea that needed backing and this was exactly why he came to see me."

Sam and Jack moved east to assist with the production, leaving competent men in charge of their film exchanges in Los Angeles and San Francisco. "I suggested we buy some news reel footage of the war to save having to pay for expensive battle scenes," said Jack. Reviewers praised the Warners for their "incredibly realistic battle scenes." Few ever knew they were seeing the real war.

Gerard asked to be present at the official opening night of *My Four Years in Germany* in March of 1918 in New York City. He went on stage to receive the thunderous applause the standing audience gave after the final scene. Gerard proved himself to be an honourable man at that moment. He held up his hand and asked for silence. He then asked Harry, Sam, Albert, and Jack Warner to join him on stage. "They," he said, "have made the very first memorable American movie from my book. I congratulate them, and you should too." He clapped as the Warners stepped on stage and the audience erupted once more with applause.

First National Pictures distributed the film. Ironically, it was their studio the Warners took over when they moved from Sunset Boulevard in Hollywood to their new 104-acre location in Burbank.

The film made more than $1.5 milion before the war ended in September. James Gerard pocketed $300,000, and the Warner Brothers, from their first commercial feature, netted more than $250,000.

Warner Brothers films were becoming a force to be reckoned with in the expanding industry. But their next film, *The Kaiser's Finish*, which appeared late in 1918, was a flop. Americans, with their sons safely home from the war, weren't inspired. They didn't want to see any more war movies.

The brothers were not downhearted with their failure. Harry, still the boss in the family, sent Sam and Jack back to Los Angles with instructions to buy the best property they could get at a reasonable price that looked suitable for conversion into a film studio.

They found an existing studio right in the heart of downtown Los Angeles that was almost out of business. Jack said later he was sold on the building because the company owning it had a mini zoo attached the studio with more than fifty wild animals that had been trained to do many things when ordered by their trainer.

Both Jack and Sam later claimed they came up with the idea to create a serial in twenty-six parts, featuring a beautiful girl who faced danger in the jungle from wild animals. Every week, the final scene left her apparently facing sure death.

These serials drew huge crowds of fans who would never dare to miss a week's episode to see how the heroine was saved before being led into even worse trouble at the end of the new episode.

Sam devised a story pattern for *The Tiger's Claw*, and Jack hired an actress who had appeared in earlier serials for other companies. Helen

Holmes was sold on Warner's serial because she said, "For the first time in my experience the company knew what it was going to do in the series many weeks ahead of production."

The films were so successful the brothers hired the same heroine to appear in a new serial, *The Lost City*.

Jack then proved that he could not only create ideas, he could direct films too. Howard Hawks, later to become a renowned director, suggested that they make a comedy film, *His Night Out*, with its star to be an Italian actor, Monty Banks.

Sam and Jack liked the story, liked Banks, and hired a director to shoot from Howard Hawks's script. After only two days on the set the director threw up his hands and walked out on the film, never to return. Without another director available, Jack told Howard Hawks not to worry, he would take over as director.

Years later he said he visited theatres where Mack Sennett films were being shown. "I jotted down every humorous idea he created and used them in our film next day," he said.

The comedy was well received, and the Warner Studio made five more films with Monty Banks, all comedies, all directed by Jack Warner. "I admit I continued to steal comedy ideas from Sennett," he said in 1945 after it was revealed that Warner was the source of the anonymous pension Sennett, in retirement, received each week until he died. "I owe him much more than he will ever know," he said.

Remembering his beloved horse, Bob, in Youngstown, Jack Warner was the founder and hardest worker toward the establishment of a set of rules for producers using animals in films. This went against the wishes of other studios who had, as their early films proved, treated animals with as much respect as sacrificial lambs.

He convinced the United States government to set a standard of animal care that all producers had to meet. Veterinarians were to be present on every film set where animals were being used. They were given the authority to close down any production if animal abuse was discovered.

In 1926 the Warner brothers were reduced to three. Sam, who had been ill for some time, was diagnosed with a brain tumour and died quickly. He had been a strong believer in support of Jack when Harry had doubted whether the money the company was spending on development of sound films was worthwhile. Sadly, he never saw *The Jazz Singer*, the only film he ever directed. When Jack, Harry, and Albert tried to arrange for him to attend the opening in New York, he was too ill to be moved. He died the day before the film was shown for the first time in New York.

In 1928 the Warners moved from their Sunset Boulevard location to the 104 acres of land in Burbank that they later developed into the most productive studio in the United States.

In 1936 Jack Warner married for the second time. Two years later Ann Boyar gave him a daughter they named Barbara. He had already adopted Joy, the daughter of his new wife from a previous marriage. It was a happy marriage that lasted to the end of his days.

To list all the superb films Warner Brothers made would fill a complete book. But never to be forgotten are films like *East of Eden* with James Dean, *Little Caesar* with Edward G. Robinson, *The Life of Emile Zola* with Paul Muni, *Angels With Dirty Faces* with James Cagney, *Casablanca* with Humphrey Bogart, *Dark Victory* with Bette Davis, *Robin Hood* with Errol Flynn, *Mildred Pierce* with Joan Crawford, *The Treasure of the Sierra Madre* with Walter Huston, and *The Hasty Heart* with Richard Todd. The list is endless.

Jack Warner took a chance on many unknowns and made them into stars. Among the unknowns were: Lauren Bacall, Joan Blondell, Jack Carson, Olivia De Havilland, Kay Francis, John Garfield, Ruby Keeler, Joan Leslie, Peter Lorre, Raymond Massey, Dennis Morgan, Dick Powell, Claude Rains, Ronald Reagan, Ann Sheridan, Alexis Smith, Ned Sparks, Jane Wyman, Loretta Young, and the first canine star of the movie world, Rin-Tin-Tin.

With his love of animals, Jack Warner used to spend his lunch hours munching on a sandwich while he took Rin-Tin-Tin for a daily walk around the studio. For some time the dog lived at the home he built on fourteen acres of land at 1801 Angelo Drive in Beverly Hills. He is said to have cried when the dog died, but was not so upset that he let the series die. "We actually used eighteen different dogs as Rin-Tin-Tin," he told the *Los Angeles Times*.

Warners, unlike other studios that concentrated mainly on one form of film (for example MGM and its successful musicals), diversified production into crime, comedy, mysteries, melodramas, and biographical movies. There was also a musical that will likely never be equalled, *My Fair Lady*, on which Jack Warner spent $17 million and grossed, in 1956, the immense sum of $150 million. So sure was Jack Warner of the success of this film that he produced and edited it himself, and during the filming was on the set every day making sure the director and actors had everything necessary to make it into the box-office bonanza it became.

When Harry Warner died in 1958, Jack was in Monte Carlo. To celebrate his brother's life and the fact that he now was president of Warner Brothers, Jack went to the casino in Monaco and came away with $41,000 in winnings. "This is a great omen for the future of Warners," he said.

Unfortunately, it wasn't a great omen for Jack Warner. A week after becoming president he was involved in a near-fatal car accident on the French Riviera. But he astounded everyone by making an amazing recovery and two weeks later was back at the studio he now totally controlled.

Albert died in 1967 but had been retired for many years, leaving Jack the undisputed king of Warner Brothers.

Adjacent to his office he had a trophy room in which he displayed the Oscars his films had won. More than one hundred other citations, medals, and honours were shown to celebrity guests he entertained from around the world. Included on three occasions were the Duke and Duchess of Windsor.

Asked what were his most prized awards he answered without hesitation. "The United States Medal Of Merit, The Irving Thalberg Memorial Award from the Academy of Motion Picture Arts and Sciences, and the medal which gives me the right to call myself a Commander of the Order of the British Empire," he said. "I received the last one from Queen Elizabeth herself in 1961."

People feared Jack Warner because of his immense power, hated him because he dictated the way their lives were to unfold, or loved him for the opportunity he gave them to become stars.

The well-publicized feud between Jack L. Warner, head of Warner Brothers Studio, and Errol Flynn, one of his studio's most important assets, spread like wildfire around Hollywood in 1943.

Actors and technicians reported many public shouting matches between the two. Workers at Warner Brothers reported that Warner and Flynn often came close to blows.

The publicity did what it was supposed to do, mislead a lot of important people. Many years later it helped a writer publish a book erroneously suggesting Errol Flynn was a Nazi spy. The truth is that these public feuds were carefully orchestrated to deal a nasty blow to the German war machine in the Second World War. The feud never existed. Warner and Flynn were great friends.

At night, Flynn and Warner often enjoyed a drink or two and a game of cards behind the closed doors of Jack Warner's office or at Errol Flynn's house in Beverly Hills.

Why and how that supposed feud helped frustrate the Germans in the Second World War has never been told before, but here is the story of the successful hoax that fooled the Nazis in 1943.

The American government, during the Second World War, suspected that actor Peter Van Eyck, an import from Germany, might be a spy for the German government. They knew his brother back in Germany was a high ranking Nazi officer.

At the request of President Franklin Roosevelt, Jack Warner was asked to see if he could prove the spy theory once and for all. Errol Flynn, who called Warner "Sporting Blood," and Warner, who called Flynn "Baron," decided to see if they could trick Van Eyck into exposing himself.

Flynn became the "Jew hater," mouthing off in public about Warner and other Jews who were ruining the world. He risked his reputation and did lose a lot of friends. Warner became the man who bore the brunt of his supposed hatred. The feud was as phoney as a three-dollar bill, but Van Eyck fell for it. He approached Flynn and they became fellow "Jew haters."

Van Eyck said he wondered if Flynn might be able to gain access to the top-secret California subsidiary of the Lukas-Harold Company of Indianapolis, which was producing the Nordern XV bombsight. The Nordern, invented by Swiss engineer Carl Nordern, was proving so accurate that it was reputed to be able to hit a target inside a hundred-foot circle from as high as four miles. The Nordern was the bombsight later used on August 6, 1945, to drop the atomic bomb from the *Enola Gay* onto Hiroshima, Japan.

Flynn promised to see what he could do, and with Warner's help and the approval of the American government, he got an invitation to visit the plant. Van Eyck gave Flynn a mini camera, small enough to be hidden behind his shirt. Flynn promised to get as many pictures as possible at the plant. Before leaving for the plant, he left the camera with Jack Warner, who carried out his part of the plot in secret at his studio. When Flynn returned to Hollywood he reported to Jack Warner.

Warner had a half-dozen studio technicians, sworn to secrecy, who were never told what was really happening. They had used the camera in a mock bombsight plant built inside the Warner studio on a closed set. They even added pictures on the roll of film of phoney papers detailing the equipment's operation.

Flynn then delivered the camera, containing its undeveloped film, to Van Eyck.

It was not until after the war that Flynn and Warner were told the phoney pictures were used by the Germans to try to build a copy of the bombsight. "They apparently spent millions of dollars and more than a year trying to get the damn thing to work," said Flynn.

Jack Warner never forgot that Flynn had placed his career on the line by pretending to be a Nazi sympathizer. When Flynn called him from England in 1956, where he was making a television series, *The Errol Flynn Theatre*, he learned that the series was in danger of folding because the producers were running out of money.

Warner flew to London and quietly, through lawyers, bought out one of the film producers and personally invested the needed funds so that the series could be completed.

Also during the Second World War, Jack Warner was contacted by the Canadian government. Prime Minister Mackenzie King asked if he could spare two of his stars to go from coast to coast in Canada helping raise money by selling War Bonds. Warner, remembering the story his parents had told him, phoned the Prime Minister and said he would send not two but twenty of his stars to criss-cross the country at Warner's expense until they had raised at least $20 million. He kept his word, and the result was sales of War Bonds exceeding $30 million. He would never admit that he had given money to his stars so they could buy $10 million in War Bonds. But he never denied the suggestion.

When television came to the United States after the Second World War, almost every major studio denied the television companies the right to use the facilities at their studios. Jack Warner, with his usual foresight, welcomed them in with open arms. Within two years his studio was producing as many as thirty different half-hour television shows every week. "They made us many millions," he said to the *Los Angeles Times*. "I don't know why other studios couldn't see the possibilities. People were staying home watching television. Every other studio but ours was was in mothballs."

When Jack Warner died in September 1978, he was eighty-six years old. Eleven years earlier he had sold his controlling interest in Warner Brothers for $32 million to Seven Arts, a New York company. He continued to work as an independent producer until he was eighty. But the massive stroke he suffered in 1972 never allowed him to speak again. His wife, Ann, tended to his every need and was with him when he died.

The special tribute held after his death to raise money for one of the charities he had given to very generously in his lifetime was attended by almost every star from his glory years who was still alive. Bette Davis spoke these words:

> Though we may have hated him at the time we must all look back today with gratitude for what those years did for everyone of us. He will never be equalled. He will be sorely missed in the industry today ruled not by excellence but by money. It is a world where there are no more men like Jack Warner who could make decisions

immediately. It is now a world where boards of directors fight among themselves for weeks or months before saying yes or no.

The fifteen hundred people present stood and applauded as Bette Davis took a bow.

After the funeral, Ann Warner told friends that her husband had only three real friends: Bill Schaefer, his secretary for forty-three years; his fitness guru, Abdul Molgan, who kept Warner fit for thirty-six years before he himself died; and Lucien Rocher, who for thirty-seven years ran the house at 1801 Angelo Drive in Beverly Hills. "He adored them because they were willing to say 'no' to him," she said. "All the others he despised because whatever he asked they always answered 'yes.'"

Epilogue

I f I have failed to include your favourite Canadian personality in my book I apologize. Many who deserve to be remembered were left out because when I had written almost ninety thousand words I was told that was my limit.

I put a lot of names on a back burner, perhaps hoping that if this book sells as well as did my first one, *Stardust and Shadows*, about Canadians in the silent era, Tony Hawke and Kirk Howard, who have been so totally cooperative at Dundurn Press, will decide to let me write one more final book before I leave this earth.

Some of those important Canadians, like Fay Wray and Glenn Ford, are still alive in California. Deanna Durbin is living in retirement in France. Many have died: Rod Cameron; Jack Cummings, MGM's greatest producer; Richard Day, the set designer from Vancouver who won more Oscars in Hollywood than any other person; John Ireland, a brilliant actor; Jay Silverheels, the Lone Ranger's Tonto; director Mark Robson; and character actor Douglas Dumbrille.

Two people who were a major part of what was supposed to be an all-American cast headed by Mickey Rooney in *The Hardy Family* film series were from Canada. Cecilia Parker from Fort William (now Thunder Bay) and Ann Rutherford from Toronto are living in retirement in Los Angeles.

I answered every one of the hundreds of letters, emails, and phone calls I received after *Stardust and Shadows* was published three years ago. I welcomed into my home those people who rang my front doorbell and said they wanted to talk to me about the book or about some of the stars from the Hollywood's silent era.

A Montreal documentary filmmaker, who this year had one of his projects nominated for an Oscar, is hoping to make *Stardust and Shadows* into a twenty-four-part series for television in the not-too-distant future.

If you have photographs or information concerning Canadians in the world of entertainment I have not yet written about, I will be happy to hear from you. Here is my address:

Charles Foster
145 Leonard Street
Riverview, New Brunswick
Canada E1B 1K7
Telephone (506) 386-8749
E-mail: Ceefos@aol.com

Index